ARGENTINE CONSTITUTIONAL LAW

NUMBER IV OF THE

COLUMBIA LEGAL STUDIES

EDITED UNDER THE AUSPICES OF THE
FACULTY OF LAW OF COLUMBIA UNIVERSITY
Edwin W. Patterson, Editor

ARGENTINE CONSTITUTIONAL LAW

THE JUDICIAL FUNCTION IN THE MAINTENANCE OF THE FEDERAL SYSTEM AND THE PRESERVATION OF INDIVIDUAL RIGHTS

By SANTOS P. AMADEO

WITH A FOREWORD BY L. S. ROWE, DIRECTOR GENERAL OF THE PAN AMERICAN UNION

COLUMBIA UNIVERSITY PRESS, NEW YORK

1943

COLUMBIA UNIVERSITY PRESS, NEW YORK

Foreign Agent: OXFORD UNIVERSITY PRESS, Humphrey Milford, Amen House, London, E.C. 4, England, AND B. I. Building, Nicol Road, Bombay, India

MANUFACTURED IN THE UNITED STATES OF AMERICA

To Maruja

FOREWORD

THE ARGENTINE Republic presents so many points of similarity with the United States both in environmental conditions and political development that a study of the constitutional system of this progressive Latin American state possesses special interest.

In many respects the history of the political organization of the Argentine Republic presents problems of special interest to the student of political science. In no other country of the Western Hemisphere has the conflict between two systems of government, viz., the centralized or unitary and the federal system, been so clearly expressed. The author has shown deep insight into this important aspect of Argentine history.

No less instructive is the author's analysis of the diverse influences that entered into the formation of the Constitution of 1853. Of special interest to readers in this country will be the clear picture of the extent to which the framers of the Argentine Constitution were influenced by the provisions of the Constitution of the United States.

An important chapter is devoted to the relation of the federal government to the provinces. The Argentine Constitution not only guarantees to each province a republican form of government but also guarantees "to each province the enjoyment and exercise of its institutions." The broad terms of this provision have made possible in many instances the extension of the control of the federal government over the provinces. The author sets forth with great clearness the numerous "interventions" under which the federal government has practically taken over for periods of short or long duration the administration of one or more provinces, thus practically displacing the local governments.

This foreword would not be complete without some mention of the author's exhaustive study of the Argentine judicial system. In some respects this is the most illuminating chapter of the work.

Students of political science owe a debt of gratitude to Dr. Amadeo for this vivid picture, not only of the structure, but also of the actual operation of the political system of one of the progressive democracies of this continent.

L. S. ROWE

Washington
April, 1943

PREFACE

IT IS the purpose of this study to consider certain features of Argentine constitutional law, with special reference to the role of the judicial department in the maintenance of the federal system and the protection of individual rights. And since the constitutional law of the United States has had a profound influence on the development of constitutional law in Argentina, emphasis has been placed upon the relationship, the similarities and the differences, between the two.

This study was commenced and carried on under the direction and with the assistance and advice of Professor Noel T. Dowling, of the School of Law of Columbia University. The study had its origin in work done by the author while attending a seminar in Comparative Constitutional Law given at Columbia in 1938 by Professors Deák, Dowling, and Rogers. The author wishes to acknowledge with special gratitude the assistance given him by Professors Dowling and Deák, whose suggestions and criticisms are responsible for whatever merit the following pages possess, although they are in no way to be held to account for the ideas here expressed. He is grateful also to Dr. Bryce Wood for his generous assistance in seeing the book through the press. The author hopes that the effort to make available in English so much of what is Spanish has not suffered unduly from the fact that English is not his native tongue.

Thanks are due also to Dr. Joseph P. Chamberlain, Professor of Public Law at Columbia University, whose kindness in permitting the use of the facilities of the Legislative Drafting Research Fund, of which he is Director, for the final preparation of this study for publication, was of invaluable aid. Moreover, the author must make special mention of the Jockey Club of the City of Buenos Aires, which afforded him the resources of its splendid library for much of the research upon which this study is based.

As a member of the Faculty of the University of Puerto Rico, the author is deeply indebted to the Board of Trustees of the University for making it possible for him to spend a year on leave of absence in furtherance of this work. The author is grateful to the John Simon Guggenheim Memorial Foundation for the financial and other assistance which permitted him as a Latin American Fellow of the Foundation, to complete the study in residence under the Faculty of Law of Columbia University. The author is, finally, grateful to His Excellency Dr. Felipe A. Espil, Argentine Ambassador to the United States, and to Mr. Nelson A. Rockefeller, Coordinator of Inter-American Affairs, for their assistance in the publication of this book.

It is the hope of the author that this work will provoke interest in the study of Argentine constitutional law on the part of students and commentators on the constitutional law of the United States, and will lead to further studies of a more specialized nature relating to Argentine public law.

SANTOS P. AMADEO

New York
April, 1943

CONTENTS

ARGENTINE CONSTITUTIONAL LAW

ABBREVIATIONS

J.A.	Jurisprudencia argentina
S.C.N.	Suprema Corte de Justicia Nacional

Part One: THE CONSTITUTION AND THE COURTS

I: THE ANTECEDENTS OF THE CONSTITUTION

THE STRUGGLE of the Argentine people to establish a federal system of government is one of the most heroic and interesting chapters of modern political and constitutional history. This struggle began when the force of historical events led the Argentine nation to declare its independence from Spain early in the nineteenth century.

THE REVOLUTION

Historians [1] have classified the causes of Argentine independence as internal and external. The internal causes were: first, the political absolutism of the Spanish government; second, the exclusion of native Argentines from governmental positions; and third, the economic system imposed by Spain on her which prevented her from trading with other countries, thus creating a monopoly in behalf of Spanish merchants detrimental to the economic interests of the colonies.

The external causes were: the invasion of Buenos Aires by the English in the years 1806 and 1807; the revolution of the English colonists in North America; and the French Revolution. The English occupation of Buenos Aires contributed to the Argentine Revolution in three ways: it made the natives conscious of their military importance, since they took an active and decisive part in the defeat of the English invaders; it made them conscious of their economic importance, because during the occupation of Buenos Aires the native population carried on commerce with the English and prospered under the liberal economic policies of the English in

[1] J. González Calderón, *Historia de la organización constitucional*, pp. 8–10.

ways impossible under Spanish control; and it enabled the Argentine intellectuals to become acquainted with the literature which was the intellectual cause of the revolutions of the English colonies and of the French people. The introduction of these books had been prohibited by Spain.[2]

The revolution of the North American colonies as well as the French Revolution had a profound effect on the Argentine Revolution, not only because they constituted an intellectual and sentimental incentive to the Argentine people, but also because the system of government created after these revolutions influenced Argentine legislators in drafting the constitution for their country. The leaders of the Argentine Revolution were fully acquainted with the English, French, and North American literatures which prepared the way for these revolutions.[3] The ideas of the French Revolution spread throughout the world through its writers and philosophers. Those ideas of liberty and sovereignty reached as far as the distant colony of La Plata. In the University of Chuquisaca the patriots studied the jurists and historians of the Indies and the French philosophers.[4]

Mariano Moreno, the youngest and most radical of the revolutionists, had translated into Spanish Rousseau's *Contrat Social* and also put at the service of the revolution his knowledge of the writings of Montesquieu, Mably, Daguesseau, Locke, Filangieri, Jovellanos, Raynal, and other encyclopedists. Bernardo de Monteagudo, the successor of Moreno as the publisher of the newspaper *La Gaceta* dedicated to the spreading of revolutionary ideas, was also a student of William Paley, Turgot, and other English and French philosophers.[5] Dean Funes, a leader of the Argentine Revolution, said that the North American and French Revolutions had stimulated the thinking of the Argentines on the natural rights of men.[6]

The Argentine Revolution crystallized into a movement which led to complete independence. It took place when Napoleon in-

[2] L. V. Varela, *Historia constitucional de la República argentina*, I, 121–24.

[3] L. A. de Herrera, *La revolución francesa y Sud América*.

[4] R. Levene, *A History of Argentina* (tr. by William S. Robertson), pp. 233–34.

[5] J. M. Guastavino and C. A. Novaro, *Elementos de derecho público argentino*, pp. 19 and 32.

[6] Cited in A. Padilla, *La constitución de Estados Unidos como precedente argentino*, p. 22.

vaded Spain and imprisoned King Charles IV and the legal heir to the throne, Ferdinand VII. The Argentine revolutionists, led by Rodríguez Peña, Belgrano, Paso, Vieytes, Alberti, Terrada, French, Berruti, Chiclana, Viamonte, Saavedra, Castelli, and others, requested Viceroy Cisneros to convoke a *cabildo abierto* or popular municipal assembly for the purpose of permitting the people to decide what was to be done with the government of the viceroyalty, inasmuch as the government which gave authority to the colonial government no longer existed. The purpose of the revolutionists was to assume control of the government on behalf of the Argentine people although acting in the name of King Ferdinand VII, then imprisoned. Although Viceroy Cisneros hesitated at first to comply with the request of the revolutionary leaders, he finally acceded to it.

On May 22, 1810, the open cabildo was held in the city of Buenos Aires and the first step toward Argentine independence was taken. The proceedings of the cabildo were described as follows by a well-known Argentine historian:

In the popular assembly of May 22 three parties met face to face. The loyalist party favored the continuance of the viceroy in his post with only the innovation of associating with him in the government the chief members of the audiencia of Buenos Aires. That audiencia was at the head of the loyalist party, and its organs were the oidors of the audiencia, supported by the moral authority of the bishop and the phalanx of Spanish officials. As already indicated the party of reconciliation, which was under the influence of the chief municipal alcaldes and regidors, and which counted upon the support of the influential Spanish general, Pascual Ruiz Huidobro, wished to harmonize the demands of the two extreme parties with the exigencies of the situation and to settle the dispute by having the cabildo temporarily assume the supreme command until a provisional government should be organized that would remain dependent upon the supreme authority of the Peninsula. This party had the support of some patriots; among others Nicolás Rodríguez Peña, Feliciano Chiclana, Vieytes, Viamonte, and Balcarce. The majority of the patriot party stood merely for the deposition of the viceroy and the formation of a suitable government invested with power conferred by the people. This party was divided into two factions: one which wished to delegate to the cabildo the duty of organizing a new government, and the other which desired that this should be done as the result of a popular vote. Cornelio Saavedra, who was one of the outstanding leaders of the revolution, belonged to the first faction, while Castelli and other more impetuous or farsighted citizens belonged to the second.[7]

The revolutionists who were in favor of the deposition of the viceroy were successful. They vested the provisional government in a body representing the people but acting in the name of the king until representatives of the provinces could be convoked to establish the form of government deemed necessary. The separatist movement spread throughout the viceroyalty, and on July 9, 1816, at the Congress of Tucumán, in which all the provinces of Argentina were represented, the revolution of the cabildo of Buenos Aires of May 22, 1810, was consecrated as a national movement and the Argentine provinces declared themselves independent and free from Spain.

The principles of the North American and French Revolutions were expounded by the revolutionists in the debates at the meetings of the cabildo as well as in the steps taken to organize the provisional governments to rule the Argentine people. These political principles were first enunciated in the debates between the revolutionists and the Spaniards who supported the colonial government. Against the allegation of the latter that the Argentines had no right to supplant the Spanish government, the leaders of the revolution argued that as the legal sovereign of the provinces had been deposed the sovereignty returned to the people of Argentina. This argument constituted in effect an affirmation of the principle of popular sovereignty. This principle was once more affirmed when the revolutionists contended that the people had the right to decide who should have the power to govern in Argentina.

The principle of a representative form of government was advocated in the revolution when it was proposed and accepted that a provisional board elected by the people should take charge of the government until a national congress was convoked. In addition, the principle of separation of powers was enunciated when it was provided that the provisional board should not exercise judicial functions but that these should be exercised by the regularly constituted courts. The enunciation of the principles of popular sovereignty, representative government, and separation of powers constituted a proclamation of the basic elements of a republican form

[7] B. Mitre, *Historia de Belgrano*, I, 241–42, as cited in R. Levene, *op. cit.*, p. 221.

of government which were later consecrated in the Constitution of 1853.[8]

The Federalist Principle

During the revolutionary period and until the nation was constitutionally organized in 1853, two principles concerned with the constitutional structure of the nation dominated Argentine political and constitutional thought, namely, the federalist and the unitary.

It has been debated in Argentina whether the federalist principle was simply an imitation of the federalism of the United States or a product of the political and constitutional history of the nation. The trouble with this debate is that those participating have failed to distinguish between the constitutional mechanism employed in the application of the federalist principle and the historical, geographical, personal, social, and economic factors which may give rise to the idea or the necessity for applying it. The truth is that although Argentine federalism may have been influenced by the federal mechanism of the United States, Switzerland, and the German Confederation, nevertheless the various factors which gave rise to the idea and the necessity of establishing a federal system of government in Argentina were not the result of the imitation of any other federal system but rather had their deep roots in the political, economic, and social history of the nation, as well as in its geographical features, and in the characteristics of the Argentine people.

Thus, in considering the origin of Argentine federalism, a distinction must be made between the factors which gave rise to the idea and the necessity of the application of the federal principle and the legal mechanism to put this principle into practice. Alberdi,[9] in an admirable discussion, classifies these factors as follows: (1) The provincial differences and rivalries which were systematically promoted by the Spanish regime and were later revived by the republican demagogy. (2) The long periods of provincial isolation and independence which took place during the revolution. (3) The local peculiarities in soil and climate and also in the character,

[8] J. González Calderón, *op. cit.*, pp. 22–27.
[9] J. B. Alberdi, *Bases y comentarios de la constitución argentina*, pp. 106–8.

habits, and language of the people. (4) The enormous distances that separated some provinces from others, and the lack of good roads. (5) The partial sovereignty acknowledged by the May Revolution as belonging to all the provinces. (6) The extensive franchises previously granted to the towns and provincial governments by the Spanish regime. (7) The powerlessness of any central government to subjugate the provinces or their governments without violence and bloodshed. (8) The treaties or compacts entered into between the provinces during the period of isolation. (9) The establishment of provincial monetary systems initiated by Buenos Aires through the issuing of paper money. (10) The Agreement of San Nicolás of May 30, 1852, ratifying the Treaty of 1831, which had authoritatively affirmed the federal principle of government.

Although when the Constitution of 1853 was drafted the federalist principle as embodied in the Constitution of the United States influenced the makers of the Argentine Constitution, nevertheless in the early revolutionary days other federal systems besides that of the United States influenced Argentine federalism. On this point Alberdi said:

> The federalist principle was well known to our revolution in 1810. North American federalism was not the only source of inspiration; the federalism of Holland and of Switzerland served also as examples to our federalism. Rousseau, Necker and Dumont brought to the French Revolution the liberalism of the Helvetic Confederation. Moreno and Paso were the Argentine exponents of the French Revolution and found inspiration in Rousseau. They translated his works and were also federalists like him.[10]

Among the most important antecedents of Argentine federalism which contributed to the adoption of the Constitution of 1853 were the treaties entered into between the different provinces during the years 1820 to 1846. In this period[11] more than thirty treaties were made between the different provinces for the following purposes: to make peace, to establish bonds of mutual friendship, to contract military alliances against other provinces and foreign countries, to establish commercial relations, and to arrange for the calling of a national convention to establish a federal system of government.

[10] *Ibid.*, p. 340.

[11] *Asambleas constituyentes argentinas*, Vol. VI, part 2, pp. 131–259.

The Treaty of del Pilar between the provinces of Buenos Aires, Santa Fe, and Entre Ríos was signed on February 23, 1820, for the purpose of ending the war between the contracting provinces and to enable them to concentrate all their efforts towards the creation of a national federal government. This treaty was the first in which a group of provinces declared the necessity of creating a federal system.

The treaty of January 25, 1822, called *El Cuadrilátero* because signed by four provinces, Buenos Aires, Santa Fe, Entre Ríos, and Corrientes, marked another step in the development of the federalist principle. This was a treaty of peace and commerce which also provided for the extradition of criminals and for the calling of a national convention to establish a national federal government.

The treaty of May 17, 1827, signed by the provinces of Córdoba, Santa Fe, Entre Ríos, Corrientes, Santiago del Estero, La Rioja, Salta, Mendoza, San Juan, San Luis, and the Banda Oriental, constituted another affirmation of the federalist principle. It was provided in this treaty, first, that the contracting provinces should form an offensive and defensive military alliance; second, that the signatory provinces should agree to reject the Constitution of 1826,[12] because, among other reasons, it was based on unitary principles in violation of the rights of the provinces; third, that the provinces should agree to pool all their resources in order to destroy the national authorities which were causing so many evils to the nation;[13] fourth, that the provinces should invite other provinces to take action for the purpose of convoking a national convention to create a federal government; and fifth, that this convention should be held in the city of Santa Fe and that the respective provinces should have the inalienable right to elect and remove the delegates sent to this convention.

By another treaty, of July 5, 1830, the provinces of Catamarca, Córdoba, San Luis, Mendoza, and La Rioja agreed that it was for the common interest of all the provinces to establish a national government and to that end the governor of the province of Córdoba should call a convention. A provision for calling a constitu-

[12] See page 18 of this chapter for a discussion of this constitution.

[13] The national authorities referred to were those established under the Constitution of 1826.

tional convention for the purpose of forming a union of the provinces was also incorporated in a treaty of August 31, 1830, signed by the provinces of Mendoza, San Luis, San Juan, Salta, Tucumán, Santiago del Estero, Córdoba, Catamarca, and La Rioja.

The last important treaty which laid the immediate foundation for the Constitution of 1853 was the Treaty of El Litoral signed by the provinces of Buenos Aires, Santa Fe, and Entre Ríos on February 15, 1831. This treaty contained many important provisions. First, the signatory provinces reaffirmed all the preceding treaties of alliance, peace, friendship, and commerce which had been signed by the parties. Second, the treaty provided that all the provinces should be invited to a national congress for the purpose of establishing the general administration of the nation under a federal system of government. Third, it contained certain provisions which were later embodied in the Constitution of 1853, namely, the extradition of fugitives from justice, the guarantee of equal privileges and immunities to the inhabitants of the several provinces, and the prohibition of discriminatory taxes on ships or products entering into one province from another. Finally, a federal authority was created, to be called the Representative Committee of the Littoral Provinces of the Argentine Republic. This Committee was composed of one delegate from each province; it had power to make war, to negotiate treaties of peace, to raise an army and appoint the officers of the same, and to invite the other provinces to join in forming a federal government. This Committee, as will be seen later, was dissolved in 1832, but it constituted a step toward the organization of the Argentine Republic as a federal state.

The Unitary Principle

As in the case of the federalist principle, there were also many factors which supported the unitary principle as a possible basis upon which a national government could be established. Once more we turn to Alberdi [14] for a discussion of these factors. He classified them under two types, those belonging to the colonial epoch and those belonging to the revolutionary period. The first were: unity of Spanish origin; unity of population; unity of religion; unity of customs and language; unity of political and govern-

[14] J. B. Alberdi, *op. cit.*, pp. 103–6.

mental organization (since all the provinces formed part of a single state); unity of civil, penal, and commercial legislation; unity of judicial administration (since there was but one court of appeals, which was in Buenos Aires); unity of territory (the Viceroyalty of La Plata); and unity of financial affairs and public expenditures; and unity of executive administration (since the viceroy was head of the Viceroyalty). Finally, another unitary factor was the city of Buenos Aires, capital of the Viceroyalty. In the struggle between federalist and unitary principles Buenos Aires was the center of agitation for a unitary system. Her claim to rule the rest of the provinces was supported not only by historical factors but also by the fact that she controlled the port of Buenos Aires, the only port through which international commerce could be carried on.

The second group of factors comprised unity of political belief (since by that time the people believed in republican principles); unity in the sacrifices of the War of Independence (since all the provinces had shed blood and suffered common sacrifices and sorrows in this enterprise); unity in the conduct and efforts in the War of Independence; the different pacts entered into between the provinces and foreign countries (of which the most important one was the Declaration of Independence since in this act all the provinces acted as a united nation); the general congresses, directories, and presidencies during the revolution and after it; the diplomatic union in international affairs as established in the treaties with Brazil, England and France; the unity of glory and reputation in the symbolic colors of the flag of the Argentine Republic, and of the coat of arms of the nation; and finally, the implied and intuitive unity increasingly revealed in the unconscious expressions of the people—Argentine Republic, Argentine territory, Argentine people, instead of Republic of San Juan, nation of Buenos Aires, or state of Santa Fe.

CONSTITUTIONAL EXPERIMENTS FROM 1811 TO 1826

From 1811 to 1826 Argentina passed through a period of constitutional experimentation. Several constitutions embodying the political and constitutional principles of the revolution were tried out. The influence of the French constitutional organization of the epoch was reflected in the measures of 1811, 1815, and 1817, which established a unicameral legislature and a plural executive; but the constitutions of 1819 and 1826 reflected more strongly the influence of the Constitution of the United States, especially in the establishment of the single executive, the bicameral legislature, and the independent judicial system.[15] Although some of these constitutions were of short duration because of political intrigue and revolution, and others were never put into operation for the same reasons, they unquestionably were antecedents of the Constitution of 1853 since many of their principles and provisions were later incorporated into that Constitution.

The Organic Regulations of 1811

The first revolutionary government of Argentina adopted the first constitution of the nation on October 22, 1811. This constitution was based upon the principle of separation of powers for it provided for the determination of the powers, prerogatives, and duties of the legislative, executive, and judicial departments of government. The legislative power was vested in a junta or committee called Junta Conservadora, composed of the deputies of the province of Buenos Aires and of the other provinces. This committee was given power to declare war, make peace and treaties, impose taxes, create courts of justice, and appoint the members of the executive power in case of death or resignation.

The instrument created a plural executive of three members called the Triumvirate, with the power to defend the state, to organize armies, to collect taxes, to enforce the laws, to appoint and remove civil and military employees and their secretaries and to try them for their public conduct. The executive was, however, prohibited from exercising judicial functions; these were vested in the courts. The judicial department was made independent of other departments; it had power to apply the general laws, municipal ordi-

[15] The influence of the Constitution of the United States was also reflected in four drafts of constitutions which were either not submitted or not approved. One was drawn up by a committee appointed by the Triumvirate, and another by a patriotic society; the other two were written by unknown authors. These were complete constitutional documents containing specific provisions embodied in the Constitution of the United States—especially one of these whose authors were unknown, half of which was based directly on the Articles of Confederation and the Constitution. For the texts of these constitutions, see *Asambleas constituyentes argentinas*, Vol. V, part 2, pp. 623–38.

nances, and proclamations, and also to try persons accused of crime.

The Organic Regulations of 1811, unlike other constitutions of later date, contained no detailed bill of rights, but it did contain a general declaration which constituted a sweeping guarantee of individual rights. This declaration provided that the powers of the Conservative Board [16] should be exercised only if not opposed to the supreme right of the civil liberties of the Argentine people. Regarding this provision Varela has said that it proves that Dean Funes, who drafted the document and who had translated into Spanish many foreign books on public law, was imbued with the principles of Magna Carta, upon which were based the civil liberties of the English people.[17]

The Provisional Statute of 1811

By a political coup d'état the former constitution was, just a month after its adoption, changed by the Provisional Statute of 1811. This new instrument provided for the establishment of a general assembly composed of the cabildo of Buenos Aires, representatives of the provinces, and a number of citizens elected by the city of Buenos Aires according to the rules prescribed by the executive branch of the government. According to the Provisional Statute, the executive could not decide any matter affecting the liberty and the existence of the provinces without the express agreement of the general assembly. But according to a decree issued by the executive, the assembly could be convoked by the executive power only twice a year, could treat only those matters submitted to it by the executive, and could remain in session only eight days unless prorogued by the executive.

The executive power under this new Provisional Statute was exercised by a Triumvirate elected by the assembly. The judicial power continued to be exercised by the established courts as under the Organic Regulations of 1811, except that the Triumvirate possessed appellate jurisdiction—thus violating the principle of separation of powers which was one of the basic principles of the Organic Regulations of 1811.

The Provisional Statute did not contain any bill of rights, but it

[16] The Conservative Board exercised the legislative functions of government.
[17] L. V. Varela, *op. cit.*, II, 26.

provided that the liberties of the individual and of the press should be protected by decree issued by the government, which decree should become a part of the statute. On November 23, 1811, the Triumvirate issued an important decree establishing the guarantees of personal liberty, many of which were later incorporated into the Constitutions of 1819, 1826, and 1853.

The Provisional Statute of 1815

As a result of another revolution the third constitution of Argentina became effective on May 5, 1815. This document, which was called the Provisional Statute of 1815, did not constitute a fundamental departure from the former provisional constitutions but it had many interesting new features. Besides being the fundamental law of the nation it was also a code of public and private morals. For example, it provided that every man must obey the law and perform the following duties: to contribute to the maintenance and conservation of the rights of other citizens and the public happiness of the state; to offer all sacrifices on behalf of the country, even the sacrifice of his life; to be worthy of being called a good man, father, brother, son, and friend. At the same time it provided that the state owed the following duties to the members of the body politic: to guarantee the enjoyment of the rights of man; to alleviate the misery and distress of the citizens and to supply them with the means of becoming prosperous and of instructing themselves. All acts and regulations promulgated by the state in violation of these rights were to be of no effect.

The Provisional Statute of 1815 provided that the legislative power resided originally in the people, and that until the national congress of the provinces was held the power would be exercised by the Board of Observation. Unlike the former constitutions, which provided that the executive power should be exercised by a Triumvirate, this statute provided that this function should be exercised by a person called the Director of the State, who should be at least thirty-five years of age, and should be elected according to regulations to be drafted. The Statute created three secretaries of state to assist the executive. It also defined the powers of the executive as well as the limitations imposed on the exercise thereof. The Statute further provided that the judicial power should be exercised by the courts then in existence. The judges were to be appointed by the Director of the State on the recommendation of the bar associations of the towns in which the courts were located. It also continued the decrees of October 26, 1811, guaranteeing the freedom of the press, and of November 23, 1811, guaranteeing the rights of personal liberty and security.

This constitution had a marked federalist tendency. For the first time the provinces were granted the power to elect their governors and fix their salaries. But the lieutenant governors of the provinces were appointed by the Director of the State on the recommendation of the municipalities in which they resided.

The Provisional Regulations of 1817

The Provisional Statute of 1815 was supplanted by another constitution called the Provisional Regulations, adopted on December 3, 1817. This document, practically a reproduction of the former constitution, was of a unitary tendency, since it provided that the governments of the provinces were to be appointed by the Director of the State.

The Constitution of 1819

The fifth constitution of Argentina, adopted on April 20, 1819, was a landmark in Argentine history since, unlike the former experiments it was not of a fragmentary nature but rather a thoroughly finished document. Although this constitution did not adopt a federal system of government, the influence of the Constitution of the United States is reflected not only in many of its provisions but also in the report of the committee which drafted it. This committee stated that in drafting the Constitution they had made use of the experience of the constitutions of England and the United States and that they had adopted from those constitutions, which they believed to be models worthy of imitation by all free people, such principles as could be adapted to the peculiar conditions of Argentina.[18]

This constitution, like that of the United States, provided that the legislative power should be exercised by a national congress composed of two houses. The principle that the representation of

[18] *Asambleas constituyentes argentinas,* I, 369.

the lower house should be based on population was incorporated. Also the principle that the state should be represented in the Senate was embodied therein. However, the document differed from the Constitution of the United States in that the Senate included representatives of the army, the church, and the universities, and the Director of the State whose term had expired. The Senate, like that of the United States, had the power to try impeachments, a two-thirds vote being required to convict. The judgment of the Senate extended merely to removal from office and ineligibility to occupy a position in the government.

The constitution vested in Congress the following powers: to enact the laws to be enforced within the territory of the nation; to declare war and make peace; to levy duties and, for a term not exceeding two years, to levy uniform taxes for the necessities of the state; to fix, on the recommendation of the executive, the size of the military and naval forces in time of war and peace and to determine the number of troops necessary in the place where Congress held its sessions; to provide and maintain a navy; to borrow money on the credit of the state; to regulate the form of trials and to establish courts inferior to the supreme court; to create and eliminate offices of all kinds; to regulate domestic and foreign commerce; to demarcate the boundaries of the provinces; to establish new ports on the coast of the nation whenever Congress should consider it expedient; to make uniform plans for public education and to provide the means for sustaining the schools; to receive annually from the executive an accounting of the public expenditures and to examine them and determine their validity; to coin money, regulate its value, and fix the standard of weights and measures; to secure for limited periods to authors and inventors the exclusive rights to their respective writings and discoveries.

As to the executive power, the constitution provided that it should be vested in a person called the Director of the State, elected for a term of five years by both houses of Congress in joint session. He was granted the following powers, many of which were based on similar powers granted to the President of the United States: to act as commander in chief of the army and the navy; to publish and execute the laws enacted by Congress; to open the sessions of Congress and inform it as to the state of the union, recommending such measures as he might judge necessary and expedient; to propose in writing bills and other necessary measures to Congress; to convoke Congress in extraordinary session during the recess of the same when the public interest required it; to declare war and make peace and direct the army for the defense of the state; to repulse foreign invasions, repress conspiracy, and suppress public riots; to appoint officers of the army and navy, ambassadors, public ministers, and consuls, and to receive those from foreign nations; to appoint and remove his ministers; to make treaties with foreign nations, with the advice and consent of the Senate, except treaties which would cede part of the territory of the nation, in which case the consent of two-thirds of the members of the House was required; to issue naturalization certificates, subject to the provisions of law; to appoint all officers of the government whose appointments were not otherwise provided for by the constitution or the laws; to pardon or reprieve sentences of capital punishment, after obtaining a report from the sentencing tribunal; and to confirm or reverse, subject to military regulations, sentences imposed on military and naval officers.

The judicial power was vested in a high court of justice composed of seven judges and two attorneys general appointed by the Director of the State with the advice and consent of the Senate. The members of the court were to hold office during good behavior and were to receive a compensation which could not be diminished by law during their continuance in office. The Supreme Court was granted original jurisdiction in cases concerning ambassadors, foreign ministers and consuls, in cases in which one or more provinces were a party, in cases between cities of different provinces concerning territorial limits, in cases based on contracts entered into by the government with other parties, and finally, in cases involving officers who were impeached by Congress. It also had appellate jurisdiction in cases based on treaties, on crimes committed against the law of nations, and in all other cases of appeal from the decisions of the courts created by Congress as might be provided by law.

One of the most interesting sections is that comprising the declarations of the rights guaranteed in the Constitution. This section divided rights into those of the nation and those of individuals. One of the rights of the nation was to amend the Constitution whenever the common interest of the Republic required it, according to the forms prescribed in the Constitution. The Constitution could be amended by ordinary legislative action, except that a two-thirds vote was required. The section dealing with the rights of the nation also provided that no officer or agency of the nation was above the law and that the officer or agency ordered, judged, or governed only according to the law. It provided, finally, that the nation delegated the power of sovereignty to the authorities to the end that the legislative department could not encroach on the powers of the executive or the judiciary, nor the executive encroach on the powers of the legislative, nor the judiciary encroach on the powers of the other two.

The rights guaranteed to the individual citizen included all civil rights relating to life, liberty, and property. The guarantee of trial by jury, unlike the provision in previous constitutional experiments, was not absolute; it gave discretion to Congress to establish trial by jury when the circumstances permitted.

The Constitution of 1826

The Constitution of 1819 never went into effect. The *caudillos* or political leaders of the provinces of Entre Ríos and Santa Fe defeated the troops of the national government in the battle of Cepeda on February 1, 1820, and Congress was dissolved. Then the province of Buenos Aires took the initiative in inviting the provinces to a national convention to draft a permanent constitution. The provinces responded to the call and sent delegates. The convention met at Buenos Aires on December 16, 1824, and on December 24, 1826, a constitution was drafted.

The influence of the Constitution of the United States is reflected not only in several of the provisions of this constitution, but also in the debates in the convention. While in the national convention of 1813 only one reference was made to the political institutions of the United States, and only four in the convention which drafted the Constitution of 1819, in this convention there were fifty such references. This constitution, unlike that of 1819 and the Constitution of the United States, declared expressly the form of government it intended to establish, namely, a representative republican form. And to assure that the form of government would be republican it further provided that the Argentine nation should never become the patrimony of any person or family. Like the former experiments, this one enunciated the principles of the separation of powers and limited government when it provided that the nation delegate its sovereignty to the three departments of government—legislative, executive, and judicial—under the restrictions expressed in the Constitution.

The legislative department consisted of two chambers, one of senators and the other of representatives. The members of the lower house were directly elected by a plurality of votes by the people of the provinces. It was composed of one representative for every fifteen thousand inhabitants elected for a four-year term, one-half of its membership being renewed every two years. Each province, and the federal capital, was entitled to one senator, elected by an electoral college somewhat similar to that used in electing the President of the United States.

As under the Constitution of the United States, Congress was vested with enumerated powers. The executive power was vested in a person called the President, to be elected by an electoral college similar to that used for electing the President of the United States. The President was granted extensive legislative, executive, and administrative powers. The judicial power was vested in a high court of justice composed of nine judges and two attorneys general. The members of the court were to be appointed by the President with the advice and consent of the Senate, were to hold office during good behavior, and were to receive compensation which could not be diminished during their continuance in office. The Supreme Court, like that of the United States, was vested with two types of jurisdiction, original and appellate. The original jurisdiction extended to cases in which a province was a party, cases between two or more provinces, cases between towns of different provinces relating to territorial limits, contract cases in which the government was a party, criminal cases in which persons impeached by Congress were accused, and cases concerning ambassadors, public ministers, and consuls. The appellate jurisdiction comprised cases appealed from the lower courts and dealing with admiralty and maritime jurisdiction, crimes against the law of nations, ecclesiastical cases, and other cases as provided by law.

This constitution, although not a federal one because the provinces were not autonomous entities but merely administrative divisions of the national government, nevertheless recognized a certain degree of self-government in the provinces and contained several provisions concerning their organization and functioning. The executive power of each province was vested in a governor appointed by the President of the Republic. He was empowered to enforce the national laws in the province as well as the regulations enacted by the council of administration of the province, and he had power to appoint employees to positions created by the same council. The legislative power of the province was vested in a council of administration elected by the people in the same manner as the members of Congress. This council had power to legislate on matters relating to police, primary education, public works, local taxes, budgets, and all matters of local concern. The judicial power was to be exercised by a superior tribunal and inferior courts to be created by law and vested with criminal, civil, and administrative jurisdiction.

The bill of rights of this constitution, included in a section called "General Dispositions," contained provisions guaranteeing all civil rights relating to the life, liberty, and property of the individual. The constitution could be amended by the ordinary process of legislation but only on a three-fourths vote of Congress. This constitution was rejected by the provinces on the ground that it deprived them of their powers and prerogatives as autonomous bodies. Thus ended the last attempt at constitutional government in Argentina until the calling of the Constitutional Convention at Santa Fe in 1852.

THE PERIOD OF CONFEDERATION

The Constitution of 1826 having been rejected, the provinces entered into a period which ended in 1851 and which has been called by the Argentine historians the Period of the Confederation. During this period the different provinces lived an autonomous institutional life. However, unlike the period of confederation in the United States during which a national Congress represented the states, in Argentina there was no political power to act in behalf of the provinces, with the exception of the governor of Buenos Aires, who represented the provinces in their relations with foreign nations. In 1832 the Committee of the provinces entrusted the management of their foreign relations to General Juan Manuel de Rosas, governor of the province of Buenos Aires. He held this position until 1852, when at the battle of Monte Caseros he was overthrown by a revolutionary army led by General Urquiza.

Urquiza's Pronunciamento

From 1831 to 1852 Rosas, governor of Buenos Aires and director of foreign relations of the Confederation, ruled with a strong hand not only the province of Buenos Aires but also the other provinces of the Confederation, through his political henchmen who were either governors of the provinces or prominent political leaders. Argentine historians have called the period of Rosas' rule the Period of Confederation and Dictatorship. Nevertheless under his rule the federalist tendency grew stronger and stronger, because the provinces became practically self-governing entities and developed, although slowly, the constitutional machinery of self-governing units of a future federal state.

Even under the Rosas dictatorship the idea of convoking a national convention for the purpose of establishing a national constitution prevailed among Argentine political leaders. As early as 1834 Facundo Quiroga, a provincial political leader, suggested the calling of a constitutional convention for organizing the nation. He was not able to achieve this aim; he was assassinated. In 1846 the governor of Entre Ríos, General Justo José de Urquiza, and Madariaga, the governor of the province of Corrientes, also suggested the necessity of reorganizing the nation under a federal government. This plan was disapproved by Rosas on the ground that the country was not prepared to take such a step.

Governor Rosas was charged by his political opponents with obstructing the establishment of a constitution for the nation, as such action on his part would have meant the end of his political and personal dictatorship. On May 1, 1851, General Urquiza, acting as governor of Entre Ríos, made his epoch-making pronunciamento against Rosas. In this declaration he stated that the province of Entre Ríos would resume the sovereign authority which it had delegated to Governor Rosas as director of foreign affairs of the Confederation, and having done so, would deal directly with its sister provinces until the calling of a national convention for the purpose of organizing the Republic. Immediately other provinces followed the example of Entre Ríos.

After Urquiza's public declaration the province of Entre Ríos made a military alliance with the Republic of Uruguay and the Kingdom of Brazil to overthrow Rosas and to obtain the independence of Uruguay. The military forces of Rosas and those led by General Urquiza clashed in the battle of Monte Caseros on February 3, 1852. Rosas' army was defeated, and Rosas took refuge in the British Embassy at Buenos Aires. He later went into exile in England.

The Meeting at Palermo

After the defeat of Rosas, General Urquiza called a meeting of the governors of Buenos Aires, Corrientes, and Santa Fe, which assembled at Palermo, in the city of Buenos Aires, for the purpose of discussing the necessity of organizing the nation in conformity with the former treaties between the provinces and with the laws of the Confederation. General Urquiza was appointed director of foreign affairs by the three above-mentioned provinces until the nation should be organized.

II: THE MAKING OF THE CONSTITUTION OF 1853

AFTER the meeting of Palermo, General Urquiza, acting in his capacity of director of foreign affairs of the Argentine Confederation, sent a message on April 8, 1852, to the governors of the different provinces. In this he asked them to attend a meeting in the town of San Nicolás de los Arroyos, in the province of Buenos Aires, on May 20, 1852. The purpose was to discuss the calling of an Argentine constitutional convention, as provided by the Federal Pact of 1831. By this step General Urquiza not only refuted the claim of his political enemies that he wanted to become a dictator like Rosas but also made possible the creation of a national constitution for Argentina, for he took counsel with the governors of the provinces who had rejected the constitutions drafted in 1819 and 1826. The governors of twelve provinces [1] attended the meeting and signed the document which is known in Argentine constitutional history as the Agreement of San Nicolás. This agreement unquestionably was one of the documents which laid the foundations of the Argentine governmental system.

THE AGREEMENT OF SAN NICOLÁS

The most important provisions of this historic document were as follows: The Federal Pact of 1831 was recognized as the basis for the constitutional organization of the Republic, and a constitutional convention was to be called in order to organize a federal system of government, as provided in that Pact. This constitutional convention was to be held in August, 1852, and its delegates were to be elected in the same manner as the members of the provincial legislatures, with each province entitled to two delegates. A majority of the votes of these delegates would suffice for the adoption

[1] The representatives of the provinces of Salta and Jujuy who had not attended the meeting at San Nicolás signed the agreement on July 1, 1852. J. González Calderón, *Historia de la organización constitucional,* p. 225.

of the constitution. The governors of the provinces obligated themselves to use every lawful means for securing the election of men imbued with patriotism and probity. The city of Santa Fe, capital of the province of the same name, was designated as the place of the convention. The constitution, once adopted, was to be sent to the provisional executive power, who would proclaim the same, with such organic laws as would be necessary for its enforcement. The convention would then elect the first president and would adjourn. Pending the election of the president, the land and naval forces would be placed at the disposal of General Urquiza, who during this period was to represent the national sovereignty and act as director of foreign affairs. The provisional executive was also empowered to form a council of state to assist him in the management of foreign affairs. The director of foreign affairs would receive the title Provisional Director of the Argentine Confederation.

THE CONSTITUTIONAL CONVENTION OF 1852–53

The men who attended the Convention of Santa Fe, like the men who attended the Philadelphia Convention of 1787 and drafted the United States Constitution, were among the ablest of the nation and represented all walks of life. An Argentine historian has thus described them:

> The men who were elected as delegates to the constitutional convention were intelligent citizens of discreet conduct. Among them were jurists, writers, economists, statesmen, ecclesiastics, former judges, politicians, and businessmen. All walks of life were represented in the constitutional convention except the army which had never been absent from other conventions. The work to be done was purely a civil one, and in such a task men who are accustomed to command are out of place. Each province sent two delegates, who brought with them to Santa Fe the fervent desires of the people they represented. All of them, regardless of their political beliefs, were in favor of a federal system of government.[2]

The delegates who attended the convention and the provinces they represented were: from Catamarca, Pedro Centeno and Pedro Ferré; from Córdoba, Juan del Campillo and Santiago Derqui; from Corrientes, Luciano Torrent and Pedro Díaz Colodrero; from Entre Ríos, Ruperto Pérez and Juan María Gutiérrez; from Jujuy,

[2] J. B. Lafont, *Historia de la constitución argentina*, II, 259.

Manuel Padilla and José de la Quintana; from La Rioja, Regis Martínez; from Mendoza, Agustín Delgado and Martín Zapata; from Salta, Facundo Zuviría; from San Luis, Delfín Huergo and Juan Llerena; from San Juan, Ruperto Godoy and Salvador del Carril; from Santa Fe, Juan F. Seguí and Manuel Leiba; from Santiago del Estero, José B. Gorostiaga and Benjamín Lavaisse; and finally, from Tucumán, Salustiano Zavalía and Fray José Manuel Pérez. As the province of Buenos Aires had rejected the Agreement of San Nicolás it did not send any representatives to the convention.

Although it was provided in the Agreement of San Nicolás that the convention should meet in August, 1852, difficulties in the selection of the delegates and poor means of communication delayed its start until November; on the fifteenth day of that month the first preliminary session was held. The convention elected as provisional president Fray José Manuel Pérez, the oldest member of the convention, and as secretary Delfín Huergo, the youngest member.

The first step taken by the provisional president was to appoint a committee to examine the credentials of the delegates and a second committee to examine the credentials of the members of the first committee. On November 16, the committees submitted their reports, which were approved by the convention. On the same day a committee was appointed to draft an oath to be taken by the members of the convention, and on November 18 the draft was made and approved by the convention. On the same date the convention elected as permanent president Facundo Zuviría, as vice-president Manuel Leiba, and as secretaries Juan Francisco Seguí and Delfín Huergo. The convention held its last preparatory session on November 19. The President informed the convention that he had received a communication from the governor of the province of Entre Ríos stating that he had been authorized by General Urquiza to represent him in the inauguration.

On November 20, 1852,[3] after the delegates took the oath approved by the convention, the National Congress of Santa Fe was officially inaugurated. Immediately thereafter Governor Domingo Crespo of Entre Ríos entered the convention, accompanied by Dr. Luis J. de la Peña, provisional minister of foreign affairs, who was

[3] General Urquiza had provided by decree that the convention should be inaugurated on that date.

to read General Urquiza's message to the convention. In his message General Urquiza referred to the events which had led to the calling of the convention and encouraged the members to finish the task which had been entrusted to them:

Delegates of this convention, the time has come for you to make use of the lessons of our history and draft a constitution which will make impossible the existence of anarchism and despotism in this country. Both monsters have devoured our national life. The first one has caused us to shed blood, the other one has disgraced us. May the grace of God and devotion to our country enlighten you.[4]

Immediately after Dr. de la Peña finished reading General Urquiza's address President Zuviría delivered a speech answering it. In his speech the president of the convention encouraged General Urquiza to continue his work on behalf of the union of the Argentine people. Then he said:

The constitutional convention which you have just inaugurated will not betray the cause which has been entrusted to it by the people. This convention will be loyal to the glory of the hero of Caseros [5] and it will not dim it nor permit it to be dimmed by injustice, slander, or ingratitude, because it is a national glory which has been entrusted to us by the suffrage of the people.[6]

On December 24, 1852, the convention appointed a Committee on Constitutional Affairs to prepare a draft constitution. It was composed of Pedro Díaz Colodrero, Manuel Leiba, Juan del Campillo, Pedro Ferré, Martín Zapata, Juan María Gutiérrez and José Benjamín Gorostiaga. The Committee rendered its report to the convention on April 18, 1853. Delegates Gutiérrez and Gorostiaga, who in the Santa Fe Convention played roles similar to those of Hamilton and Madison in the Philadelphia Convention, defended the committee's report. Unlike the Philadelphia Convention, where rival plans were presented, one by the larger states and another by the smaller states, the Convention of Santa Fe was confronted with no antagonistic plans.

Two fundamental problems were before the Santa Fe Conven-

[4] E. A. Ibarra, *Congreso constituyente de 1852*, p. 18.

[5] General Urquiza is called the "hero of Caseros" because of his victory over the army of Rosas in the battle of Monte Caseros.

[6] E. A. Ibarra, *op. cit.*, p. 21.

tion: first, whether it should draft a federal constitution as provided in the Agreement of San Nicolás, and second, whether it should approve or reject the draft constitution submitted by the Committee on Constitutional Affairs. As to the first, the convention was almost unanimous in favor of adopting a federal constitution. A small minority argued that the occasion was not the proper one for adopting the proposed constitution. President Zuviría voiced the opinion of this minority in a speech which was read to the convention.[7] Delegate Gutiérrez, replying to President Zuviría, refuted the thesis that the constitution should not be drafted at that time. He said that if, as was argued, the country was in chaos, the constitution presented the only means to save it, that the people were eagerly demanding the establishment of a constitution because they saw in it their salvation, and that to defer its establishment would constitute an action he would not dare to call by its right name.[8]

As to the second problem, the convention approved in principle and with unimportant amendments the draft constitution which the committee brought in. In its report the committee gave a brief outline of the proposed system of government. The main provisions of the report were: The constitution would establish a federal system of government according to the provisions of the Agreement of San Nicolás and of the Federal Pact of 1831. Under this system the provinces would preserve their sovereignty and independence, and would be governed by their own institutions and elect their legislatures and governors freely by the votes of their inhabitants. Besides the provincial governments there would be a central government which would represent the provinces in their foreign relations and would exercise all the powers of the provinces in matters relating to their general welfare. The report also explained that the central government would be divided into three departments, namely, the legislative, the executive, and the judicial, which would exercise the powers granted to them by the constitution. Finally the report explained that the constitution would establish certain rights and guarantees in behalf of the citizens and inhabitants which would constitute at the same time limitations on the powers of the national government.

[7] *Asambleas constituyentes argentinas,* IV, 470.
[8] *Ibid.,* p. 479.

Sources of the Constitution

What were the sources drawn upon by the authors of the Argentine Constitution? It is interesting to know that the framers of both the Argentine and the United States Constitutions were influenced by the same social and political principles. In discussing this question, a distinguished Argentine legal scholar has said that the spiritual influences were the same because through Montesquieu, who was the indirect legislator of the United States, the legislators of that country and of Argentina conceived the principle of the separation of powers.[9] He also said that the ideas of liberty and democracy expounded by Rousseau influenced the political ethics of the United States, as they did the revolutionary leaders of Argentina and the men who drafted the Argentine Constitution.

The Founding Fathers of the Argentine Constitution, like those of the United States, drew upon two different kinds of sources in drafting their respective constitutions, namely, national and foreign. The foreign sources which the makers of the United States Constitution followed were English. As to the national sources, the makers of the United States Constitution were influenced by the principles and precedents of constitutional government embodied in the colonial constitutions. These, although based originally upon English constitutional principles, were modified by the peculiar political, social, and economic conditions prevailing in the colonies to such an extent that they became quite different from the early English sources.[10]

The members of the Convention of Santa Fe were also influenced by the legislative and constitutional sources discussed in the previous chapter dealing with the constitutional attempts before the Constitution of 1853. Other sources were two drafts of a constitution prepared by Juan Bautista Alberdi and Pedro de Angelis.[11] This is especially true of the draft prepared by the first author, which had a profound and definite influence on the Argentine Constitution. A well-known Argentine student of the life of Al-

[9] R. Bielsa, *La protección constitucional y el recurso extraordinario*, pp. 141–42.

[10] For a discussion of the sources of the United States Constitution considered in relation to colonial and English history, see C. E. Stevens, *Sources of the Constitution of the United States*, 2d ed., London, 1927.

[11] J. González Calderón, "El setenta y cinco aniversario de la constitución argentina," in *Doctrina Constitucional*, p. 41.

berdi has said that his books [12] are to Argentine law what the works of Blackstone and Kent are, respectively, to English and to American law.[13] And another student of Argentina's political institutions has said that Alberdi's writings constitute a remarkable example of the application of the scientific method to the study of social, economic, political, and legal problems.[14]

The role played by Alberdi's *Bases* in the convention is described by an Argentine historian [15] who lived in the period when the constitution was drafted:

Delegate Gutiérrez, during the preparatory sessions of the Convention, had seen and looked over, in the office of the secretary of the Convention, a copy of *The Federalist,* by Hamilton, which belonged to Rivera Indarte, but when the moment came to draft the Constitution the book had disappeared. The loss of such a book was considered irreparable in Santa Fe. Then the delegates to the convention learned of the existence of Dr. Alberdi's book *Bases and Points of Departure for the Political Organization of the Argentine Republic,* and the reading of that scholarly, philosophical, and practical book fixed the path to be followed in drafting the constitution. Everyone then considered the constitutional organization of the republic feasible. Many delegates were anxious to introduce constitutional projects which would have caused much jealousy and discussion and would in practice have resulted in dissension among the members of the convention, due chiefly to literary jealousy and conflicting ideology. The happy suggestion of Delegate Gutiérrez prevented this when he petitioned the convention to request Dr. Alberdi for a project of constitution adapted from his book *Bases and Points of Departure for the Political Organization of the Argentine Republic.* Dr. Alberdi did not delay in sending to the convention a second edition of his book, together with a project which was to guide the committee in charge of drawing up the constitution. The convention began immediately to discuss the framing of the constitution, a task which took them more than four months. The committee ap-

12 *Bases y puntos de partida para la organización política de la República argentina* (*Bases and Points of Departure for the Political Organization of the Argentine Republic*); *Estudios sobre la constitución argentina* (*Studies on the Argentine Constitution*); *La República Argentina consolidada* (*The Unified Argentine Republic*); *Derecho público provincial argentino* (*Argentine Provincial Public Law*); *El gobierno en Sud-América* (*South American Government*); *El sistema económico y rentístico de la Confederación Argentina* (*The Economic and Financial System of the Argentine Confederation*), in which the author explains what should be the economic and financial foundations of the government he proposed in his *Bases.*

13 M. García Merou, *Alberdi; ensayo crítico,* p. 23.

14 J. N. Matienzo, *Juan Bautista Alberdi,* p. 10.

15 M. A. Pelliza, *Historia de la organización nacional,* pp. 67 and 68.

pointed to the task followed Alberdi's project, modifying certain details and altering the order of some of the articles. The committee also modified the wording of the project, not to improve it but to eliminate a certain academic style which was spontaneous in Alberdi but which would have been of no practical value to the future interpreters of the constitution.[16]

In his *Bases* Alberdi expounded three main ideas concerning the constitutional organization of the Argentine nation. First, he said that the powers of the delegates to the convention should be extensive and without limitations in order that they might accomplish effectively the task that had been entrusted to them. If their task was to draft a constitution it had to be left to their discretion to determine what should be the form of the constitution.[17]

In the second place, he strongly condemned the extreme radical views of the old federalist and unitary political parties, whose antagonism had previously prevented the constitutional organization of the Republic. After stating that the federalist and the unitary tendencies should be harmonized in order to reach a satisfactory solution of the Argentine constitutional problem, he said:

> Fortunately, events have led us to the solution of our constitutional problem by the adoption of an intermediate position between a pure federal and a pure unitary system of government. This solution represents peace between the provinces and the nation, between the part and the whole, and finally, between localism and the idea of the creation of the Argentine Republic. Thus, our form of government will be a mixed one representing a compromise between federalism and unitarism, and based upon the unity of the nation. But unlike that form prescribed by the Constitution of 1826, this system will be divided into provincial governments with limitations imposed upon them by the federal constitution, as is provided in the case of the central government.[18]

In order to make feasible the establishment of the constitutional scheme which he proposed, Alberdi suggested that the convention adopt the constitutional mechanism of the United States, making

16 Professor González Calderón has said that the Constitution of 1853 is far superior to Alberdi's project. He has also stated that the convention rejected several formulas and suggestions of the illustrious writer because they were neither adequate nor convenient. "El setenta y cinco aniversario de la constitución argentina," in *Doctrina constitucional*, p. 39.

17 J. B. Alberdi, *Bases*, pp. 52–54.

18 *Ibid.*, pp. 138–39.

such changes as might be necessary in order to adapt it to Argentina. In advocating this, he said:

The mechanism of the general government of the United States offers us an idea of how to make practicable the association of the principles upon which the organization of the national government should be based. In that country, as in ours, the unitarian and federal tendencies fought for the control of the national government, and the necessity to consolidate them in a mixed system of government suggested to them the idea of creating a mechanism which may be applied to similar situations, with the modifications required by the special circumstances of each case. The discreet assimilation of a system when it is adaptable to analogous circumstances does not mean that it has been servilely copied. . . . The establishment of the mixed system of government which we propose will be made effective by the division of the legislative department into two chambers: one representing the provinces as sovereign entities, the members of which will be elected by the provincial legislatures; the other representing the people of the republic in general as if the provinces formed a single Argentine state. In the first chamber the provinces will have equal representation and in the other they will be represented according to population.[19]

In the third place, Alberdi contended that the prevailing constitutional law of Argentina and of South America in general was opposed to the material and moral progress of the people. Throughout his work he pleaded for the establishment of a constitutional system which would foster the economic, intellectual, and moral progress of the nation. In advocating such a constitutional system he presented as an example the constitution of the state of California adopted in 1849.

I am fortunate in being able to cite, in behalf of the constitutional system which I propose, the last constitution of California which is the confirmation of our constitutional bases. The constitution of the new state of California, approved in Monterey on October 12, 1849, by a convention of delegates elected by the people of California, is an example of how the constitutional law now prevailing in the United States was applied to the government of a new state when admitted into the Union. . . . Five years prior to the adoption of the constitution there were excluded from the territory of California non-Catholics, foreigners, and all commercial enterprises. Under the republican regime of Spanish-America there was only isolation and poverty in California until the

[19] *Ibid.*, pp. 143–44.

neighboring civilization, provoked by these unjustifiable exclusions and conditions, took possession of this territory and implanted upon its soil its institutions and laws, bringing the blessings of liberty to the people. In four years, a country which had been for three hundred years an obscure and miserable territory, became a state of the first republic of the world. The constitution of California represents the traditions of liberty of the United States and will make of the state of California a great country in a few years.[20]

For Alberdi the drafting of a constitution for Argentina was not only a scientific pursuit but also a patriotic and an apostolic mission. Through his writings one can feel his intense desire and passion for seeing Argentina a united and prosperous nation with a stable constitutional system. For this reason when writing his *Bases* he maintained a scientific and patriotic attitude and drafted a constitution based upon the historical and constitutional antecedents of Argentina as well as upon the most advanced principles of constitutional law prevailing in the period in which he wrote.[21]

The foreign sources which influenced the drafters of the Argentine Constitution were the Chilean Constitution of 1833, the Swiss Constitution of 1848, the Constitution of the United States, the German Confederation, and the French Constitution of 1791. But the political and constitutional institutions of the United States exercised a greater influence on the men of the Santa Fe Convention than any of the others mentioned. This influence was exercised directly and indirectly. The indirect influence was exercised through the constitutions of 1819 and 1826 in which many of the provisions of the Constitution of the United States were incorporated and also through Alberdi's *Bases,* which, as has been said, was influenced by the Constitution of the United States. The direct influence was exercised by the literature dealing with the Constitution of the United States with which the framers of the Argentine Constitution were acquainted independently of the writings of Alberdi.[22]

The influence of American political institutions on the framers of the Argentine Constitution is demonstrated by statements made

20 *Ibid.,* pp. 52–54.

21 *Ibid.,* pp. 145–46; C. A. Aldao, *Errores de la constitución nacional,* pp. 248, 249.

22 In 1811, Mr. Manuel García de Sena, a Venezuelan, published in Philadelphia a book entitled *La Independencia de la Costa Firme justificada por Tomás Paine treinta años ha: Extracto de sus obras* (*The Independence of Costa Firme Justified*

in the convention by the members of the committee which drafted the constitution, and by references to the Constitution of the United States when the different articles of the Argentine Constitution were discussed in the convention. Delegate Gorostiaga, who with Delegate Gutiérrez defended the report of the committee, said: "The Constitution of the Argentine Republic must be federal. The Committee has strictly observed this principle when organizing a national government for the republic, by leaving in existence the sovereignty and independence of the provinces. The project of this Constitution is modeled on that of the Constitution of the United States, the only model of a true federation existing in the world today." [23] And Gutiérrez said: "The Constitution is eminently federal, it is modeled on that of the United States, the only federation in the world which is worthy of being copied." [24]

Delegate Zavalía, when discussing the status of the provinces in

by Thomas Paine Thirty Years Ago: An Extract from his Works). This edition contained, first, a translation of *The Federalist;* second, a translation of Paine's book *Common Sense* and his dissertation *The Government and its Relation to Financial and Banking Affairs;* third, translations of the Declaration of Independence of the United States, the Articles of Confederation, the Constitution of 1789, and the constitutions of Massachusetts, Connecticut, New Jersey, and New Hampshire. In 1812 the same author also published in Philadelphia a Spanish translation of a book entitled *Historia concisa de los Estados Unidos desde el descubrimiento de la America Latina hasta el año 1807* (*A Concise History of the United States from the Discovery of Latin America to the Year 1807*). This book contained an explanation of the organization and functioning of the Philadelphia Convention, and a summary of the local and national institutions of the United States, as well as a comparative study of the constitutions of the various states in regard to the appointment and election of the different officers of government.

Other important books dealing with the political institutions of the United States which were known to the framers of the Argentine Constitution were: a Portuguese translation of *The Federalist* made in Rio Grande, Brazil, in 1835; a French translation of *The Federalist,* published in France in 1792, entitled *Le Fédéralist, ou Collection des quelques écrits en faveur de la constitution proposée aux Etats-Unis de l'Amérique par la convention convoquée en 1787;* a book, published in Philadelphia in 1778, dealing with the American colonies and the Articles of Confederation, entitled *Recueil des loix constitutives des colonies angloises confédérées sous la dénomination d'États-Unis d'Amérique septentrionale, . . . traduit par Regnier;* a Spanish translation of the work of de Tocqueville entitled *De la democratie en Amérique,* published and translated by Antonio Sánchez de Bustamante in Buenos Aires in 1837; and finally, a French translation of Justice Story's *Commentaries on the Constitution of the United States,* by Paul Odent, published in 1843. The information concerning this literature was obtained from J. González Calderón, "Como se hizo la constitución argentina," in *Estudios y dictámenes en derecho público,* pp. 25–55, and "El setenta y cinco aniversario de la constitución argentina," in *Doctrina constitucional,* pp. 39–43; C. A. Aldao, *Errores de la constitución nacional,* pp. 246–50.

[23] *Asambleas constituyentes argentinas,* IV, 468. [24] *Ibid.,* p. 479.

the federal system created by the proposed constitution, said that the centralizing features incorporated in the draft constitution are also found in the Constitution of the United States, the greatest model of all confederations, which the members of the committee followed when drafting the Constitution.[25] The president of the convention, closing the debates, said:

> The federation will be well comprehended if it is interpreted in the light of the federation of the United States, the best example of a federation in the civilized world. Neither the Helvetic nor the German confederation could be taken into consideration when drafting the Argentine Constitution in as much as the first one is artificial and permanently anarchical, and the second is a decrepit one under which so many abuses have been perpetrated.[26]

When different articles of the proposed constitution were discussed in the convention, constant reference was made to the Constitution of the United States. For example, it was noted that: the national government imposes the taxes on imports; [27] when a state is a party to a controversy the Supreme Court has original jurisdiction; [28] the Constitution of the United States does not specifically state what city shall be the capital of the republic; [29] in the United States there are two sovereignties, namely, national and state, exercising their powers within the same territory; [30] the governors of the states are not subject to impeachment by Congress; [31] the national government, not the state governments, has the power to coin money, and the states are expressly forbidden to exercise this power; [32] each state creates its own institutions and laws; [33] the codes of substantive law are enacted by the states and not by the national government.[34]

Other Functions of the Convention

The Convention of Santa Fe, unlike that of Philadelphia, besides adopting a constitution, also exercised legislative, executive, and electoral functions. This practice of having constitutional conventions exercise other than constituent powers has been a characteristic feature of Argentine public law since the early con-

[25] *Ibid.*, p. 520. [26] *Ibid.*, p. 539. [27] *Ibid.*, p. 502. [28] *Ibid.*, p. 521.
[29] *Ibid.*, p. 496. [30] *Ibid.*, p. 521. [31] *Ibid.*, p. 522. [32] *Ibid.*, p. 328.
[33] *Ibid.*, p. 528. [34] *Ibid.*, p. 529.

stitutional assemblies. Under the terms of the Agreement of San Nicolás the convention was authorized to enact the organic laws which were necessary for the enforcement of the Constitution. Thus, the convention, besides adopting the Constitution, enacted a statute organizing the municipality of the federal capital; [35] a national customs statute; [36] and a law organizing the finances and the public credit of the nation.[37] The convention also approved treaties made by the provisional executive of the Confederation with the United States and France.[38] Finally, on February 20, 1854, it counted the votes for the first president and vice-president of the Republic, namely, General Urquiza and Dr. del Carril.[39]

Adoption of the Constitution

On May 1, 1853, the members of the Constitutional Convention signed the new Constitution. The president of the convention made the following remarks: "On May 1, 1851, the Hero of Caseros terminated the era of terror and despotism in the nation. On May 1, 1853, we have terminated the epoch of anarchy by establishing the principles of law and order when adopting this constitution. May God permit that we shall be as successful in our task as the Hero of Caseros was in performing his." [40]

On May 5, 1853, the convention notified the provisional director of the Confederation that it had drafted the Constitution. In this communication the convention stated that it had decided that the Constitution should be presented for examination and approval to the province of Buenos Aires, which had not taken part in the convention. Together with the communication to the chief executive of the Confederation the convention sent to him the original copy of the Constitution signed by all the members as well as copies of the statutes it had enacted for the enforcement of the Constitution and of the decrees issued by the convention. The message finally said: "Sir, the Constitution of the Argentine Confederation has legalized your revolution. The Convention bestows upon you the glory of Washington, since there is no greater glory to which you can aspire." [41]

The Constitution adopted by the Convention of Santa Fe was

[35] *Ibid.*, p. 543. [36] *Ibid.*, p. 551. [37] *Ibid.*, p. 611. [38] *Ibid.*, p. 570.
[39] *Ibid.*, pp. 670–78. [40] *Ibid.*, p. 538. [41] *Ibid.*, pp. 548–49.

not submitted to provincial conventions for approval or rejection, as the Constitution of the United States was submitted to the conventions of the several states. The reason was that, according to the Agreement of San Nicolás, the Constitution was to become effective when approved by the convention and proclaimed by the provisional director of the Confederation. On May 25, 1853, the provisional director, by executive decree, ordered that the Constitution should become effective in all parts of the nation.

PROVINCIAL CONVENTION OF BUENOS AIRES OF 1860

In the United States the state of Rhode Island, the smallest in the Union, refused to ratify the Constitution of 1789. This fact did not affect fundamentally the strength and unity of the government established by the Constitution. But in Argentina the situation was different, because the province of Buenos Aires which did not become a part of the federation created by the Constitution of 1853, was the most important of the provinces in size and wealth. The Argentine nation could not become a strong and united republic without the province of Buenos Aires. There were no fundamental reasons why this province should not be a part of the Argentine federation with the exception of the political differences existing between the leaders of the province and those of the federation. The Convention of Santa Fe had appointed a committee to submit the Constitution to Buenos Aires and asked that it be examined and ratified;[42] but the authorities of the province refused to do so.

After several years of conflict and even of war between the federation and the province, Buenos Aires finally agreed to ratify the Constitution, subject to the provisions of a treaty signed by the province with the federal authorities on November 9, 1859, in the town of San José de Flores in the province of Buenos Aires. This treaty is one of the several pacts to which the preamble of the Constitution refers. It provides, among other things: that the province of Buenos Aires is declared to be an integral part of the Argentine Republic and will become a part of the same after ratifying the Constitution; that twenty days after the signing of the treaty the province will call a constitutional convention to ex-

[42] *Ibid.*, p. 548.

amine the Constitution; that if the provincial convention accepts the Constitution of 1853 without making any objection to it the province of Buenos Aires will ratify the Constitution on the date set forth by the convention; that in case the provincial convention proposes amendments to the Constitution the said amendments shall be submitted to the Congress of the federation in order that they may decide on the necessity of convoking an *ad hoc* national convention for the purpose of considering the amendments proposed by the provincial convention; that the province binds itself to send delegates to the said convention in proportion to its population and to accept what the national convention shall decide, except that its territory cannot be divided without the consent of its legislature.[43]

Amendments Proposed by Provincial Convention

Pursuant to the provisions of the Treaty of San José de Flores, the province of Buenos Aires held its constitutional convention in the city of Buenos Aires on January 5, 1860. The convention did not accept the Constitution of 1853; it appointed a committee to draft amendments which should be made. The committee was composed of Bartolomé Mitre, the great Argentine historian and political leader; Domingo Faustino Sarmiento, the Argentine educator and admirer of United States institutions; Dalmacio Vélez Sársfield, the most distinguished jurist at that time and later author of the Argentine Civil Code; José Mármol, one of the greatest poets of Argentina; and Antonio Cruz Obligado, one of the most prominent public men of the province of Buenos Aires.

Even to a greater extent than in the case of the Santa Fe Convention the Constitution of the United States influenced the men of the provincial convention of Buenos Aires.[44] As a matter of fact, the purpose of the reforms proposed by the committee was to incorporate in the Argentine Constitution those provisions of the Constitution of the United States which had not been considered

[43] *Ibid.*, Vol. VI, part 2, p. 562.

[44] While in the Santa Fe Convention only seventeen references were made to the Constitution of the United States and its political and economic history, in the provincial convention of Buenos Aires there were more than a hundred and sixty-eight. These references were made to demonstrate the necessity of adopting the provisions of the United States Constitution on the ground that the political and economic conditions prevailing in Argentina were similar to those in the United States.

at Santa Fe. This purpose was expressed by the committee in several parts of its report.

Since then [the Santa Fe Convention], the national government, which was modeled on that of the United States, has gone through a process of consolidation which reveals the deficiencies in those provisions in which the national Constitution departed from its model. At the same time the constitutional law of Buenos Aires, which was the expression of the provincial sovereignty and which had its roots in the constitutional antecedents of the province, has perfected itself through the influence of democratic ideas. The first fact proves that national peculiarities did not have a great influence in the organization of the federal republic, and that although it is true that the federation had been already established, nevertheless its present constitutional organization is exclusively based upon the Constitution of the United States, and therefore its antecedents must be traced prior to 1853. The second fact clearly shows that the only true national constitutional antecedents belong to the provincial governments. Therefore, the province of Buenos Aires, before becoming a part of the federation, should and ought to propose, as the general formula of reform, the reëstablishment of the text of the Constitution of the United States of North America, the only authoritative constitution in the world whose essence cannot be altered without violating the basic principles of federalism.[45]

The purpose of the reforms proposed by the committee was materialized when the convention, on the recommendation of the committee, approved thirty-four amendments to the national Constitution. Eighteen of these were based on provisions of the Constitution of the United States which were not originally embodied in the Constitution approved by the Santa Fe Convention. These eighteen amendments were: three to eliminate certain provisions under which the provincial constitutions were made subject to the approval of Congress before becoming effective; [46] one to repeal a provision which imposed upon the Provinces the duty of pro-

[45] In another part of its report the committee said: "The reforms formulated by the committee are based on the science and experience of the constitution which is most analogous to ours, namely, that of the United States. The committee bases its reforms on this constitution because it is the one most applicable to our political conditions, and because it is the model upon which the Constitution of the Confederation is based. Therefore the committee has appealed to its text, to its supplementary statutes and also to the doctrines interpreting it, when revising the Argentine Constitution because if the revision is not done in the light of such precedents many parts of the Argentine Constitution would have no meaning whatsoever." *Asambleas constituyentes argentinas,* IV, 769.

[46] These amendments were proposed in order to incorporate the principle of the Constitution of the United States under which the constitutions of the states are not

viding for free primary instruction; [47] one to eliminate a provision which authorized the federal government to intervene in the provinces without the request of the provincial authorities for the purpose of establishing the public order; [48] two to add new articles to the Bill of Rights to provide, respectively, that Congress shall have no power to dictate laws restricting the liberty of the press or establishing federal jurisdiction thereon,[49] and that the declarations, rights, and guarantees which the Constitution enumerates shall not be considered a denial of other rights and guarantees not enumerated but which arise from the principle of the sovereignty of the people and of the republican form of government; [50] one to provide that members of Congress must have three years of residence previous to their election in the provinces from which they are elected; [51] one to eliminate the requirement that the judges of the Supreme Court shall permanently reside in the federal capital; [52] two to provide for changes in the institution of impeachment, the first of which was to repeal the provision authorizing Congress to impeach the members of each house and the governors of the provinces, and the second to provide that Congress shall have the power to impeach civil officers for crimes and misdemeanors; [53] one to amend the amending procedure by providing that either

subject to the approval of Congress, except when a territory is admitted into the Union. *Ibid.*, pp. 773–74.

[47] This amendment was proposed because the former provision was considered an encroachment upon the self-government of the provinces. *Ibid.*, p. 773.

[48] The purpose of this amendment was to incorporate the provision of the Constitution of the United States under which the federal government cannot intervene in the states to restore the public order unless requested to do so by the state authorities. *Ibid.*, pp. 810–11.

[49] The purpose of this amendment was to incorporate the First Amendment of the Constitution of the United States which provides that Congress shall make no law abridging the freedom of speech or of the press. *Ibid.*, pp. 773–74.

[50] The object of this amendment was to embody the Ninth Amendment of the United States Constitution which provides that the enumeration in the Constitution of certain rights shall not be construed to deny or disparage others retained by the people. *Ibid.*, pp. 772, 841.

[51] This amendment was adopted in order to incorporate the provision of the United States Constitution which requires that senators and representatives must be inhabitants of the states from which they are elected. *Ibid.*, pp. 775, 971, 972.

[52] The object of this amendment was to eliminate this requirement in order that the Supreme Court judges could hear cases in the territory of the provinces as the judges of the Supreme Court of the United States did under the early circuit court statutes. *Ibid.*, pp. 775, 978, 979.

[53] This amendment was adopted in order to incorporate the impeachment provisions of Art. I, § 2 and § 3 of the United States Constitution. *Ibid.*, p. 778.

chamber of Congress and not the Senate alone shall have the power to propose amendments to the Constitution; [54] one providing that appointments made by the president during the recess of the Senate shall expire at the end of the next session of the legislature, so that the executive shall be compelled to submit them to the approval of the Senate; [55] one to amend the judiciary article of the Constitution so as to deprive the federal courts of the power to entertain jurisdiction in cases involving conflicts between the departments of government of the several provinces; [56] one to provide that Congress shall not, by any regulation of commerce or revenue, give preference to the ports of one province over those of another; [57] two to limit the taxing power of Congress by providing that tariff duties shall be uniform throughout the nation,[58] and that Congress shall not levy taxes on exports; [59] one to eliminate a provision which declared that the city of Buenos Aires shall be the capital of the Confederation and to provide instead that the authorities of the federal government shall reside in the city which is declared to be the capital by a special law of Congress, after cession made by one or more provincial legislatures of the territory to be federalized.[60]

The amendments adopted by the convention which had no relation to the Constitution of the United States were those providing: that slaves entering Argentine territory shall become free men;

[54] The committee said that the provision of the Article establishing the amending procedure was based on the theory that as the Senate represents the provinces this legislative body should propose the amendments, but that this was a false theory, because the act of amending the Constitution is a legislative act which in other countries, especially in the United States, is exercised by the people. *Ibid.*, p. 779.

[55] The convention adopted this amendment in order to incorporate a provision of the Constitution of the United States under which the recess appointments made by the president shall expire at the end of the next legislative session. Art II, § 2. *Ibid.*, p. 869.

[56] The object of this amendment was to establish the judiciary article of the Constitution of the United States under which the federal courts cannot entertain jurisdiction in this type of controversy. *Ibid.*, p. 781.

[57] This amendment was adopted in order to introduce a similar provision (Art. I, § 9) of the United States Constitution. *Ibid.*, pp. 783–84, 829.

[58] This provision, like the former, was adopted to incorporate a similar provision (Art. I, § 8) of the United States Constitution. *Ibid.*, p. 784.

[59] This amendment was added for the purpose of adopting a provision of the Constitution of the United States which prohibits Congress from taxing the products of the states by means of export duties. *Ibid.*, pp. 784, 894–900.

[60] This amendment was adopted in order to embody a similar provision (Art. I, § 8) of the United States Constitution. *Ibid.*, pp. 793–98.

that neither the Supreme Court nor the lower federal courts shall have jurisdiction in cases arising from the interpretation of ecclesiastical laws; that the members of the federal judiciary shall not act at the same time as judges of the provincial courts; that the number of judges of the Supreme Court shall be reduced from nine to four and the number of attorneys general from two to one; that Congress when enacting citizenship and naturalization statutes shall not violate the principle of *jus solis;* that the power of Congress to enact code legislation and the power of the provincial courts to apply the codes enacted by Congress shall be clarified; [61] that the official name shall be changed from The Argentine Confederation to The United Provinces of La Plata River; [62] that the province of Buenos Aires shall be entitled to twelve members in the Chamber of Deputies instead of six; that the provision of the Constitution that it would not be subject to amendment until ten years after its adoption shall be repealed; that the phrase referring to the execution of criminals by spear and knife shall be eliminated, but without amending the rest of the clause which prohibited the infliction of cruel and unusual punishment; that a section which authorized the President to suspend individual constitutional guarantees in cases in which the public safety was endangered without notifying Congress of his action shall be repealed; that the phrase "without the previous consent of the President of the Confederation" shall be eliminated from the article which stated that the ministers cannot in any case take decisions on their own account without the previous consent of the President of the Confederation except in regard to matters concerning the economic and administrative regime of their respective departments.[63]

[61] The object of this amendment was to preserve the power of the provincial courts to apply the codes enacted by Congress and thus maintain the principle of federalism by establishing a dual system of courts applying the same law. *Ibid.*, p. 782.

[62] Sarmiento expressed himself as follows when speaking in behalf of this amendment: "Like Argentina, the United States was a confederation during nine years without achieving any practical results. As in our case, they found the word that saved them. They named their country 'The United States of North America.' We, after nine years of war and hesitation, will name our country 'The United Provinces of La Plata River.' It seems to me that these circumstances and this comparison are worthy of being mentioned on this occasion." *Ibid.*, p. 937.

[63] This amendment was enacted in order to establish the responsibility of the ministers in accordance with the parliamentary system created by the Argentine

In addition, several other amendments were adopted for the special benefit of the province of Buenos Aires. An amendment provided that the power of Congress to regulate the free navigation of the rivers, to establish ports which it may consider to be necessary, and to establish custom houses shall not extend to suppress those custom houses which existed in each province at the time of their incorporation. Another amendment provided that export duties imposed by Congress shall not extend beyond the year 1866, on which date these duties shall cease to be national taxes. An amendment was made in Article 31 which, when originally drafted, provided as follows: "The Constitution, the laws of the nation promulgated by Congress in accordance with it, and the treaties made with foreign nations shall be the supreme law of the land and the authorities of each province must conform thereto, nothwithstanding any provision in the provincial laws or constitutions which may be contrary to them." The amendment added the following clause to the article: "Except that in the case of treaties, those provinces which were not represented in the Convention when the Constitution was approved and which had not been given such representation afterwards through their legislatures shall not be required to conform with them." An amendment to Article 101, which provided that the provinces shall preserve all powers not delegated to the federal government, added the clause that the provinces shall also preserve all powers expressly reserved to them by special pacts made at the time of their incorporation.

NATIONAL CONVENTION AD HOC OF 1860

The Congress of the Confederation, having been officially notified of the reforms proposed by the provincial convention of Buenos Aires, enacted, on June 23, 1860, a statute authorizing the calling of a national convention *ad hoc* for the purpose of considering these reforms. The statute also authorized the President of the Confederation to take all necessary steps in order that the con-

---

Constitution by preventing a minister from acting in important matters without the consent of the other ministers. *Ibid.*, pp. 780–81.

vention be held as soon as possible. On September 14, 1860, the convention met at Santa Fe, and all the provinces, including Buenos Aires, sent delegates.

The convention appointed a committee to consider the amendments proposed by Buenos Aires, composed of the leaders of the Convention of Santa Fe of 1853 and of the provincial convention of Buenos Aires. The members of this committee were Salvador María del Carril, Dalmacio Vélez Sársfield, José Mármol, Rufino de Elizalde, Juan Francisco Seguí, Luis Cáceres, and José B. Gorgostiaga. The committee rendered its report on September 23, 1860. The report recommended the approval, with some minor changes, of all the amendments which the convention of Buenos Aires had considered essential in order to incorporate those provisions and principles of the Constitution of the United States which had not been included by the Santa Fe Convention.

Certain changes in the amendments were proposed by the committee and approved by the convention. One was that the official names of the Republic should be United Provinces of La Plata River, Argentine Republic, and Argentine Confederation, instead of The United Provinces of La Plata River as proposed by the convention of Buenos Aires; the name Argentine Nation was to be used by Congress when enacting laws. The amendment proposed by Buenos Aires providing that the Supreme Court should be composed of four judges and one attorney general was eliminated in order that Congress should have power, as does the Congress of the United States, to determine the size of the court.

Another modification proposed to the reforms submitted by the Buenos Aires convention related to the qualifications of the members of Congress. The Buenos Aires convention proposed that the members should have three years of residence in the province from which they were elected; the national convention reduced the number to two, or, as its equivalent, that the members should have been born in the province from which they were elected.

The national convention also proposed the elimination of the last clause of Article 31 as amended by the Buenos Aires convention, which provided: "Except that in the case of treaties, those provinces which were not represented in the Convention when the Constitution was approved and which had not been given such representation afterwards through their legislatures shall not be required to conform with them." As a substitute the following clause was added: "except for the province of Buenos Aires, under the treaties ratified after November 11, 1859." Finally, the convention proposed to substitute for a clause of Article 97 which provided that "the federal courts shall have jurisdiction in cases between a province and its inhabitants, and between a province and a foreign state or citizens or subjects of a foreign state" the following: "the federal courts shall have jurisdiction in cases between a province or its inhabitants against a foreign state or citizens or subjects of a foreign state."

THE AMENDING PROCEDURE

Although the procedure for amending the Argentine Constitution differs in many respects from the amending procedure of the United States Constitution,[64] nevertheless the Founding Fathers of the Argentine Constitution incorporated into it the United States principle of separating the constituent power from the ordinary legislative power.[65] In other words, the Argentine Constitution, like that of the United States, cannot be amended simply by an act of Congress. The framers of the Argentine constitutions of 1819, 1826, and 1853 did not follow exactly the same process as that employed for amending the United States Constitution. A leading Argentine authority on constitutional law has remarked that Story's theory that the amending of the Constitution should

[64] Article V of the United States Constitution provides: "The Congress, whenever two-thirds of both houses shall deem it necessary, shall propose amendments to this Constitution, or, on the application of the legislatures of two-thirds of the several states, shall call a convention for proposing amendments, which, in either case, shall be valid to all intents and purposes, as part of this Constitution, when ratified by the legislatures of three-fourths of the several states, or by conventions in three-fourths thereof, as the one or the other mode of ratification may be proposed by the Congress; provided, that no amendment which may be made prior to the year one thousand eight hundred and eight shall in any manner affect the first and fourth clauses in the ninth section of the first article; and that no state, without its consent, shall be deprived of its equal suffrage in the Senate."

[65] In Municipalidad de la Capital v. Elortando, 33 S. C. N. 162 (1888), the Court stated that the Constitution makes a clear distinction between the legislative and the constituent power of government and that the legislative power is subordinated and limited by the constituent power.

be feasible but not too easy has been incorporated in Article 30 of the Argentine Constitution of 1853.[66]

The Argentine Constitution provides that the Constitution may be amended entirely or in any of its parts. The necessity for a constitutional reform must be declared by Congress by a vote of two-thirds of its members, but it shall not be effected except by a convention called for that purpose.

There are three steps necessary for amending the Argentine Constitution. First, the declaration by Congress that it is necessary to amend the Constitution, and a resolution of the same body convoking a national convention for the purpose of amending it. Second, the election of the members of the constitutional convention. Third, the adoption of the amendment by the national convention.

When the Constitution was amended for the first time, in 1866, Congress put into effect the steps above-mentioned in the following manner. The Senate and the Chamber of Deputies passed a resolution on June 9, 1866,[67] convoking a national convention for the sole purpose of amending Article 4 and section 1 of Article 67 of the Constitution.[68] Then, on June 14, 1866,[69] Congress enacted another statute to provide how and when the delegates of the convention should be elected and when the convention should meet, and to specify other details regarding the organization of the convention.[70]

66 M. A. Montes de Oca, *Lecciones de derecho constitucional,* I, 497.

67 *Colección de leyes nacionales,* II, 271.

68 This amendment was to eliminate the provisions of this article which prohibited Congress from taxing exports after 1866.

69 *Colección de leyes nacionales,* II, 271.

70 The provisions of this statute are: The Convention shall consider the reform of Article 4, and section one of Article 67 of the Constitution as declared to be necessary by Congress; the Convention shall be composed of the same number of delegates and in the proportion that is fixed by Article 38 of the Constitution; the qualifications of the delegates of the Convention shall be the same as those required by the members of Congress; the Convention shall take place in the city of Santa Fe, on September 1, 1866; the election of the delegates for the Convention shall take place on July 22, 1866; the delegates shall receive a compensation of one thousand pesos and the travelling expenses paid to the members of Congress; the election of delegates to the Convention shall be held in accordance with the general election laws; the counting of the votes for the election of delegates shall take place fifteen days after their election; the executive power is authorized to spend the necessary money for the enforcement of this law.

In 1898, when the Constitution was amended for the second time, Congress made some changes in the procedure. Instead of enacting two statutes, as it did before, it passed only one statute embodying all the provisions of the two statutes enacted in 1866. This statute [71] provided for the calling of a constitutional convention and declared the necessity of partially reforming the Constitution in relation to the number of inhabitants which Article 37 fixes as the basis for the election of the members of the Chamber of Deputies.[72] The statute also declared the necessity of amending Article 87 relative to the number of ministers that shall compose the President's cabinet.[73]

In both instances the laws were passed by more than two-thirds of the entire membership of each house, so that no question has been raised as to whether the two-thirds to which Article 30 makes reference means two-thirds of the members present or two-thirds of the entire membership of each house.[74] The question has not been decided by the Argentine Supreme Court, but Argentine writers [75] agree that it should be two-thirds of a quorum of each house, as in the United States. Another question was whether the President should sign the laws. When the laws of 1866 and 1898 were passed the President was notified by Congress, but the laws were not submitted for his signature. A leading Argentine commentator has maintained that the President's approval of the law is not necessary; [76] he holds that the principle expounded by the Supreme Court of the United States in *Hollingsworth v. Virginia*, 3 Dallas 378 (1798), and *Hawke v. Smith*, 253 U. S. 221 (1920), is applicable to the Argentine Constitution. In these two cases the

[71] *Colección de leyes nacionales*, XI, 339.

[72] The amendment made to this article provided that the number of representatives shall be one for every 33,000 inhabitants instead of one for every 20,000, and that Congress may increase but not diminish the ratio of representation provided in the article.

[73] The amendment adopted provided that the number of ministers shall be eight instead of five, and that Congress shall have the power to determine the organization of the administrative departments under the direction of these ministers.

[74] *Cámara de Diputados, Diario de sesiones*, 1866; pp. 70–80; *ibid.*, 1897, p. 695; *Cámara de Senadores, Diario de sesiones*, 1866, p. 105; *ibid.*, 1897, p. 294.

[75] J. González Calderón, *Derecho constitucional argentino*, I, 362; M. A. Montes de Oca, *Lecciones de derecho constitucional*, II, 496–98; J. M. Estrada, *Curso de derecho constitucional federal y administrativo*, p. 30.

[76] J. González Calderón, *Derecho constitucional argentino*, III, 34.

United States Supreme Court held that a resolution of Congress proposing an amendment does not require executive approval.

After the delegates to a national convention are elected there are two important problems: first, the organization and functioning of the convention, and second, its powers and limitations. The procedure observed in organizing the conventions of 1866 and 1898 was as follows: the convention held three sessions, one called the preparatory session, a second called the inauguration session, and a third called the closure session. In the first, the provisional president was appointed, and two committees, the Committee on Powers and the Committee on Rules. In the second, another committee was appointed to draft the reform projects. In the closure session, this committee brought in its report for approval or disapproval.

The problem as to the powers and limitations of national conventions in Argentina may be stated as follows: First, such conventions can consider only those matters which are included in the law enacted by Congress providing for the calling of the convention. Second, they have the power to approve or disapprove the reforms proposed by Congress in the act declaring the necessity to amend the Constitution, but they cannot make any amendment or amendments not included in the law passed by Congress.

This problem was discussed in 1866. It was argued that the convention had the power to consider only the subject matter submitted to it by Congress. Thus, in order to prevent the convention from considering other matters than those submitted by Congress, the first article of the law provided that the convention was convoked for the *sole* purpose of reforming Article 4 and that part of section 1 of Article 67 which limits the power of Congress to tax exports.[77] In the Convention of 1898 the same question was presented, and the convention itself agreed that it could consider only those matters submitted to it by Congress.[78]

That the practice of Argentine legislators of limiting the power of conventions was adopted from United States precedents as reflected in Story's *Commentaries on the Constitution of the United*

[77] *Cámara de Diputados, Diario de sesiones,* 1866, pp. 67–70.
[78] *Asambleas constituyentes argentinas,* V, 781–82.

States is demonstrated by the debate that took place in the Argentine Senate in 1897, when the law providing for calling a convention was under discussion. Thus Senator Guiñazú, referring to the remarks of the chairman of the committee, said:

> The member of the committee who has reported the bill to the house in his interesting and scholarly speech has reminded us that in North America, when it is intended to convoke a constitutional convention with more or less limited powers, special care is taken in defining and limiting with precision and clearness the powers which the convention may exercise. This is a healthy precedent worthy of taking into consideration.[79]

[79] *Cámara de Senadores, Diario de sesiones,* 1897, pp. 277–78.

III: THE JUDICIAL FUNCTION IN CONSTITUTIONAL CASES

ONE of the phases of the Argentine constitutional system which has been especially influenced by United States principles is the organization, structure, and functioning of the federal judiciary. When the statute for organizing the federal courts was under discussion Argentine legislators had before them the legislative precedents relating to the organization of the federal judiciary of the United States. The committee of the Argentine Senate stated: "The legislative and executive departments are very easy to organize because there are many precedents and practices concerning their organization in our constitutional history, but in regard to the judiciary it is different, especially in a federal system of government. And for this we found only one model in the judicial history of all nations and that is the judicial history of the United States." [1]

THE NATIONAL JUDICIARY

The drafters of the Argentine Constitution of 1853 gave constitutional status to the federal judiciary. Thus the Constitution provides, first, that the judicial power shall be vested in one Supreme Court of justice and in such inferior courts as Congress may establish (Art. 94); and second, that Congress shall have power to constitute tribunals inferior to the Supreme Court (Art. 67, § 7).[2]

The Supreme Court

A statute organizing the Argentine federal judicial system, enacted in 1858, provided that the Supreme Court should be composed of nine justices and two attorneys general; but it was never put into operation. In 1862 Congress enacted another statute which, with the exception of a few minor changes in 1902, has

[1] *Cámara de Senadores, Diario de sesiones,* 1862, p. 447.

[2] "The judicial Power of the United States, shall be vested in one supreme Court, and in such inferior Courts as Congress may from time to time ordain and establish" (U.S. Constitution, Art. III, § 1).

since remained the law.[3] It provided that the Supreme Court shall be composed of five judges and one attorney general—a number which has not been changed. In this respect Argentina differs from the United States, where the number of justices of the Supreme Court, starting at six, was reduced to five, increased to six, seven, nine, and even to ten, then reduced to eight and, in 1869, fixed at nine where it has remained. A distinguished Argentine writer has criticized the United States and Argentine constitutional methods of allowing Congress to change the size of the Court on the ground that it may lead to the modification of the majority of the Court in order to prevent the Court from declaring statutes unconstitutional.[4]

A feature in the Argentine Constitution which is absent from that of the United States relates to the requirements as to age, legal education, and practice of the profession that the judges of the Supreme Court must have in order to be eligible for appointment. The Constitution of 1819 provided that no one could be a member of the high court of justice unless he was a graduate in law, had practiced eight years, and was forty years of age. The Constitution of 1826 had a similar provision but it required in addition the qualifications of senators. The Constitution of 1853 provides that no person can be a judge of the Supreme Court unless he is a lawyer with eight years of practice and possesses the qualifications required of senators (Art. 97), namely, thirty years of age, citizenship in the nation for six years and enjoyment of an annual income of two thousand pesos or an equivalent salary (Art. 47).

There is great similarity in the United States Constitution and that of Argentina regarding the method of appointment of national judges and the means of securing the independence of the judiciary from the legislative and executive departments. The Constitution of 1853 declares that the President shall appoint the members of the Supreme Court and of the inferior federal courts with the advice and consent of the Senate (Art. 86, § 5). It further provides that the justices of both the Supreme Court and the inferior courts of the nation shall hold their office during good behavior, and shall receive for their services a compensation which shall be de-

[3] *Colección de leyes nacionales,* II, 52.

[4] H. Alsina, *La justicia federal,* p. 50.

termined by law and which cannot be diminished in any manner whatsoever during their continuance in office (Art. 96).

The provision that the compensation of the national judges cannot be diminished during their continuance in office was interpreted by the Supreme Court for the first time in *Fisco Nacional v. Medina,* 176 S. C. N. 73 (1936). Congress had enacted an income tax statute which applied to the salary of the defendant, who was a member of a lower federal court. The defendant refused to pay, contending that the tax was unconstitutional because it constituted a diminution of his compensation. His contention was upheld. The Court stated that Article 96 of the Constitution, although modeled on a like provision in the Constitution of the United States, was more specific because it provided that the compensation could not be diminished *in any manner whatsoever.* The Court then discussed the practical importance of such provisions and said that they were placed in the Constitution to guarantee the economic independence of the judges from possible interference by the stronger departments of government, the legislative and the executive. For support of the point that a tax on the compensation of a national judge constitutes a diminution of his salary the Court cited several decisions of the United States Supreme Court.[5]

The Constitution of the United States is silent on the subject of a Chief Justice. By statute it is declared that there shall be a chief justice of the United States and eight associate justices appointed by the President with the advice and consent of the Senate.[6] On the other hand, neither in the Argentine Constitution nor in the statute organizing the Supreme Court is there anything as to whether there shall be a Chief Justice or who shall appoint him. By constitutional usage accepted by the Senate, however, the President assumed the power to appoint the Chief Justice from 1862

[5] Evans v. Gore, 253 U. S. 245 (1920); Miles v. Graham, 268 U. S. 501 (1925); O'Donoghue v. United States, 289 U. S. 516 (1933). Subsequently, in O'Malley v. Woodrough, 307 U. S. 277 (1939), the Supreme Court of the United States disapproved the doctrine of Evans v. Gore. Mr. Justice Frankfurter, speaking for the Court, stated: "To subject them [the federal judges] to a government tax is merely to recognize that judges are also citizens and that their particular function in government does not generate an immunity from sharing with their fellow citizens the material burdens of government whose Constitution and laws they are charged with administering."

[6] 28 U. S. Code § 321.

to 1930. On October 16, 1862, President Mitre appointed to the Supreme Court Doctors Valentín Alsina, Francisco de las Carreras, Salvador María del Carril, Francisco Delgado and José Barros Paz, but he did not specify which of these persons was to be the Chief Justice. On October 17, 1862, the following discussion took place in the Senate:

THE PRESIDENT OF THE SENATE: The Minister told me that he wanted to come to this session but I forgot to call him. But I will communicate to the Senate that he wishes the Senate to know that Dr. Alsina will be the Chief Justice of the Supreme Court and that Mr. Pico will be the Attorney General.

WHEN THE MINISTER OF JUSTICE CAME TO THE SENATE HE STATED: I have nothing else to add to what the President of the Senate has said. I only want to say that by mistake these two appointments were not made in the notes sent to the Senate.

SENATOR URIBURU: The power of appointment of the Chief Justice belongs to the President and the only power of the Senate is to approve it.[7]

On January 6, 1863, Chief Justice Alsina resigned and the President appointed Justice de las Carreras to succeed him.[8]

The practice by which the President appointed the Chief Justice was abandoned in 1930 when the Supreme Court itself assumed the power of appointing its Chief Justice. In that year a revolution overthrew the government of President Hipólito Irigoyen, and the National Congress was dissolved. The Court, after having received a communication from the provisional government recognizing the power of the Court to appoint its Chief Justice, immediately assumed the exercise of the power. The Court stated in a resolution of September 19, 1930—158 S. C. N. 292 (1930)—that although former precedents did not support the action of the Court, it was evident that the practice under which the President had made the appointments had no constitutional or legal basis and affected in no justifiable way the principle of the separation of powers. The Court also said that in permitting the President to appoint the Chief Justices it had wished to observe a conciliatory and harmonious attitude toward the other departments of government in order to prevent possible conflicts which would have

[7] *Cámara de Senadores, Diario de sesiones,* 1862, p. 525.

[8] C. Zavalía, *Historia de la Corte suprema de justicia,* p. 559.

been very hard to solve by legal means. The Court thereupon appointed Roberto Repetto as Chief Justice.

The Constitution of Argentina, unlike that of the United States, provides that the Court shall promulgate its own internal and economic regulations and shall have the power to appoint its subordinate employees (Art. 99). The law which organized the Supreme Court also provided that it should have the power to appoint and remove its subordinate employees. This law also provided that the Court should have the power to make rules and regulations not only for its internal administration but also for the sectional federal judges. In August, 1863, the Court drafted the rules and regulations for its internal organization. According to those rules the Argentine Supreme Court is in session from February to December. Unlike the practice in the United States, Supreme Court hearings are held very seldom, but the parties may submit written arguments to the Court in which they state the facts and legal questions involved in the case.

The Argentine Supreme Court cannot render any decision or any other judicial pronouncement except by vote of the absolute majority of the members of the Court.[9] There is a difference between the Argentine and the United States Supreme Court in respect to the method employed in giving opinions. In Argentina the opinion is not rendered by a single judge in the name of the Court, but *per curiam*.[10] But dissenting or concurring opinions may be rendered. The opinions of the Supreme Court of Argentina are given as much publicity as those of the United States Supreme Court, and are widely discussed by legal writers in the newspapers and law journals.[11] No decision of the Argentine Supreme Court has, however, been the subject of such great public opposition as when the United States Supreme Court handed down the opinions in *Marbury v. Madison*, 1 Cranch 137 (1803), and in *Scott v. Sandford*, 19 How. 393 (1857).

Before the Supreme Court of Argentina decides a case the at-

[9] Art. 9, Law No. 27.

[10] The opinions of the Court are published officially under the direction of the clerks of the Court. At present there are one hundred and eighty-nine volumes containing the decisions since 1863.

[11] The leading law journals published in Argentina are *La Ley*, *Jurisprudencia argentina*, *La Gaceta del Foro*, and those published by the Universities of Buenos Aires, La Plata, Córdoba, El Litoral, and by the Bar Association of Buenos Aires.

torney general renders an opinion in which he states whether or not the Court has jurisdiction and his opinion on the merits. In many cases the Court has adopted the opinion of the attorney general as the opinion of the Court.[12] The attorneys general of the Argentine Supreme Court have played in many cases as important a role as the judges themselves.[13] The Argentine Supreme Court, following the tradition of the civil law, prefers to cite as authorities text-writers rather than judicial decisions. For this reason it may be said that the Argentine Court cites more frequently the commentators on the Constitution of the United States than does the United States Supreme Court itself.

There is an interesting feature in the organization of the Argentine Supreme Court which is not found in the United States. It consists in the appointment by the Supreme Court of a number of substitute judges for the Supreme Court, the federal chamber of appeals, and the sectional federal courts, who act as judges of these courts when the regular members are unable to act. *Fisco Nacional v. Medina,* already referred to (p. 51), was decided by these special judges because the regular members of the Supreme Court felt that in an indirect way they were parties to the controversy. The substitute judges are appointed in December of each year and receive compensation for their services when acting as judges.

The Supreme Court is given power by statute to supervise the federal chamber of appeals, the federal sectional courts, and the federal territorial courts. In order to exercise this power the Court is authorized to issue rules and regulations. The Supreme Court also has power to impose fines for the violation of these rules, not to exceed two hundred pesos. Should the members of the lower courts commit faults or acts of negligence of a serious character, the Court may inform the Chamber of Deputies of the nature of these violations for possible impeachment proceedings. If the faults or acts of negligence are committed, not by the judges but by the

12 An example of this practice is Ferrocarril Central del Sud v. Municipalidad de Juárez, 183 S. C. N. 190 (1939).

13 The attorney general performs other functions similar to those of the attorney general of the United States. He is the administrative head of the federal judicial system, he is the legal counsellor of the President of the Republic, and he also prosecutes suits in behalf of the nation and defends it when it is sued.

federal prosecuting attorneys or the public defenders, the Court may suspend them and notify the President.[14]

There is great similarity between Argentina and the United States in regard to the process through which the Supreme Courts have passed before becoming important factors in the institutional life of the two nations. The Argentine Supreme Court, like that of the United States, was in the early stages of its existence without large influence or popular prestige.[15] But such has not been the case in the later stages, and especially at present.

The growth in importance and prestige of the Argentine Court has been one of the most significant characteristics of the development of the nation. Speaking of the success of the Argentine Supreme Court as a public institution, the able historian of the Court, Professor Clodomiro Zavalía, has said that of all the Argentine institutions which were taken from the Constitution of the United States, the Supreme Court is the one which has established itself most profoundly in the public conscience and most perfected itself in actual practice.[16]

The institutional importance and prestige of the Argentine Court is due to the ability, impartiality, and wise statesmanship with which its members have faced and solved the grave constitutional, political, and economic problems brought before the Court since it began to function in 1862. As in the United States Supreme Court, eminent justices have contributed to the prestige of the Court. This is especially true in the case of Chief Justice Antonio Bermejo, who served for twenty-five years, and who, because of his long tenure and his distinguished services in constitutional development, has been called the John Marshall of the Argentine Supreme Court.

The judges of the Argentine Supreme Court have demonstrated throughout the history of the Court a profound knowledge and understanding not only of the Constitution but also of the political and constitutional history of the United States. How have they acquired such a knowledge of the political institutions of the

[14] Art. 10 and Art. 11, Law No. 4055.

[15] J. González Calderón, "La obra constructiva de la Corte Suprema," in *Doctrina constitucional,* p. 223.

[16] C. Zavalía, *op. cit.,* p. 11.

United States? In the Argentine law schools no courses in United States constitutional law are taught except in a general way as part of the courses given in comparative law. Thus, knowledge of such constitutional law has to be acquired through research by the judges and lawyers. The sources of information have been mainly the literature dealing with the political institutions of the United States and the decisions of the federal and state tribunals.[17]

Federal Chambers of Appeals

The federal chambers of appeals occupy in the Argentine federal judicial system the same position that the circuit courts of appeals do in the United States. They were created by statute in 1902. Like the circuit courts of appeals in the United States, they were created in order to reduce the appellate jurisdiction of the Supreme Court, and they exercise appellate jurisdiction exclusively.

Only four of these courts were created originally, but at present there are eight. They function in the following places: One is in the federal capital, and this hears the appeals in cases decided by the federal sectional judges of the federal district and of the provinces of San Luis and San Juan. Two are in the cities of La Plata and Bahía Blanca, in the province of Buenos Aires; these hear appeals in cases decided by the federal sectional courts located in the province and also exercise jurisdiction over the decisions rendered by the federal territorial judges of La Pampa, Neuquén, Río Negro, Chubut, Santa Cruz, and Tierra del Fuego. One is in the city of Paraná, in the province of Entre Ríos, with jurisdic-

[17] When the Argentine Court decided its first cases, the authorities cited were *The Federalist*, Story, *Commentaries on the Constitution of the United States*, and Kent, *Commentaries on American Law*. But as time went on the Court began to cite other authorities on the public law of the United States and England, such as Desty, Curtiss, Fisk, Cooley, Cushing, Tiffany, Goodnow, Burgess, Bryce, Blackstone, Dillon, Freund, Tiedman, Gray, Page and Jones, Lewis, Watson, Garett, Seligman, Black, Redfield, Sedgwick, Wilson, and others. Some of these works were translated into Spanish and French. The Court also cited decisions of the Supreme Court and other courts of the United States, particularly from two collections of decisions of the federal courts of the United States, edited by Paschal and Bump. The works of these two authors were translated into Spanish by Nicolás Calvo and Clodomiro Quiroga, two Argentine legal writers, in the year 1886. At present the Supreme Court and the lower federal courts have fairly complete libraries containing reports of the United States Supreme Court and lower federal courts as well as the leading treatises dealing with public law in the United States.

tion over cases decided by the sectional judges of this province and by the federal judges of the territories of El Chaco, Formosa, and Misiones. One is in the city of Córdoba, in the province of the same name, which hears appeals from the sectional courts in this province and from sectional courts of other provinces not included within the jurisdiction of any other chamber of appeals. One is in the city of Rosario, in the province of Santa Fe, which hears cases decided by the federal sectional judges of this province. Another is in the city of Mendoza, in the province of the same name, which hears cases decided by the federal judges of this province. Finally, one is in the city of Tucumán, in the province of the same name, which hears decisions rendered by the federal sectional judges of this province.

The chambers of appeals, like the circuit courts of the United States, are composed of three judges, with the exception of that of the federal capital which is composed of five judges. The other officers of the courts are the attorneys general, public defenders, and clerks. The judges and the attorneys general are appointed by the President with the advice and consent of the Senate, and hold office during good behavior. The judges must have the same qualifications as judges of the Supreme Court. Each court has the power to appoint its Chief Justice, but the clerks and other subordinate officials are appointed by the Supreme Court.

Federal Sectional Courts

The federal sectional courts, like the federal district courts of the United States, are the courts of original jurisdiction. The judges of these courts, like those of the other federal courts, are appointed by the President with the advice and consent of the Senate, and hold office during good behavior. The judges and the attorneys general must be twenty-five years of age, and must be lawyers with at least three years of practice. The judges have power to make rules and regulations for the internal organization of the courts and to appoint subordinate officials with the approval of the Supreme Court. Among the most important subordinate officials of these courts are the clerks and public defenders of insolvent and absentee parties.

The statute creating the federal sectional courts provided for one or more sectional courts in the provinces as the Executive shall determine. The present distribution is as follows: three in the federal capital, two exercising civil and commercial jurisdiction and the other exercising criminal jurisdiction; four in the province of Buenos Aires; three in the province of Santa Fe; two in the province of Entre Ríos; two in the province of Córdoba; and one each in the provinces of Corrientes, Santiago del Estero, Tucumán, San Juan, San Luis, Mendoza, La Rioja, Catamarca, Salta, and Jujuy.

Territorial Courts

As in the United States, the Argentine Congress has established a system of courts in the national territories and in the federal capital. This resembles the judicial organization of the territories and the capital of the United States, but also differs from it in many respects. The sixteen territorial judges are distributed as follows: two in El Chaco, two in Chubut, one in Formosa, four in La Pampa, two in Misiones, one in Neuquén, three in Río Negro, and one judge who exercises jurisdiction in the territories of Santa Cruz and Tierra del Fuego. These judges are appointed for a four-year term by the President with the advice and consent of the Senate. They must be Argentine citizens, graduates of one of the national university law schools, and they receive a compensation which cannot be diminished during their continuance in office. They are removed not by impeachment but by the procedure employed to remove the judges of the federal capital, which will be discussed later. They exercise jurisdiction in commercial, civil, and criminal cases.

Jurisdiction over civil and commercial cases where the amount in controversy is less than three hundred pesos is exercised by justices of the peace elected by the respective municipalities for a two-year term. These judges can be removed by a two-thirds vote of the municipal council. Appeals from the decisions of the justices of the peace may be taken to the federal territorial judges, whose decisions are final. The justices of the peace are the only judges of the federal judicial system who are popularly elected.

The system of courts in the federal capital differs in one respect from the system of courts in the United States in the District of

Columbia. While in the District of Columbia the Supreme Court and the court of appeals exercise federal and local jurisdiction, in the federal district of Argentina there are two branches, one exercising federal jurisdiction and the other local jurisdiction. Local jurisdiction is exercised by the following courts: the justice of the peace courts, which exercise civil jurisdiction in minor cases; a chamber of appeals, to which are brought appeals from the justice of the peace courts; the courts of commerce, which exercise jurisdiction in cases arising under the code of commerce; the civil courts of original jurisdiction, which have power to decide cases not subject to the jurisdiction of the justice of the peace courts; the criminal courts, which have jurisdiction over minor and serious offenses; and finally, two chambers of appeals, one for civil cases and the other for criminal and commercial cases. The judges of these courts are appointed by the President with the advice and consent of the Senate, hold office during good behavior, and receive a compensation which cannot be diminished during their continuance in office. The judges of the chambers of appeals can be removed by impeachment proceedings, but the justices of the other courts can be removed only by a special court composed of two members of the civil chamber of appeals and one member of the criminal and commercial chamber of appeals.

Legislative Courts

In *Ex Parte Acevedo,* 30 S. C. N. 102 (1886), the Argentine Supreme Court incorporated into the Argentine law the United States classification of courts into constitutional and legislative.[18] The petitioner was charged with criminal libel against the President

[18] Since American Insurance Co. v. Canter, 1 Pet. 508 (1828), the courts of the United States have been classified as constitutional and legislative. In Ex Parte Bakelite Corporation, 279 U. S. 438 (1929), the Supreme Court, after holding that the Court of Customs Appeals is a legislative court and that Congress can impose upon it the duty of giving advisory opinions, stated that the constitutional courts are those created under Article III, while legislative courts are those created by Congress in the exercise of other constitutional powers. The first type of court shares in the exercise of the judicial power defined in Article III, it can be vested with no other jurisdiction, and it has judges who hold office during good behavior, with no power in Congress to provide otherwise. On the other hand, Congress can impose on the second type of courts functions directed to the execution of one or more of its powers, and their judges hold for such term as Congress prescribes, whether it be for a fixed period of years or during good behavior.

through the publication of a newspaper article, and the federal sectional court and the criminal court of the federal capital claimed jurisdiction. The attorney general maintained that neither had jurisdiction, his theory being based on Article 32 of the Constitution which prohibits Congress from enacting legislation restricting the liberty of the press and from vesting the federal courts with jurisdiction over such offenses. Both the federal sectional court and the criminal court of the federal district were courts created by Congress.

The Supreme Court upheld the power of the criminal court on the ground that it was a legislative and not a constitutional court and that Article 32 did not prohibit Congress from vesting in it jurisdiction over crimes committed through the press. The Court then stated that the courts of the nation are constitutional courts while those of the territories are legislative and that the former are created under the constitutional grant of power to create inferior tribunals to the Supreme Court, while the latter are created under the power to organize and administer the government of the national territories. The Court cited a passage from Story [19] to support the view that Congress had power to give the courts of the federal capital jurisdiction over press offenses.

Argentine writers on public law have criticized this decision. Dr. Felipe A. Espil has suggested that the passage from Story, which was based on *American Insurance Co. v. Canter,* 1 Pet. 511 (1828), was not applicable to the local courts of the Argentine federal district, because that case involved a court created by Congress for the territory of Florida and not in the District of Columbia; and further that the principle expounded by Story that the ter-

[19] "The judges of the inferior courts spoken of in the Constitution do not include the judges of the courts appointed in the territories of the United States under the authority of Congress to regulate the territories of the United States. The courts of the territories are not constitutional courts, in which the judicial power conferred by the Constitution on the general government can be deposited. They are legislative courts created in virtue of the general sovereignty which exists in the national government over its territories. The jurisdiction with which they are invested is not a part of the judicial power which is defined in the third article of the Constitution, but arises from the same general sovereignty. In legislating for them, Congress exercises the combined power of the general and of a state government. Congress may, therefore, rightfully limit the tenure of office of the judges of the territorial courts, as well as their jurisdiction, and it has been accordingly limited to a short period of years." J. Story, *Commentaries on the Constitution of the United States,* 5th ed., Boston, 1891, IV, 445.

ritories of the United States do not form a part of the nation is not applicable in Argentina in as much as under the preamble of the Argentine Constitution the territories are a part of the Republic.[20]

In *Ríos v. García,* 99 S. C. N. 283 (1904), the Argentine Supreme Court settled the question whether Congress had power to vest in the local courts of the federal capital the judicial power provided for in Article 100. The defendant was convicted in the criminal courts of the federal district for having violated a national election law which prohibited federal employees from participating in political activities. The law provided for an appeal from the decision of the local court to the federal chamber of appeals of the federal district. The defendant alleged that the law vesting the local courts with jurisdiction over a case based upon the Constitution and the laws of Congress was unconstitutional because the local courts were not federal tribunals. The Supreme Court, nevertheless, upheld the statute on the ground that Congress, when legislating for the federal capital, exercises the combined power of a national and of a local government.

JURISDICTION OF FEDERAL COURTS

Article 100 of the Argentine Constitution, following a practically identical provision of the United States Constitution, provides as follows:

The Supreme Court and the inferior courts of the nation shall decide all cases not enumerated in clause 11 of Article 67 which arise under the

20 *La inamobilidad de los jueces,* XVIII J. A. 25 (1928). Dr. Espil's thesis of a difference between the territorial court and those of the federal district was confirmed by the Supreme Court of the United States in O'Donoghue v. United States, 289 U. S. 516 (1933), in which the Court held that the Supreme Court and the Court of Appeals of the District of Columbia are constitutional courts. The question in this case was whether the judges of these courts were subject to federal taxation without violating the provision of the Constitution that the compensation of the federal judges shall not be diminished during their continuance in office. The Court, after discussing the differences between constitutional and legislative courts, stated that the former are ordained and established under Article III, that their judges hold office during good behavior, and that their compensation cannot be diminished during their continuance in office. The Court then stated that these courts are permanent establishments of the United States and a part of the federal judicial system because the District of Columbia, unlike the territories, is a permanent part of the United States—the very heart of the Union. The Court finally stated that although these courts are constitutional courts, nevertheless Congress can impose upon them other duties which it could not impose upon the federal courts located in other parts of the nation.

provisions of this Constitution, the laws of the nation, or treaties with foreign powers; cases concerning ambassadors, public ministers, and consuls; cases of admiralty and maritime jurisdiction; in controversies to which the nation is a party; cases which arise between two or more provinces, between one province and citizens of another province, between citizens of different provinces, and between a province or its citizens and a foreign state or its citizens.

According to Article 101:

In the above-mentioned cases the Supreme Court shall have appellate jurisdiction, under such rules and exceptions thereto as Congress may establish, but in all cases concerning foreign ambassadors, ministers, and consuls, and in those to which a province may be a party, the jurisdiction of the Supreme Court shall be original and exclusive.[21]

The Argentine Congress has enacted several statutes prescribing the nature, extent, and limitations of the jurisdiction of the federal courts. The first was Law No. 17, of October 16, 1862,[22] which established the principle that the federal courts never act officiously, that they exercise jurisdiction only in judicial controversies, and that their chief purpose is to maintain the objects of the national Constitution. Then came, on September 14, 1863, Law No. 49,[23] vesting the federal sectional courts with criminal jurisdiction, and Law No. 50,[24] establishing the rules applicable in civil and criminal procedure. Finally, on September 3, 1878, Congress enacted Law No. 927,[25] which excluded from the jurisdiction of the federal sectional courts all civil cases involving less than five hundred pesos

21 The Constitution of the United States provides: "The judicial Power shall extend to all Cases, in Law and Equity, arising under this Constitution, the Laws of the United States, and Treaties made, or which shall be made, under their Authority; to all Cases affecting Ambassadors, other public Ministers and Consuls; to all Cases of admiralty and maritime Jurisdiction; to Controversies to which the United States shall be a Party; to Controversies between two or more States; between a State and Citizens of another State; between Citizens of different States; between Citizens of the same State claiming Lands under Grants of different States, and Between a State, or the Citizens thereof, and foreign States, Citizens or Subjects.

In all Cases affecting Ambassadors, other public Ministers and Consuls, and those in which a State shall be party, the supreme Court shall have original Jurisdiction. In all the other Cases before mentioned, the supreme Court shall have appellate Jurisdiction, both as to Law and Fact, with such Exceptions and under such Regulations as the Congress shall make" (Art. III, § 2).

22 *Colección de leyes nacionales,* II, 52.

23 *Ibid.,* p. 70.

24 *Ibid.,* IV, 410.

25 *Ibid.,* II, 70. This law continues to be enforced in civil cases with the modifications that were made to it in Law No. 3981, *ibid.,* XII, 472, which provides that the Code of Civil Procedure of the federal capital shall supplement the rules of pro-

and also all cases relating to bankruptcy and testamentary proceedings. Under the provisions of this law the provincial courts could exercise jurisdiction over these cases.

The legislative history of these statutes shows that the Argentine Congress made use of precedents of the United States. In the debates reference was made to the United States judicial system, especially in regard to the jurisdiction of the federal courts.[26] When the question whether a province could be sued in a lower federal court was under consideration, Senator Navarro, chairman of the committee reporting the bill, said:

> In view of the doubt as to whether a province could be sued in the lower federal courts, the Commission has conferred with the members of the Supreme Court in order to determine how to decide this matter. The members of the Court have informed us that after studying the organic laws they have found that in that country [the United States] the lower federal courts have jurisdiction in cases in which the states are parties. The reasons why the federal courts have been given jurisdiction in this type of case are, first, because it is very inconvenient for the states located far away from the Supreme Court to come to it to defend their cases, and second, because in the last instance the Supreme Court would hear these cases in the exercise of its appellate jurisdiction.[27]

When Law No. 27 was being discussed the legislative committee of the Senate which drafted the bill reported:

> The American statute of 1789 regulating the jurisdiction of the federal courts provided that the circuit courts could exercise jurisdiction in diversity of citizenship and nationality cases and in cases between foreigners and citizens only when the amount of the controversy exceeded five hundred dollars. The courts of the states exercise jurisdiction in cases in which the amount involved is less than five hundred dollars. But later on the law was modified so as to give to the federal courts jurisdiction in cases in which the amount of the controversy was less than five hundred dollars provided that the United States was a party to the controversy.[28]

In *Gómez v. La Nación*, 2 S. C. N. 36 (1865), in which the issue was whether the nation could be sued without its consent, the

cedure established by it. The rules of criminal procedure provided in Law No. 50 were repealed by Law No. 3981, which declared that the Code of Criminal Procedure of the federal capital shall be applied in all the federal courts.

[26] *Cámara de Senadores, Diario de sesiones,* 1863, p. 193; *Cámara de Diputados, Diario de sesiones,* 1863, pp. 74–463.

[27] *Cámara de Diputados, Diario de sesiones,* 1863, pp. 183–249.

[28] *Cámara de Senadores, Diario de sesiones,* 1878, pp. 81–82.

Court stated that United States and not Spanish precedents were the sources to be followed. The Court dismissed the suit for damages on the ground that the national government, like that of the United States, could not be sued without its consent, and that when the Constitution says that the Supreme Court shall exercise jurisdiction in cases to which the nation is a party this means that the Court shall exercise jurisdiction only in those cases to which the nation is a party plaintiff. In support of this holding the Court stated:

> There is nothing that will induce us to believe that the makers of the Constitution, when drafting the articles dealing with the jurisdiction of the federal courts, took into consideration Spanish constitutional and legislative precedents. On the other hand, it is evident that when they drafted these articles they tried to imitate, with slight changes, the Constitution of the United States in this particular respect, as they did in others. For this reason, in order to understand the nature, extent, and limitations of the jurisdiction of our federal courts, we must interpret them in the light of United States principles and precedents and not in the light of Spanish constitutional and legislative precedents.[29]

Federal Sectional Courts

The jurisdiction of the federal sectional courts, like that of the district courts of the United States, is subject to Congressional regulation. The Argentine Congress has vested these courts with original jurisdiction over three different types of controversies. First, cases based upon the character of the controversy, which include those arising under the Constitution, the laws of Congress, treaties with foreign nations, and cases relating to admiralty and maritime jurisdiction. Second, cases based upon the character of the parties to the controversy, in which are included civil controversies between aliens and citizens of Argentina [30] and between

[29] On September 27, 1900, Congress enacted Law No. 3952, allowing suit against the national government, without congressional approval, for acts done by the national government in a private capacity. In Sepp Hermanos v. Gobierno Nacional, 100 S. C. N. 103 (1904), the Court held that the civil actions against the nation authorized by this statute are those derived from the artificial capacity of the federal government when acting as a private person and therefore subject to the relations of private law.

[30] In Vignale v. Albarracín, 36 S. C. N. 394 (1889), the question was whether Congress had power to provide that civil suits between Argentine citizens and foreigners where the amount of the controversy was less than five hundred pesos should

residents of different provinces; [31] cases affecting the private affairs of consuls; [32] cases to which the nation is a party; cases dealing with the administrative acts of the national government, including cases between private parties originating from administrative acts of the national government; cases concerning fiscal actions against persons or corporations, whether these are based on debts or on contractual obligations entered into between persons or corporations and the national government; and finally, cases in which a collector of revenue of the nation is a party, provided the case is related to the collection of revenue and the public services concerning it. The third and last type of case is based on the place where the controversy occurred. These include cases related to the criminal jurisdiction of the federal sectional courts, which extends to crimes committed on the high seas, or on board national ships, or by foreign pirates; crimes committed within the jurisdiction of the provinces in violation of the national laws; crimes committed on the rivers, islands, and ports of the Republic, and crimes of any kind committed within places in which the national government has exclusive jurisdiction.

The sectional courts, unlike the district courts of the United States, exercise appellate jurisdiction in several types of cases. These consist in appeals from decisions by administrative officials in the enforcement of the sanitary police laws, internal revenue statutes, tariff laws, Agricultural Defense Act and the Vegetation Conservation Statute. These courts also exercise appellate jurisdiction in cases decided by the captains of merchant vessels in which the amount of the controversy is less than fifty pesos and which have arisen between members of the crew themselves or between them and the officers of the ship.

Although a habeas corpus proceeding is not, technically speaking, an appeal, yet in its practical effect it amounts to an appeal because the court to which the petition is made may annul or

be tried in the provincial courts instead of in the federal sectional courts. The Supreme Court, citing United States precedents, upheld the validity of the law.

[31] In Gaché v. Martínez, 20 S. C. N. 163 (1868), the Argentine Supreme Court held, on the authority of Morris v. Gilmer, 129 U. S. 315 (1889), that the phrase "controversies between residents of different provinces" was equivalent to "controversies between citizens of different states" as provided in the Constitution of the United States.

[32] Gorostiola de Angulo v. Maylin, 178 S. C. N. 401 (1936).

declare void the arrest or sentence imposed upon the petitioner. The federal sectional courts, similar to the federal district courts of the United States, have the power to issue writs of habeas corpus under certain conditions. Thus, it is provided by statute that when a person is arrested or imprisoned by a national authority, or when a member of Congress or any person acting in behalf of the national government shall have been arrested or imprisoned by a national authority, or when a member of Congress or any person acting in behalf of the national government shall have been arrested or imprisoned by any provincial authority, the Supreme Court or any of the federal sectional courts shall, on petition of the person arrested or imprisoned or on the petition presented in his behalf by any member of his family or any of his friends, inquire into the reasons for his arrest or imprisonment, and if it is found that such arrest or imprisonment is illegal, the petitioner shall immediately be freed by the court.[33]

Federal Chambers of Appeals

The federal chambers of appeals, like the circuit courts of appeals of the United States, are exclusively courts of appellate jurisdiction. They exercise jurisdiction in the following types of cases: first, in cases decided by the federal sectional courts, except that in commercial and civil cases the amount involved in the controversy must exceed five hundred pesos; second, in cases decided by the federal territorial courts even when related to common law matters; third, in cases appealed from the federal sectional and federal territorial courts where it is alleged that there has been a denial or a delay of justice; fourth, in cases where questions are certified by the territorial courts relating to minors, incompetent persons, and matters concerning fiscal controversies. Also like the circuit courts of appeals of the United States, they review decisions of certain administrative tribunals.

[33] In Ex Parte Alem, 54 S. C. N. 432 (1893), the petitioner, a national senator who had been arrested by the President during the declaration of a state of siege, was freed on habeas corpus proceeding by a federal sectional court on the ground that the President had no constitutional power to arrest a member of Congress even during the state of siege, because such an action of the President constituted an unwarranted interference with the legislative department of government.

The Supreme Court

The original jurisdiction of the Argentine Supreme Court, like that of the United States Supreme Court, is expressly provided for in the Constitution, and Congress has no power to alter it.[34] It includes the following: first, suits between two or more provinces; [35] second, civil suits between a province and one or more of its residents,[36] or residents of other provinces,[37] or citizens or subjects of foreign states; third, suits between a province and a foreign state; fourth, suits concerning ambassadors, or other public ministers or their families, members of the legation or domestic servants; and fifth, cases concerning the privileges and immunities of consuls and vice-consuls.

[34] See Ex Parte Sojo, discussed infra, p. 75.

[35] The jurisdiction in this type of case is not only original but exclusive, regardless of the nature of the controversy. The only exception is a case concerning boundary disputes, because in the Argentine Constitution (Art. 67, § 14), unlike the United States Constitution, Congress is authorized to fix the territorial limits of the provinces. Thus, in Cárcano v. Santiago del Estero, 98 S. C. N. 107 (1903), the Court held that it had jurisdiction in a case between two provinces relative to lands which they possessed within their respective limits provided that the resolution of the Court did not fix new boundaries between the provinces nor alter those already established by Congress. And in Pereyra Iraola v. Buenos Aires, 133 S. C. N. 312 (1921), involving the question whether the Court could alter the boundaries of two provinces which had been fixed by Congress but which had been changed because the river establishing the boundaries had changed its course, the Court, on the authority of Nebraska v. Iowa, 143 U. S. 359 (1892) and Missouri v. Nebraska, 196 U. S. 23 (1904), declared itself without jurisdiction and stated: "Even under the reign of the American institutions under which the Supreme Court determines the limits of the different states, the decisions of that Court have declared that when it is provided by statute that a river which separates two states constitutes the boundary between them, such a boundary is not altered even when the river happens to change its course."

[36] In Mendoza Hermanos v. San Luis, 1 S. C. N. 485 (1865), and Avegno v. Buenos Aires, 14 S. C. N. 425 (1874), this provision was attacked as unconstitutional on the theory that as the Argentine Constitution was adopted after the Eleventh Amendment of the Constitution of the United States, it was the intention of the framers of the Argentine Constitution that the Argentine provinces, like the states of the United States, under the provisions of the Eleventh Amendment, could not be sued without their consent. But the Court, on the authority of Chisholm v. Georgia, 2 Dallas 419 (1793), held that the provinces, like the states of the United States before the adoption of the Eleventh Amendment, could be sued without their consent by their own citizens, citizens of other provinces, or by citizens or subjects of foreign nations. In Coronado v. Buenos Aires, 1 *Gaceta del Foro* 9 (1916), the Court held that the provinces can be sued only in civil suits arising from contractual obligations.

[37] In Molina v. Santa Fe, 57 S. C. N. 337 (1896), the Court held that execution or attachment may be issued against the property of the provinces to enforce judgments against them. But in Bank of Boston v. Corrientes, 182 S. C. N. 498 (1938), the Court held that the revenues of a province cannot be attached or levied upon to such an extent as to cripple essential governmental activities.

The appellate jurisdiction of the Argentine Supreme Court is conferred by the Constitution but is subject to such exceptions and regulations as Congress shall make. In *Gobierno Nacional v. Eiriz,* 137 S. C. N. 345 (1922), this power of Congress was questioned by the petitioner, who had been denied an appeal to the Supreme Court from his conviction in a military court for embezzlement. He was refused appeal on the ground that the Court had not been given appellate jurisdiction in cases from military tribunals except those in which a constitutional or federal question had been raised. The petitioner attacked the statute as in conflict with Articles 100 and 101 of the Constitution, giving the Court power to hear on appeal all cases arising under the Constitution and the laws of Congress with the exception of those mentioned in Article 67, § 11. But the Court denied his contentions and held that the clause granting to Congress power to regulate the appellate jurisdiction of the Court was based on the Constitution of the United States. "As Campbell Black has observed," said the Court, "the appellate jurisdiction of the United States Supreme Court may be regulated, restricted or broadened as Congress may deem necessary, and since the creation of the circuit courts of appeals, in which Congress has vested considerable appellate jurisdiction, the Supreme Court exercises appellate jurisdiction only in certain enumerated types of cases." [38]

The ordinary appellate jurisdiction of the Supreme Court extends to all decisions, and all interlocutory judgments causing irreparable damage, rendered by the federal chambers of appeals

[38] The power of the Congress of the United States to regulate the appellate jurisdiction of the Supreme Court is discussed in Ex Parte McCardle, 7 Wallace 506 (1869). The petitioner, who was not in the military service of the United States, was arrested by military authorities for publishing an alleged libelous article against the federal authorities stationed in the state of Mississippi. He petitioned the circuit court for the southern district of that state for a writ of habeas corpus, but the court having denied the writ, he appealed to the United States Supreme Court under a statute which authorized such appeals. After the case had been argued before the Supreme Court and while the Court had it under its consideration, Congress repealed the statute under which the appeal had been taken. The Court dismissed the appeal on the ground that since Congress had repealed the statute which authorized it, the Court no longer had jurisdiction over the case, and stated: "The exception to appellate jurisdiction in the case before us, however, is not an inference from the affirmation of other appellate jurisdiction. It is made in terms. The provision of the Act of 1867, affirming the appellate jurisdiction of this Court in cases of habeas corpus, is expressly repealed. It is hardly possible to imagine a plainer instance of positive exception."

in those cases over which these courts do not have final jurisdiction. Jurisdiction is exercised through the ordinary procedures of appeal and nullity. The method of appeal through certiorari is unknown in Argentine practice. The method of appeal is employed to review the decisions of the lower courts on the merits of the controversy. The second method—that of nullity—is used to review the decisions of the lower courts on account of violation of procedural rules. If there has been no violation of the rules of procedure but error in rendering the judgment, the Court may annul the judgment and render one according to the merits of the case. If the procedure is void the Court will remand the case to the lower court to proceed according to the law.

The ordinary appellate jurisdiction includes the following: first, cases in which final judgments have been rendered against the nation for acts done when acting as a private person; second, fiscal actions in which final judgments have been rendered against persons or corporations either for debt, or for breach of contract, or for violation of national tax laws or administrative regulations, and in general in all cases in which the nation or a collector of revenue is a party,[39] provided that the amount involved in the controversy exceeds five thousand pesos; third, cases involving final judgments relating to admiralty matters; fourth, cases where final judgments have been rendered dealing with the extradition of criminals requested by foreign nations under treaty provisions; fifth, cases in which final judgments have been rendered in certain types of criminal conduct.[40]

One of the most important functions of the Argentine and of the United States Supreme Courts is to maintain the supremacy of the Constitution, the laws of Congress, and treaties made with foreign nations. The Argentine Supreme Court maintains this

[39] In González v. Compañía de Tranvías Eléctricos de Rosario, 139 S. C. N. 209 (1923), the Court held that the right to appeal in this type of case belongs to the nation only because the appellate jurisdiction is for the purpose of protecting the interest of the nation and not that of the parties suing it.

[40] Cases dealing with fraud against the national revenue, provided the amount involved exceeds five thousand pesos, Fiscal v. Brusafferri Cía., 97 S. C. N. 289 (1903); cases dealing with the violation of administrative regulations, Law No. 4055, Art. 3, § 2; cases dealing with the crimes of treason, rebellion, sedition, homicide, arson, piracy, and shipwreck committed on the high seas on board a national ship or by foreign pirates; and in general all crimes whose penalty exceeds ten years of imprisonment in the penitentiary, Law No. 4055, Art. 3, § 5.

supremacy through the exercise of its extraordinary appellate jurisdiction by means of the writ of error.[41] Through this writ are brought to the Supreme Court the records of final judgments rendered by the supreme courts of the provinces and the lower federal courts which are challenged as contrary either to the Constitution, the laws of Congress, or treaties made with foreign nations. The Argentine statutes establishing the writ of error provide that once a suit [42] has been filed in the provincial courts, the decision of these courts will be final and can be appealed to the Supreme Court only in the following cases: when the validity of a treaty or a law of Congress or of an authority exercised in the name of the nation [43] has been drawn in question and the decision is against

[41] In Pereyra v. Pacific Steam Navigation Co., 119 S. C. N. 422 (1914), the Court explains as follows the origin and purpose of the writ of error: "The writ of error authorized by statute is designed to guarantee the supremacy of the national Constitution, the laws of Congress, and treaties, as provided in Article 31 of the Constitution. This writ was reproduced from Section 25 of the American Judiciary Act of 1789 (§ 709, Revised Statutes) and lies only according to the terms of the statute and the constant jurisprudence of the American and Argentine courts against final judgments of provincial and federal tribunals in which a federal question has been discussed and the decision is contrary to the right, privilege, or exemption alleged to be based upon the Constitution, the laws of Congress, or treaties."

[42] In In re Francioni, 110 S. C. N. 391 (1907), the Court held that for a suit to exist it is necessary that there shall be adversary parties and justiciable issues involved so that the Court may render a final judgment which can be judicially enforced. But in defining the word "suit" the Court has not limited its meaning to a purely judicial controversy. Thus, in Ex Parte Manuel González Maceda, 155 S. C. N. 356 (1929), the Court held that the writ of error lies from the final decision of a chief of police prohibiting the holding of a public rally. The Court stated: "It is not an obstacle to the issuing of the writ that the judgment has been pronounced by an administrative officer, inasmuch as the constitutional guarantees may be violated in this type of proceeding as in a judicial proceeding." And in In re Schuster, 113 S. C. N. 294 (1910), the Court held that a writ of error lies against the resolution of the supreme court of a province which denies validity to a license of expert penman issued by a national authority. The Court stated that for the purpose of issuing the writ of error it is not necessary that the judgment shall have been rendered in an ordinary judicial proceeding but it is sufficient that it is a final judgment and that the judicial authority which rendered the same is a superior tribunal of a province. But in Bavastro v. Junta Electoral, 128 S. C. N. 314 (1918), in which the plaintiff requested the Supreme Court to review the decision of an electoral board, the Court stated that the writ did not lie because the board is not a court of justice within the meaning of the writ of error statute.

[43] By the term "authority exercised in the name of the nation" is meant those titles, privileges, or authorities which emanate from the national Constitution, laws or treaties. Thus, in Ferrocarril de Buenos Aires v. Senac, 109 S. C. N. 239 (1908), the Court held that the writ of error lies when a provincial court denies validity to a property granted to the defendant by a judicial decision of a federal court when the said title is set up as a defense in an ejectment proceeding against the holder of such title. A decree of the President issued to enforce a law of Congress has the

its validity;[44] when the validity of a law decree or authority of a province has been drawn in question on the ground of its being repugnant to the Constitution, or treaties, or laws of Congress and the decision is in favor of its validity; when the meaning of some clause of the national Constitution, a treaty, a law of Congress, or a commission exercised in the name of the national government[45] has been drawn in question and its validity is denied, provided that such title, right, privilege or exemption upon which such clause is based[46] is involved in the controversy. The statute also provides that when an appeal is taken to the Supreme Court the complaint against the decision of the Court must be pleaded according to the terms of the statute[47] so that the grounds of the

---

same status as the law which it attempts to enforce, Duguid y Cia. v. Muñoz, 22 S. C. N. 450 (1880).

[44] By the term "drawn in question" is meant that the federal question presented in the trial must be the subject of discussion before the superior tribunal from whose decision it is appealed to the Supreme Court, González v. Buenos Aires, 23 S. C. N. 249 (1881). But in In re Stoddard, 102 S. C. N. 356 (1905), the Court held that the validity of the Constitution, laws, or treaties is also drawn in question when the lower court has taken into consideration in rendering its decision the constitutional clause, treaty, or law of Congress upon which the federal claim is based, although the parties have not invoked them expressly. In this case the plaintiff, the consul of Great Britain, petitioned the lower court to be appointed testamentary executor of an English subject under the provisions of a treaty entered into by Argentine and Great Britain. Although the plaintiff never invoked during the trial the provision of this treaty, the Court nevertheless based its decision upon the treaty and denied plaintiff's claim. The Supreme Court granted the writ on the ground that, although the treaty was not invoked by the party, nevertheless the Court based its decision upon the treaty. The rule in the United States is different, Howard v. Fleming, 191 U. S. 126 (1903). For a discussion of this problem see F. A. Espil, *La Suprema Corte federal y su jurisdicción extraordinaria*, p. 55.

[45] In Glickman v. Puppo et al, 120 S. C. N. 175 (1914), the Court held that the writ of error lies when a lower court has refused to recognize the validity of a license granted by the National Commission of Patents and Inventions.

[46] In Banco Nacional Argentino v. Granelli, 101 S. C. N. 70 (1904), the Court stated that according to the national jurisprudence as well as that of the United States Supreme Court the writ of error does not lie unless the decision of the lower court is adverse to the federal or constitutional question pleaded in the inferior court. But the decision of the lower court does not have to be expressly adverse to the federal or constitutional question in order that the writ of error may lie. In Melo de Cané v. Buenos Aires, 115 S. C. N. 111 (1911), the Court held that if in a case it is alleged that a local statute is in conflict with the Constitution and the Court does not categorically decide the question but impliedly sustains the statute the writ of error lies. And in In re Gascón, 115 S. C. N. 411 (1912), the Court also held that the silence of the Court on the federal question may amount to a rejection of the federal question and thus be subject to review by writ of error.

[47] In order that the writ may lie it is held necessary that the federal question should be pleaded during the period of trial. Thus, in Ex Parte Rosenwald, 151 S. C. N. 48 (1925), the Court held that the federal question must be pleaded be-

appeal appear on the record,[48] which shall show that it has a direct and immediate relation to the constitutional clause, treaty, law of Congress, or commission which has been invoked.[49] It is also provided that the writ of error does not lie from the decisions of the lower courts when interpreting or applying the civil, commercial, penal, or mining codes.[50] The statute finally provides that in case

fore final judgment is rendered. And citing Cooley, *Treatise on Constitutional Limitations,* the Court stated: "The Supreme Court of the United States has arrived at the same conclusion when interpreting the Judiciary Act from which we adopted Article 14 of the statute which establishes the writ of error in this country." The Court has held also that the writ of error does not lie in the following cases: when the federal question is not debated during the course of the trial and is set up as a result of the judgment of the Court, Rocatagliata v. Graña, 75 S. C. N. 183 (1898); when the federal question was pleaded for the first time in the petition for appeal, Castro v. Aubone, 104 S. C. N. 407 (1906). In Rodríguez Bernabe v. Impuestos Internos, 183 S. C. N. 396 (1939), the Court held that the writ of error lies if the federal question is pleaded orally during the course of the hearing.

48 The requirement that the federal question shall appear on the face of the record has no importance in Argentine federal procedure and does not give rise to as much litigation as it does in the United States, due to the difference between the civil and criminal procedure applied in the two countries. An Argentine author has explained this difference as follows: "This requirement does not have among us the importance that it has in the federal procedure of the United States because in Argentina we have followed, with few exceptions, the written procedure of Spain and therefore in our procedure the federal question must necessarily appear on the record. In the United States, on the other hand, the question has provoked a great number of conflicts and interpretations because the oral nature of the civil and criminal procedure makes it difficult to determine when the federal question does appear on the record." F. A. Espil, *op. cit.,* p. 65.

49 In Aredondo v. Calaza, 85 S. C. N. 395 (1900), the Court denied a writ of error on the ground that it is not sufficient to make general allegations of unconstitutionality; the party affected must specify what provision of the Constitution, statute, or treaty is violated by the decision of the court. And in Etcheart v. Méndez Cía., 112 S. C. N. 79 (1910), the Court held that an implied invocation of a constitutional provision, statute, or treaty is not sufficient. The principle that the federal question must stand by itself independent of nonfederal questions was discussed in Bemberg y Cía. v. Roca, 133 S. C. N. 298 (1921). In this case the Court, on the authority of Cooley, *Treatise on Constitutional Limitations,* held that when the decision of the court can be based on questions not of a federal character the Court will not review the case even when the federal question has been raised in the trial.

50 In Otta v. Banco Hipotecario Nacional, 183 S. C. N. 287 (1940), the Court stated that under Article 67, § 11, of the Constitution, and Article 13 of Law No. 48, the Supreme Court cannot review on writ of error the judgment of the local courts interpreting the codes of substantive law enacted by Congress. The same principle applies to the interpretation of the bankruptcy statute which forms part of the code of commerce, In re Silva, 122 S. C. N. 46 (1915), and the laws supplementing the general codes, such as the civil marriage statute, Grossi v. Pérez, 114 S. C. N. 70 (1910), and the special criminal statutes, In re Díaz, 102 S. C. N. 112 (1905).

The Court will not review decisions of the provincial courts interpreting the constitutions and statutes of the provinces as long as in their interpretation no right guaranteed by the Constitution, treaty, or law of Congress is violated. Thus, in the Supreme Court reverses the decision of the lower court it shall have power to make a declaration concerning the question in dispute and remand the case to the lower court to proceed according to its judgment, or it may decide the case on its merits, or it may award execution on the judgment, especially if the case had been once before remanded by the Court.

THE DOCTRINE OF JUDICIAL REVIEW

As in the constitutional system of the United States, the power of judicial review is the outstanding characteristic of the Argentine system. In the exercise of this power the federal courts may declare void any executive, legislative, or judicial act which is in conflict with the Constitution. The provincial courts have a corresponding power over all acts in conflict with the national Constitution or with their provincial constitution.[51]

The Argentine Constitution, like that of the United States, does not expressly authorize judicial review. But the absence of express authority has never been deemed a denial to the Supreme Court of the power to pass on the constitutionality of the laws enacted by Congress.[52] In Argentina there is stronger historical evidence than in the United States that the framers of the Constitution intended the Supreme Court to exercise the power. First, the framers of the Argentine Constitution modeled the constitutional system on that of the United States; and since the power of judicial review had al-

---

Sociedad Anónima Frigoríficos Anglo v. Buenos Aires, 172 S. C. N. 149 (1934), the Court, on the authority of Cohen v. Virginia, 6 Wheat. 264 (1821), and of Dillon's edition of *John Marshall: Complete Constitutional Decisions,* stated: "Since the first decisions rendered by judges who had been members of the Constitutional Conventions of 1853 and 1860, this Court has had the opportunity to examine carefully the extent and limits of its jurisdiction in matters relating to the interpretation of the provincial constitutions and laws. These judges came to the conclusion that under Law No. 48, the Supreme Court had no power to review the decisions of the provincial courts interpreting the provincial constitutions and statutes when their interpretation did not conflict with the national Constitution, laws, or treaties."

[51] In Argentina, as in the United States, the Supreme Court is not the only tribunal which has the power to declare laws unconstitutional. Thus, in Chaparrone v. Juez de la Capital, 149 S. C. N. 122 (1927), it was held that a justice of the peace has such power.

A fundamental difference between the Argentine and the United States procedure in raising questions of constitutionality is that in Argentina there is no injunctive relief nor declaratory judgment.

[52] The constitutions of the provinces expressly authorize their supreme courts to declare laws unconstitutional.

ready been established under that Constitution it may be assumed that they adopted this principle also. Indeed the Argentine Supreme Court has stated:

The system of government which rules us today is not our own creation. We found it functioning and tested by long years of experience, and we adopted it. And it has been rightly said that one of the great advantages in having adopted it is that we have come into possession of a whole body of doctrine, practice, and case law which illustrates and completes the fundamental principles of our government and which we can and should utilize in all those constitutional aspects which we have not altered by express provisions of the Constitution.[53]

Second, the Conventions of Santa Fe in 1853 and 1860 accepted the power of judicial review as a matter of fact; it was not an issue brought to the consideration of the conventions.[54] Third, in the Convention of Buenos Aires in 1860 the power of judicial review was recognized, in as much as it was stated that the jurisdiction of the Supreme Court of Argentina was modeled upon that of the United States Supreme Court, and it was also explained how and in what circumstances the power would be exercised.[55]

The doctrine of judicial review has been expressly recognized in statutes as well as by the opinions of the members of Congress who drafted these statutes, many of whom had been members of the Conventions of 1853 and 1860. When the first of these laws was discussed in Congress in 1857, Senator Zapata, chairman of the committee which drafted the law, after stating that the Argentine statute [56] was based on the United States Judiciary Act of 1789 and on the commentaries of Story and Kent, said:

The federal courts have the power not only to refuse to apply laws which they believe are in violation of the Constitution, but also to determine the validity of executive action when it is contended that it infringes the rights guaranteed by the Constitution. This immense political power, which at first sight may appear to be dangerous, does not become so because the federal judges will always exercise their functions within the sphere of action which the Constitution has reserved to them.[57]

53 Ex Parte de la Torre, 19 S. C. N. 231 (1877).

54 *Asambleas constituyentes argentinas,* IV, 535, 1037–52.

55 *Ibid.,* pp. 985–86.

56 This law was never applied but served as a precedent for laws upon which the jurisdiction of the national courts is based.

57 *Cámara de Senadores, Diario de sesiones,* 1857, p. 222.

This was so recognized in the laws enacted in 1862. It was then provided that one of the objects of judicial power is to preserve the supremacy of the Constitution, ignoring any acts of other departments of government in conflict with the Constitution. This provision is an authorization to the national courts to declare unconstitutional not only acts of the governments of the provinces but acts of the national government as well. When this statute was discussed in Congress, Congressman Vélez, chairman of the committee, said:

> The judiciary in the United States is a special power, as it should be among us. When the judiciary passes on the constitutionality of any act, it may be said that it is above Congress because it has the power to declare that the law enacted by Congress is in violation of the Constitution. In this case the judiciary is superior to Congress because it leaves without effect a law passed by this department of government. But when the Supreme Court, as well as the other courts of the nation, decide that a law is unconstitutional they do this in a particular case and do not declare the law unconstitutional in general. For this reason, although the judiciary has the power to declare laws of Congress unconstitutional, it does not become superior to Congress.[58]

One of the most interesting coincidences in the history of Argentine constitutional law is that the first case in which the Supreme Court declared an Act of Congress unconstitutional was very similar to *Marbury v. Madison,* 1 Cranch 137 (1803), in which the Supreme Court of the United States for the first time invalidated a national statute. In that case the Supreme Court of the United States held that Congress had no power to enlarge the original jurisdiction of the Supreme Court as established in the Constitution. *Ex Parte Sojo,* 32 S. C. N. 120 (1887), was Argentina's first case. The petitioner had been imprisoned by the Chamber of Deputies after having been convicted by that legislative body for publishing a libelous article against one of its members. He petitioned the Supreme Court for a writ of habeas corpus under a law of Congress. Although the Court, in several previous cases, had assumed original jurisdiction in similar controversies, it raised the question whether Congress had power to authorize original jurisdiction in cases not mentioned in the Constitution. The attorney general had

58 *Cámara de Diputados, Diario de sesiones,* 1863, I, 301.

reported that the matter had been settled by former decisions. The Court ordered him to make another report on the question. In his second report he contended that the Court had jurisdiction, because as the petitioner had been imprisoned by order of the Chamber of Deputies the writ involved the exercise of appellate, not original, jurisdiction, and that it was unnecessary to raise the issue whether Congress had power to alter the original jurisdiction.

The Court, however, declared itself without jurisdiction. As to the argument on appellate jurisdiction, it held that as the petitioner was not convicted by a court but by a legislative body the case could not be considered as an appeal. On the authority of decisions of the United States Supreme Court [59] it was held that a case could not be considered as on appeal unless a decision or decree rendered by an inferior court is brought before a superior tribunal for review. The Court further said that the Chamber of Deputies could not be considered an inferior court and its decisions could not be subject to judicial review because that would constitute a violation of the principle of separation of powers.

On the fundamental issue the Court said that as Article 102 of the Constitution, unlike the Constitution of the United States, provides that in certain matters the Court shall have original and *exclusive* jurisdiction, Congress could not change the original jurisdiction in any manner whatsoever. But instead of holding, as in other cases, that the act of Congress was in conflict with Article 31 of the Constitution, the Court based its decision on *Marbury v. Madison,* 1 Cranch 137 (1803), and on the commentaries of Kent and Story. The Court stated:

It is timely to cite also the case of William Marbury v. James Madison, Secretary of State of the United States, in confirmation of the doctrine irrevocably established by the United States Supreme Court that Congress cannot assign original jurisdiction to the Supreme Court over cases other than those specified in the Constitution. In this case it was held that a law of Congress repugnant to the Constitution is not a law; that when the Constitution and a law of Congress are in conflict the Constitution must prevail. It was finally held that Congress cannot confer upon the Supreme Court any type of original jurisdiction which has not been already conferred upon it by the Constitution.

59 The Alicia v. United States, 7 Wall. 571 (1869); Ex Parte Bunford, 3 Cranch 448 (1806); United States v. Hamilton, 3 Dallas 17 (1795); and Ex Parte Barry, 2 Howard 65 (1844).

But this decision, unlike that of *Marbury v. Madison,* was not unanimous. Of the five members of the Court, Chief Justice Victorica and Associate Justices Frías and Ibargúren held the statute unconstitutional; Associate Justices de la Torre and Zavalía delivered dissenting opinions. The dissenting opinion of Justice de la Torre denied the power to declare the law unconstitutional, on the ground that there was nothing in the Constitution expressly prohibiting Congress to enact the statute.

When the fundamental law has not expressly limited the powers of Congress these cannot be restricted because something has been discovered in the spirit of the Constitution which nevertheless is not mentioned in the instrument. It is only when there are express constitutional limitations on the legislative power that the courts are justified in declaring unconstitutional the acts of the legislative department.

Within a year after *Ex Parte Sojo* the Supreme Court declared another law of Congress unconstitutional in *Municipalidad de la Capital v. Elortondo,* 33 S. C. N. 162 (1888). The national statute authorized the municipality of Buenos Aires to expropriate private property for the purpose of constructing an avenue, and the municipality instituted eminent domain proceedings for land in excess of what was needed. The defendant contended that she could not be compelled to sell the excess; that the statute constituted a violation of property rights guaranteed by the Constitution. The lower court sustained the statute. On appeal, the Supreme Court reversed, holding that Congress had exceeded its power.

The Court thus explained the constitutional and statutory basis of the power to declare laws unconstitutional:

It is an elemental principle of our constitutional organization that the courts shall have the power and the duty to examine the laws in the specific controversies brought before them in order to determine if they are in conflict with the Constitution, and the courts can refuse to apply them if they are in conflict with the fundamental law. The exercise of such power by the judiciary constitutes a protection of the rights guaranteed in the Constitution, and at the same time it prevents the possible commission of abuses by the other two departments of the government. The exercise of the power of judicial review by the courts is derived from the separation of the legislative from the amending power made by the Constitution and from the essentially subordinate and limited nature of the legislative power as compared with the constituent power. This principle is expressly established in the laws of April 16, 1862, and September 14, 1863. The first of these laws declares that one of the objects of the federal judiciary is to maintain the supremacy of the national Constitution, ignoring in the decision of cases any acts of the other departments of government which conflict with the national Constitution. The second law provides that the federal and the provincial courts shall apply, as the supreme law of the land, first the Constitution, and then, in the following order, the laws enacted by Congress, the treaties entered into between the national government and foreign nations, the laws of the provinces, the general laws enforced before the formation of the Union, and the principles of international law.

After discussing the power of Congress to determine what is and what is not a public purpose, the Court continued:

Although there is not a precise line distinguishing what is a public purpose and what is not, when the legislature exercises the power of eminent domain, under which Congress has a wide discretion in determining when property is needed for a public use, nevertheless when Congress exceeds its functions in the execution of this power the courts have the power to protect the rights of property where these have been invaded by Congress. Such is the doctrine established by the Supreme Court of the United States in relation to the taxing power of Congress,[60] under which the legislative department has a wider discretion than under the power of eminent domain. The Supreme Court of the United States has said that the legislative department, in the exercise of its taxing powers, as in the exercise of its other powers, is subject to the control of the courts, and as a matter of fact the courts have declared unconstitutional taxes which were not imposed for purely public purposes.

As in the former case, Associate Justice Zavalía dissented on the ground that as there was no express provision in the Constitution defining what is a public use the Court should respect the congressional declaration.

The power of judicial review had been exercised by the Supreme Court before the Sojo and the Elortondo cases, but none of the earlier cases overturned an Act of Congress. Indeed the first case was decided shortly after the Court was organized. This was *Gobierno Nacional v. Ríos,* 1 S. C. N. 32 (1863). Defendants were charged with the commission of the crimes of homicide and piracy aboard an Argentine ship on the Paraná River, one of the navigable

[60] Citing Steel v. Smelting Co., 106 U. S. 447 (1882); and Cole v. La Grange, 113 U. S. 1 (1885).

waterways of Argentina. When the crime was committed the federal sectional courts were not yet organized, and the President issued a decree authorizing the captain of the port of the city of Rosario to try the offenders. Upon conviction they appealed to the Supreme Court, contending that the sentence imposed upon them was null and void because the decree authorizing their trial was unconstitutional: first, because under the Constitution, Congress and not the President had power to create tribunals inferior to the Supreme Court; second, because the captain of the port was not a judge within the meaning of the Constitution; third, because according to the Constitution neither the President nor his subordinate officials could exercise judicial functions. The decree was held unconstitutional as an encroachment by the President upon the powers vested in Congress, and the sentence imposed upon the defendants was adjudged null and void.

A year later the Court declared another presidential decree in conflict not only with the Constitution but also with a law of Congress. This was *Gobierno Nacional v. Tomkinson and Co.*, 1 S. C. N. 62 (1864), in which a fine imposed on the defendants by customs authorities was confirmed by the chief executive. All proceedings were authorized by an executive decree, not by a law of Congress. The defendants appealed to the Supreme Court and contended that the procedure was unconstitutional: first, because the Constitution prohibited the President from exercising judicial functions, and second, because by statute the federal sectional courts had jurisdiction over the alleged crime for which the defendants were fined. The decision was reversed. This case is significant because it is the first one in which the Court exercised the power of judicial review without specifying that it was acting under Article 31 of the Constitution, from which may be drawn the implication that the Court possessed such power.

In *Ex Parte Mendoza,* 1 S. C. N. 350 (1864), where the Court for the first time declared unconstitutional a decision of a lower federal court, no reference was made to Article 31. The issue was whether a person accused of crime could be questioned under oath concerning the offense and compelled to answer under pain of criminal prosecution for contempt. The defendant successfully contended that such procedure was contrary to the provision of the Constitution that no person can be compelled to testify against himself. This was the first case in which the Court exercised the power of judicial review to protect the rights guaranteed to persons in criminal prosecutions.

The first cases in which the Argentine Supreme Court protected property and contractual rights against encroachment by the provincial governments were *Ituraspe v. Montaldo,* 8 S. C. N. 45 (1869), and *Procurador Fiscal de San Juan v. Sociedad Benéfica de Señoras,* 11 S. C. N. 139 (1871). They are somewhat parallel to two early United States Supreme Court cases, *Fletcher v. Peck,* 6 Cranch 87 (1810), and *Dartmouth College v. Woodward,* 4 Wheat. 518 (1819). In the first, with an issue similar to that in *Fletcher v. Peck,* the Court declared unconstitutional a provincial statute which dispossessed plaintiff of property bought from the province under the provisions of a statute enacted by the provincial legislature which declared void the sale of land made under the former statute. The Court held this statute in violation of Article 17 of the Constitution which provides that property is inviolable and that no inhabitant of the nation can be deprived thereof without due process of law.

The second case, somewhat similar to the Dartmouth College case, involved a women's philanthropic society which had been created by an executive decree of the governor of the province of San Juan. The society adopted rules and regulations which were approved by executive decree. They provided that the society would be supported by its own resources and by contributions from the provincial and national governments and that the society would appoint its governing body in the future when vacancies occurred. Some years later the governor of the province by decree ordered the dissolution of the society and provided that a similar institution composed of men should take and administer the funds of the organization. The president of the defendant society attacked the validity of the decree, alleging that, as the defendant was a juristic person which could not be dissolved except as provided by law without violating the contractual relationship between the defendant and the government, the decree was in conflict with Article 14 of the Constitution, which guarantees the right of association for useful purposes, and also in violation of Article 17 above mentioned. The provincial courts upheld the decree. Five grounds were assigned: first, there was no contract between the defendant and the government; second, the defendant had ceased to be a juristic person when dissolved by the branch of the government which created it; third, the defendant was a public and not a private institution; fourth, the right of association for useful purposes is subject to governmental regulation; fifth, the rights of the members of the association were not prejudiced by the dissolution of the society, since the funds of the organization were to be used for charitable purposes. On appeal the Supreme Court reversed, saying that the defendant society was not a public institution nor a branch of the government but a juristic person which could only be dissolved according to the provisions of the law authorizing dissolution, and further that, even if the defendant were not a juristic person, its funds could not be taken by the government without violating Articles 14 and 17 of the Constitution. In these two cases, as in the Mendoza and Tomkinson cases, the Court refrained from stating under what constitutional or statutory provision it had the power to pass on the constitutionality of the provincial statutes.

The Argentine Constitution reserves to the provinces the power to legislate concerning press offenses and to vest the provincial courts with jurisdiction to try these offenses (Art. 32). In *Procurador Fiscal v. Moreno,* 10 S. C. N. 361 (1871), the Court made use of the power of judicial review to prevent the national government from exercising jurisdiction over such offenses. The defendant was accused of the crime of libel committed against a national judge. A federal sectional court took jurisdiction, and the Supreme Court reversed its decision on the ground that it violated Article 32 of the Constitution.

Under the Argentine Constitution, Congress has power to levy taxes on exports and imports. In *Mendoza Hermanos v. San Luis,* 3 S. C. N. 131 (1885), in which for the first time the Argentine Supreme Court declared unconstitutional a provincial statute, the Court prevented the provincial government from taxing exports. The defendant province had imposed a tax on all products exported to other provinces, but the Court declared the statute unconstitutional on the ground that the power to tax exports is given exclusively to the national government. In this case the Court based its decision on Article 31 of the Constitution.

By statutes as well as by rules of the Supreme Court itself, certain general principles have been established limiting the exercise of the power of judicial review in order that the courts shall not interfere with other departments of government. The necessity for such limitations has been recognized by the Court in *Ex Parte Bonevo*, 155 S. C. N. 248 (1929):

> The most delicate mission of the judiciary of the nation is to know how to maintain itself within its proper sphere of governmental action reserved to it by the Constitution without encroaching upon the functions which belong to other departments of government, inasmuch as it is the duty of the judiciary to maintain the observance of the national Constitution. For this reason it is a matter of grave concern for constitutional harmony and public order that the judiciary should not encroach upon the powers vested by the Constitution in the other departments of government.[61]

The first statute dealing with the judicial system declared that the courts shall never assume jurisdiction officiously but only in specific controversies involving adversary parties and justiciable issues.[62] The Court has uniformly adhered to this principle. Thus in *Ex Parte Moores*, 30 S. C. N. 281 (1886), in which the petitioners requested a lower federal court to declare an act of Congress null and void, the petition was dismissed on the ground that it did not contain the essential elements of a case or controversy. On appeal the lower court was sustained, and the Court stated:

> There cannot be a suit unless there is a party defendant. The way to proceed when a person wants to recur to a court is very simple. If a person believes that his constitutional rights have been violated by a law of Congress he must first obey and comply with the law under protest or with reservations, and then sue the officer who executed the law or demand the repayment of that which has been illegally taken away from him. The federal courts cannot make general declarations, but must apply legal principles to a specific and concrete controversy. The

[61] In In re Gallino, 160 S. C. N. 247 (1931), Associate Justice Sagarna, citing Willoughby, *Constitutional Law*, 2nd ed., I, 5, said: "In every government which has a written constitution it is understood that the power to give a final decision in governmental matters must be vested in some one of the departments of government, but from this it does not necessarily follow that the court shall have the final say in all public affairs. Not all constitutional questions are reviewable by the judges nor even by the highest court, because each department of government has its own sphere of governmental action in which the exercise of its functions is not subject to review by this or by any other court."

[62] Law No. 27, Art. 2.

court that should declare a law unconstitutional without reference to a specific controversy would be acting outside of its sphere of action and would invade that of the legislative power.[63]

In the process of constitutional interpretation the Court has established several principles which are closely related to the one just discussed. Only parties affected by the alleged unconstitutional statutes or acts of the executive can question their constitutionality.[64] No person can attack the constitutionality of a statute unless his economic interests or legal rights have been violated by the enforcement of the statute in question.[65] The Court shall determine if it has jurisdiction of the case before declaring it unconstitutional.[66] The Court will limit its decisions to the issues and parties involved in the controversy and will not decide the question abstractly.[67] When a statute is declared unconstitutional, the Court does not repeal it but merely refuses to apply it, and the decision of the Court will affect only the parties and the issues involved in the specific controversy.[68] The Court will not render advisory opinions to the President, to Congress, or to any executive officer.[69] The Court will not declare a law unconstitutional unless such a declaration is necessary in order to decide the case.[70] Once an issue has been settled by the Supreme Court, the lower courts as well as the Supreme Court itself are bound by such

[63] In In re Bravo, 115 S. C. N. 163 (1911), the Court, on the authority of Muskrat v. United States, 219 U. S. 346 (1911), and of Miller, *Lectures on the Constitution of the United States*, p. 315, stated: "The decisions of the Supreme Court of the United States, applying principles analogous to those already cited, hold that the power to declare a law unconstitutional can be exercised only when there is a case or controversy in which there are conflicting parties and justiciable issues involving legal rights which the Court has the power to protect according to the Constitution and the laws of the Republic."

[64] Seré v. La Capital, 181 S. C. N. 362 (1938).

[65] Villanueva v. La Capital, 24 S. C. N. 248 (1882); S. A. Territorial Río de La Plata v. La Nación, 182 S. C. N. 276 (1938).

[66] Araoz v. Compañía Jujeña de Kerosene, 3 S. C. N. 139 (1866).

[67] Fisco Nacional v. Comerciantes de Mendoza, 5 S. C. N. 74 (1868).

[68] In Ex Parte Zumba de Tramberti, 183 S. C. N. 76 (1939), the Supreme Court stated: "One of the great achievements of the makers of the Constitution of the United States of North America consisted in limiting the effects of the judgments of the courts in cases where statutes had been declared unconstitutional to the facts, issues, and parties involved in the same, without affecting the normal application of the statute and the rights of persons not involved in the case in which the law was declared unconstitutional."

[69] Pintos v. Sosa, 28 S. C. N. 411 (1885).

[70] Mignaquy v. Gobierno Nacional, 129 S. C. N. 93 (1919).

decision,[71] even in common law cases.[72] The laws,[73] as well as the acts of government officials,[74] are presumed to be valid until they are declared unconstitutional by a court of competent jurisdiction. A law will not be declared unconstitutional unless there is a clear and undoubted opposition between the law and the Constitution.[75] The Court, when examining whether or not a law is unconstitutional, will not consider the soundness or unsoundness of its economic or social theories but only whether the statute is in conflict with the Constitution.[76] The Court will not declare a law unconstitutional because the legislators were not wise in the selection of the means to solve the social or economic problems which the law attempted to solve.[77] The Court will not consider the purely moral aspects of the issues involved.[78] The Court will not consider whether the law will be efficient or inefficient from the point of view of its economic operation.[79] The Court will always give full

[71] Videla v. García, 9 S. C. N. 53 (1870).

[72] In Barreta v. Córdoba, 183 S. C. N. 409 (1939), in which the question was whether it should follow the doctrine of a previous case or abandon it, the Court declared that there was no reason why it should not follow the principle of the former cases, and, citing Cooley, *Treatise on Constitutional Limitations,* stated: "It would be extremely inconvenient for the community if judicial precedents were not taken into consideration and consequently followed by the courts." And again, citing Willoughby, *Constitutional Law,* the Court explained the nature and limitations of the doctrine of *stare decisis,* especially in constitutional cases, saying: "And although it does not mean that the authority of precedents may be decisive in the decision of all cases, nor that the principle of *stare decisis* is applied without any reservation in constitutional matters, it does not necessarily follow that the precedent should not be applied when it does not clearly appear that there was no error or inconvenience in the decision of the question involved in the case. And if this does not appear from the previous case there is no reason why its doctrine should not be followed."

[73] Schmidt v. Banco de Santa Fe, 25 S. C. N. 347 (1883).

[74] The River Plate Fresh Meat Co. v. Buenos Aires, 100 S. C. N. 318 (1903).

[75] In Avegno v. Buenos Aires, 14 S. C. N. 432 (1874), in which the question was the constitutionality of a law of Congress providing that the Supreme Court shall exercise original jurisdiction in cases between a province and its residents or residents of other provinces, or citizens or subjects of foreign states, the law was upheld, and the Court stated, on the authority of *The Federalist,* No. 80: "In order that a law duly enacted and promulgated shall be declared unconstitutional it is essential that the provision of the law shall be absolutely incompatible with the Constitution and that there shall be an evident opposition between them. This must be so because of the respect to which the legislative department that enacted the law is entitled. The incompatibility between the law and the Constitution may be based on the letter of the Constitution, or on the spirit of the same when the letter of the Constitution is obscure or gives room for different interpretations."

[76] Grosso v. Mendoza, 128 S. C. N. 435 (1918).

[77] Ercolano v. Lanteri, 136 S. C. N. 161 (1922).

[78] Aparicio v. Salta, 135 S. C. N. 113 (1921).

[79] Guardian Assurance Co. v. Gobierno Nacional, 150 S. C. N. 89 (1927).

effect to the intentions of the legislators as evidenced from the letter and the spirit of the laws.[80] A tax law will not be declared unconstitutional on the ground that it is unjust or inconvenient to the taxpayer as long as it does not violate the rights guaranteed by the Constitution.[81] The Court will not question the motive [82] or errors of the legislators in enacting the statute. Finally the Court will not permit a party who has previously waived the right to test it to attack the constitutionality of a statute.[83]

The Court will not entertain jurisdiction of cases where the subject matter is of a political nature. The Court has refused to take jurisdiction in the following: a suit to declare unconstitutional a law of Congress and a presidential decree authorizing intervention in a province to restore the republican form of government [84] and to guarantee to the people the enjoyment of their institutions; [85] a suit to review the president's discretion in declaring a state of siege in the nation; [86] a suit to test the legality of the composition of Congress; [87] a controversy to test the validity of the proceedings of an electoral board in charge of counting the votes for members of Congress.[88]

In 1930 there was presented to the Supreme Court a very interesting juridical and political problem closely related to the principles under consideration. It had to do with the recognition by

80 Compañía Azucarera Tucumana v. Tucumán, 150 S. C. N. 150 (1927).

81 Ramos v. Municipalidad de la Capital, 181 S. C. N. 266 (1935).

82 In Ferrocarril del Sud v. Draque Cía., 131 S. C. N. 105 (1920), the Court stated: "The power of the courts to interpret the Constitution and the laws does not have any other limitations than those which result from their own condition as judges. Therefore the judges, in the exercise of their judicial functions, may make use of their intelligence and other means of investigation, either legal or scientific, if the judicial precedents already established conflict with their own convictions. But in the process of interpreting the Constitution and the laws they should see the issues of the controversies as judges and should not take into consideration the motives or intentions behind the makers of the laws or the intentions of the parties when attacking the statutes, nor should they assume any attitude which may tend to impair the reputation and dignity of the judiciary which they represent."

83 Departamento Nacional del Trabajo v. Sassone Robene, 187 S. C. N. 6 (1940).

84 The Court cited Luther v. Borden, 7 Howard 1 (1849), in which the United States Supreme Court held that it had no jurisdiction in a case in which the subject matter was political in nature.

85 Gobernador Provisorio de San Juan v. Interventor Nacional, 54 S. C. N. 180 (1893).

86 Ex Parte Tamborini, 167 S. C. N. 25 (1933).

87 S. A. Azucarera Concepción v. Tucumán, 143 S. C. N. 131 (1925).

88 Varela v. Arizú, 23 S. C. N. 257 (1881); Peña v. Presidente Senado, 47 S. C. N. 191 (1892).

the Court of the revolutionary government which came into power on September 6, 1930, when the government of the late President Irigoyen was overthrown by a successful revolution. On September 10, 1930, the president of the provisional government, General Uriburu, addressed a communication to the Supreme Court in which he stated that a provisional government had been established as a result of the revolution, that the provisional government was in possession of the military and police forces necessary to preserve peace, safety and order, and that it was ready to defend property, liberty, and life, and to maintain the supremacy of the Constitution and the laws of the country. In a resolution of September 30, 1930,[89] the Court, on the basis of that communication, recognized the provisional government as a de facto government on two fundamental grounds: first, that the facts stated in the communication unquestionably characterized it as a de facto government; second, that, according to national and international doctrines concerning de facto officers, their acts were valid no matter what defects or vices were inherent in their appointment or election, and that no one could test the validity of their appointment when they were in apparent possession of the powers and functions of government. But although the Court recognized the provisional government as a de facto one, it also stated in its resolution that the acts of such government would be subject to judicial review as if it were a de jure government, if any of its officers should violate the rights of personal liberty and property which the Argentine Constitution guarantees to all persons.[90]

This resolution of the Argentine Court, by which it solved the most difficult juridical and political problem ever confronted by it since the establishment of the Constitution in 1853, demonstrates that even in times of crisis the Constitution is the point of departure for the solution of all national problems. In other words, even the gravest political situations may have a solution within the framework of the constitutional system, and it is unnecessary to appeal to extralegal methods. This was shown by the communication of the provisional government which stated that that government would

[89] 158 S. C. N. 290 (1930).

[90] In Cahiza v. Gobierno Nacional, 177 S. C. N. 238 (1937), the Court declared unconstitutional a decree of the provisional government and stated that it had the same constitutional powers as a de jure government, but no greater powers.

support the Constitution and the laws enacted in pursuance of the same, and also by the resolution of the Court which, although recognizing such a government as a de facto one, nevertheless advised it that it had no more powers than a de jure government and that its acts would be subject to judicial review in order to maintain the supremacy of the Constitution.

Part Two: DIVISION OF POWERS IN THE FEDERAL SYSTEM

IV: FEDERAL-PROVINCIAL AND INTER-PROVINCIAL RELATIONSHIPS

ON A general and somewhat preliminary view two sets of relationships within the federal system must be observed.[1] They are, first, the relationships between the central government and the provinces, and second, those among the provinces themselves. In respect to the former the Argentine system reveals some wide and significant differences from the practices prevailing in the United States; as to the latter a note of similarity runs through the doctrines of both countries.

FEDERAL-PROVINCIAL RELATIONSHIPS

Four features will be discussed under this head: the guarantee of a republican form of government; provincial governors as natural agents of the national government; protection against invasion and domestic violence; and intergovernmental tax immunities.

Republican Form of Government

Here occurs the most notable difference between the two systems. The Argentine Constitution, following that of the United States, imposes upon the central government the obligation of guaranteeing to the provinces a republican form of government.[2] But it goes further in that it provides that "the federal government shall intervene in the territory of the provinces to guarantee such form of government" (Art. 6).

[1] In subsequent chapters detailed consideration will be given to the division of powers between the central government and the provinces.

[2] "The United States shall guarantee to every State in this Union a Republican Form of Government . . ." (U. S. Constitution, Art. IV, § 4).

Article 5 defines the essential elements of a republican form of government and under what conditions the federal government guarantees its enjoyment. "Each province shall adopt for itself a constitution under the republican representative system, which shall accord with the principles, declarations, and guarantees of the National Constitution, and which shall insure the administration of justice, municipal government, and primary education. Under these conditions the federal government guarantees to each province the enjoyment and exercise of its own institutions." Under these provisions the federal government has power to intervene for two purposes, first, to support or re-establish the authorities deposed by sedition or invasion, and second, to guarantee the enjoyment and exercise of provincial institutions. In this second situation the federal government intervenes not to protect the authorities from sedition or invasion, but to protect the people if the provincial authorities prevent them from enjoying a republican form of government.

The first type of intervention is called executive, and takes place when the local authorities of the provinces request it on their own behalf. It is called "executive" because the federal government does it peremptorily in compliance with the constitutional mandate, with the object of protecting the province against invasion and domestic violence. The executive orders such intervention in the exercise of his power as commander in chief of the army and the navy. The second type of intervention is called "reconstructive," or "political," and takes place when the republican form of government and the enjoyment and exercise of the institutions of the provinces have been subverted for any reason whatsoever, especially when the authorities of the provinces have been responsible for this subversion.

In *Ex Parte Orfilia*, 154 S. C. N. 192 (1929), which involved the validity of the arrest of the petitioner by order of the National Commissioner during a period of intervention, the Supreme Court explained the differences between the Argentine and the United States constitutions and stated:

The Constitution of the United States only guarantees a republican form of government to the states. The Argentine Constitution, on the other hand, guarantees two things, both a republican form of government, and the enjoyment and effective exercise of the provincial institutions. Thus, while in North America the federal government is obliged to protect a State only when its form of government has been subverted, the Argentine federal government must protect a province when the form of government has been corrupted—that is, when the exercise and enjoyment of the republican institutions have been interrupted.

The question as to what branch of the federal government has power to decide if a province has or has not a republican form of government, and to intervene, was discussed for the first time in the Argentine Congress in 1869,[3] when a bill was introduced by the minister of the interior authorizing the President to intervene in the province of San Juan. In the debate two theories were advanced: one, that the executive had the power to intervene in order to restore the republican form of government; the other, that only Congress had the power to authorize such an intervention. Senator Mitre, exponent of the latter theory, cited *Luther v. Borden,* 7 How. 1 (1849), and United States statutes of 1792 and 1795, authorizing the President to intervene in a state in cases of rebellion or insurrection. On the other hand, the minister of the interior, Dr. Mariano Varela, argued that the executive department could also exercise such power without the authorization of a statute, the power being executive in nature. He also contended that in *Luther v. Borden* Chief Justice Taney did not specifically hold that such a power could be exercised by Congress only.

Twenty-odd years later, in *Cullen v. Llerena,* 53 S. C. N. 420 (1893), the question was presented to the Supreme Court. The plaintiff alleged that the federal statute authorizing the President to intervene in the province of Santa Fe was unconstitutional on the ground that it violated Article 105 of the Constitution, which provided that provinces should establish their own local institutions and should govern themselves and elect their governors and legislators without interference by the federal government. The Supreme Court declared itself without jurisdiction and held, citing *Luther v. Borden, supra* and *Texas v. White,* 7 Wall. 700 (1869), that the determination whether a state has a republican form of government is a political, not a judicial, question. Only Congress has the power, the Court held, to declare whether a prov-

[3] *Cámara de Senadores, Diario de sesiones,* 1869, pp. 174, 210, 239, 281, 315, 346, 370, 398.

ince has a republican form of government and whether the federal government should intervene in order to restore the authorities and republican institutions. *Sociedad Anónima Azucarera Concepción v. Tucumán,* 143 S. C. N. 271 (1924), presented the question from another angle. The plaintiff corporation attacked the constitutionality of a statute of the province of Tucumán on the ground that the local government was not republican in form, because when the legislature passed the statute some legislators were prevented by force from attending and a quorum was formed by compelling other legislators to attend the session by force. The Court, citing the former case, held that the question was political and that the Court had no authority to decide the controversy.[4]

Argentina has no general law authorizing the President to intervene in the provinces, but whenever necessary a special law has been passed to meet the individual situation. On May 30, 1869,[5] President Sarmiento sent a message to Congress recommending the enactment of a general law regulating federal intervention, similar to the United States statute of February 28, 1795, by which the President was authorized under certain conditions to use the military forces to intervene in the states in order to guarantee their republican form of government and protect them from insurrection and invasion. In his message he cited the interpretation given to the statute by the United States Supreme Court in *Luther v. Borden, supra.* Congress, however, passed a different statute, and the President vetoed it. Sometimes the President has authorized intervention while Congress was in recess, and when Congress reconvened he notified it of this action, which was approved. Such was the case in the interventions in the provinces of Entre Ríos, in 1873,[6] and those of Santa Fe, Buenos Aires, Corrientes, and Entre Ríos, in 1880.[7] In 1878 Congress ordered the cessation of the intervention in the province of Corrientes authorized by the President while Congress was in recess.[8]

Federal intervention is effected by an agent of the federal government called the national commissioner or "interventor." He is

[4] In San Luis v. Donovan, 54 S. C. N. 180 (1893), and Ex Parte Orfilia, 154 S. C. N. 192 (1929), the same principle was applied.

[5] *Cámara de Diputados, Diario de sesiones,* 1869, p. 360.

[6] *Colección de leyes nacionales,* III, 371.

[7] *Ibid.,* IV, 522.

[8] *Ibid.,* IV, 401.

appointed by and is subject to the President and performs merely those duties which the President or the laws of Congress authorize. His appointment, as well as the purpose of the intervention, is specified in the President's decree, countersigned either by the minister of the interior or by all the ministers of the President's cabinet, depending on the nature of the intervention. If it is for the purpose of reorganizing the entire government of the province, the national commissioner takes charge of the government of the province until it is reconstructed and the new legislative, executive, judicial or municipal authorities are duly elected or appointed. The national commissioner exercises both legislative and executive power. In regard to the judicial department of the province, it is the general practice for national commissioners to appoint the members of the judiciary provisionally without following the provincial constitution or laws. This practice of the commissioner, although it has been alleged to violate Article 18 of the Constitution, has been upheld by the Supreme Court in *Ex Parte Orfilia,* already discussed (p. 89). The power of the federal government to reorganize the government of the provinces through the national commissioner has been uniformly sustained by the Court, on the theory that the power has been impliedly delegated by the provinces to the federal government by the clause of the Constitution which authorizes the federal government to make effective the guarantees established by the Constitution.[9]

Regarding the powers of the national commissioner, the Supreme Court has established the following principles: First, that although the intervention is a political act of the federal government and by this very nature is limited to the objects provided in Article 6 of the Constitution, yet impliedly the federal government has the power, when the provinces have no regularly constituted authority, to provide for the economic, social, and administrative necessities of the provinces.[10] Second, that the powers exercised by the national commissioner are vested in him not by the provinces but by the national government and limited only to the objects of the intervention and according to the Con-

[9] Laborde Hermanos v. Mendoza, 143 S. C. N. 11 (1925); Anvaria v. Buenos Aires, 127 S. C. N. 122 (1918).

[10] Laborde Hermanos v. Mendoza, 143 S. C. N. 11 (1925).

stitution and the laws of Congress.[11] Third, that as the powers of the commissioner are limited by the law of Congress or the decree of the President authorizing the intervention, and as these powers are thus delegated ones, he cannot represent the province in a suit against it in the Supreme Court.[12] Fourth, that "interventions have been instituted not to abridge the rights of the inhabitants of the provinces but fully to guarantee their exercise; not to do away with the juridical personality of the provinces, which is of vital importance, nor to create a moratorium not authorized expressly by law." [13] The Court established this doctrine in a case where a creditor sued the province for a debt contracted before the intervention. The plaintiff obtained a judgment, but the national commissioner refused to pay it because, he stated, as representative of the federal government he could not recognize any debt contracted by the province before the intervention. The Court ordered the payment of the debt on the ground that the intervention does not suspend rights guaranteed by the Constitution.

A study of the reconstructive or political interventions reveals that these interventions have taken place for the following reasons: violation of the principle of separation of powers; corruption of the electoral franchise through the use of fraudulent tactics on the part of provincial officials or through the enactment of election laws which tend to prevent impartial elections; deadlock between the branches of the governments of the provinces which have made it impossible for the government to function; usurpation of public offices by the governor and the legislators after their tenure of office has expired or after electoral defeat; corruption in the administration of the public funds of the provinces which has brought the government into bankruptcy; arbitrary acts on the part of the legislators, such as refusing to permit the members of the minority parties to assume their seats; the enactment of laws in violation of the Constitution, and other forms of governmental irregularities which, according to the President and Congress, destroy the republican form of government in the provinces or

11 Moreno v. Interventor Nacional de Buenos Aires, 55 S. C. N. 192 (1894).
12 Sarmiento v. Interventor Nacional de Buenos Aires, 54 S. C. N. 550 (1893).
13 Puebla v. Mendoza, 156 S. C. N. 126 (1929).

prevent their inhabitants from enjoying and exercising the rights and institutions guaranteed by the Constitution.[14]

Speaking of the difference between the United States and the Argentine conceptions of what constitutes a republican form of government, a distinguished United States authority has said:

> In both cases the obligation is placed upon the federal government to guarantee to each constituent part of the federal system (States or Provinces) a republican form of government. In the United States, this has been construed to mean nothing more than a guarantee that the people shall "choose their own officers for governmental administration and pass their own laws in virtue of legislative power reposed in representative bodies, whose acts may be said to be those of the people themselves." *Duncan v. McCall,* 139 U. S. 449 (1891).
>
> In Argentina, a totally different view has been taken of the power which this clause confers on the federal government. Instead of drawing a line, as indicated in this decision, the thesis maintained and successfully enforced by the Argentine government has been that this guarantee involves more than the right of the people to choose their own officers and to make laws through a representative assembly. It also includes the lawful conduct of elections, strict compliance with the preliminary requirements in the formation of the registry rolls and, finally, the guarantee of an accurate counting of the election returns.[15]

Since 1853 there have been more than a hundred of these interventions in Argentina,[16] and through them it is possible for the national government to encroach upon the self-government of the provinces. Many times there has been justification for this intervention, but in many other cases political expediency has dictated them.[17] In the United States, the only somewhat similar interventions took place after the Civil War, when the constitutions and governments of the southern states were reconstructed in line with the policy laid down by the national government.

Here lies a fundamental difference between the practice of federalism in Argentina and in the United States. In the United States, no matter how irregular the functioning of the state government may be, and how corrupt or arbitrary the holding of elections, the federal government does not intervene. The federal

[14] L. H. Sommariva, *Historia de las intervenciones federales en las provincias de la República argentina,* II, 351–60.

[15] L. S. Rowe, *The Federal System of the Argentine Republic,* pp. 87–88.

[16] L. H. Sommariva, *op. cit.,* I, 180.

[17] J. González Calderón, *Por la libertad y el derecho,* pp. 153, 164, 198.

government leaves the people of the states to solve their own political problems. In Argentina, the federal government intervenes and solves the conflicts in behalf either of the people or of one of the conflicting political factions. The explanation for this difference lies in great part in the different political traditions of the two peoples. Although the tradition of local self-government is stronger in the people of the United States, this fact is not the fundamental one in determining the differences in policy in regard to intervention. The chief reason underlying this difference is that in Argentina, much more than in the United States, there has been a conflict between federal and unitary principles and practices of government. Although the Argentine Constitution was a compromise between these conflicting theories and practices, the policy and methods followed by the government are a manifestation of the unitary principles which the framers incorporated expressly and impliedly in the Constitution.

Provincial Governors as Natural Agents of the National Government

An interesting feature of the Argentine Constitution, not found in the Constitution of the United States, is that the governors of the provinces are declared to be the natural agents of the federal government for the enforcement of the Constitution and of the laws of the nation (Art. 110). For example, the governors of the provinces have the power and duty to enforce the resolutions or decrees of any of the departments of the federal government.[18] If a federal judge in a province, or the Supreme Court of the nation, wishes to enforce a decision of the Court, he requests the executive of the province to secure its execution. Thus, in *Burmeinster v. Iriondo*, 26 S. C. N. 119 (1883), where a court of the province of Santa Fe refused to obey an order of the Supreme Court to send to it certain documents needed in a suit pending before the federal tribunal, the Supreme Court requested from the executive of the province the use of the police in order to take the documents from the provincial court and bring them before

[18] The constitutions of several provinces provide that the governor is the direct and immediate agent of the national government in the provinces for the enforcement of the national Constitution and laws.

the Supreme Court. In the United States the federal courts employ their own officers to enforce their orders.

The wisdom of this feature of the Constitution has been widely discussed by Argentine authors. Those who condemn it maintain that it is contrary to the principle of federalism, in that it converts the governors of the provinces into mere employees of the federal government, lacking the necessary means to carry out the duties imposed upon them.[19] On the other hand, those who favor it argue that it prevents the existence within the nation of magistrates with great authority who might consider themselves equal to the governors of the provinces, and that it makes it easier to enforce the national laws within the provinces, since they are enforced by governors who represent the people. Finally, they say that if the governors do not enforce the federal laws, the national government may choose other agents; because, although the Constitution makes the governors the natural agents of the national government, yet they are not the only agents that government may employ.[20]

Protection against Invasion and Domestic Violence

The obligation imposed by the United States Constitution on the federal government to protect the states in case of invasion and domestic violence[21] was reproduced in the Argentine Constitution, although with certain changes in terminology. The Argentine Constitution provides that the federal government "shall intervene in the territory of the provinces in order to repel foreign invasions and, at the request of their constituted authorities, to support or re-establish them, should they have been deposed by sedition or by invasion from another province" (Art. 6).

There is a difference in regard to what authority has the power to request intervention. While the United States Constitution says that the legislature of the state or the executive, if the legislature cannot be convened, may request the protection of the federal government, the Argentine Constitution merely says that the con-

[19] J. M. Montes de Oca, *Lecciones de derecho constitucional,* II, 463.

[20] A. de Vedia, *La constitución argentina,* pp. 578–80.

[21] "The United States . . . shall protect each of them [the states] against Invasion; and on Application of the Legislature, or of the Executive (when the Legislature cannot be convened) against domestic Violence" (U. S. Constitution, Art. IV, § 4).

stituted authorities may request the intervention. But in Argentina this has been interpreted to mean that any authority, executive, legislative, or judicial, may make the request.[22]

There is also a precedent established by President Sarmiento on April 25, 1870, when the federal government intervened in the province of Entre Ríos without being asked by the constituted authorities, because they had been overthrown by a revolutionary movement. In justification President Sarmiento maintained that the assassination of the governor, the intimidation of the legislature, and the inability of the judicial power to function because the assassins were protected by the revolutionaries, made a request impossible. In these circumstances, considering the notoriety of the events which had occurred, a request to the federal government must be taken for granted.[23]

Intergovernmental Tax Immunities

Argentina has developed a rather sweeping doctrine that as between the provinces and the national government neither shall tax the instrumentalities of the other. This reciprocal immunity is not expressed in the Constitution but has been judicially created. The same is also true in the United States where the doctrine originated,[24] and where, it should be added, the doctrine has been weakened in recent years.

As in the United States,[25] the doctrine that the provinces cannot tax the instrumentalities of the national government arose in relation to the power of the provinces to tax the notes issued by the

[22] A. de Vedia, *op. cit.*, p. 56; J. M. Montes de Oca, *op. cit.*, I, 253–54; Argentine Constitution, Art. 6.

[23] J. N. Matienzo, *El gobierno representativo federal en la República Argentina*, p. 272.

[24] "The judicial history of this doctrine is a striking illustration of an occasional tendency to encrust unwarranted interpretations upon the Constitution, and thereafter to consider merely what has been judicially said about the Constitution, rather than to be primarily controlled by a fair conception of the Constitution. Judicial exigencies are unavoidable with reference to an organic act like our Constitution, drawn in many particulars with purposed vagueness so as to leave room for the unfolding future. But the ultimate touchstone is the Constitution itself, not what we have said about it."—Mr. Justice Frankfurter, concurring, in Graves v. New York ex rel. O'Keefe, 306 U. S. 466 (1939).

[25] In McCulloch v. Maryland, 4 Wheat. 316 (1819), the Supreme Court of the United States declared unconstitutional a state tax imposed on the issue of notes by the Bank of the United States on the ground that it constituted an unwarranted interference with an instrumentality of the national government.

National Bank. In *Buenos Aires v. Banco Nacional,* 18 S. C. N. 340 (1876), the Court declared unconstitutional a provincial statute imposing a tax on the notes issued by the National Bank, and said:

The National Bank has been created by a law of Congress in virtue of an expressed authorization of the Constitution and for the purpose of public administration and general welfare. For this reason it has the character of a national institution and is subject to the exclusive jurisdiction of the national authorities and consequently is not subject to the jurisdiction of the provinces. The taxing power of the provinces must extend over everything that is subject to their jurisdiction, but it cannot extend to institutions authorized by Congress for the purpose of exercising the powers conferred on the general government. The provisions of Article 25 of the law creating the bank, which exempt it from national or provincial taxation, are nothing more than an application of the principles previously mentioned. The tax imposed affects and obstructs the operation of the bank and is therefore unconstitutional.

A similar issue, having a different angle, came up in *Banco Nacional v. San Juan,* 18 S. C. N. 345 (1876). In this case the defendant province imposed a license tax on the National Bank. As in the former case, it was alleged that the tax was void because the bank was an instrument of the national government, and that Congress had exempted it from provincial taxation. The Court held that since Congress had the power to create a bank by express constitutional authorization, it had also the implied power to exempt it from provincial taxation.[26]

The doctrine under consideration has been applied not only to national instrumentalities of a purely governmental character but also to private institutions which Congress has recognized as fostering the prosperity and general welfare of the nation, as provided by Article 67, § 16, of the Constitution. In *Banco Británico v.*

[26] In the recent case of Pittman v. Home Owners' Loan Corp., 308 U. S. 21 (1939), the Supreme Court of the United States upheld the power of Congress to exempt from a state tax the activities of the Home Owners' Loan Corporation (a federal instrumentality). The Court stated: "Congress has not only the power to create a corporation to facilitate the performance of governmental functions, but it has also the power to protect the operations thus validly authorized. 'A power to create implies a power to preserve' (McCulloch v. Maryland, 4 Wheat. 426). This power to preserve necessarily comes within the range of the express power conferred upon Congress to make all laws which shall be necessary and proper for carrying into execution all powers vested by the Constitution in the government of the United States (U. S. Constitution, Art. 1, § 8)."

Santa Fe, 121 S. C. N. 255 (1915), the issue was whether a province could tax the operations of the plaintiff bank, a private institution established under the laws of Congress. The Court declared the provincial statute unconstitutional on the basis of several decisions of the United States Supreme Court,[27] saying:

> There is no merit in the allegation that the exemption of the national banks from state and national taxation is unconstitutional because they are created as federal institutions similar to the National Bank, the Bank of the Argentine Nation and the railroads of the nation, which are likewise exempted from taxation, because Congress has judged that such exemptions are necessary in order to secure their functioning and stability.

But the Court has refused to extend the benefits of the doctrine to sales to the national government by independent contractors. Thus in *Pérez v. Torres,* 18 S. C. N. 103 (1876), contractors who supplied the national army with meat were compelled to pay a tax on these sales and contended that it was unconstitutional as being a tax on the national government. The Court sustained the tax: "Undoubtedly the Provinces have no power to tax the things, or property, or agencies of the national government because that would be contrary to the very existence of the national sovereignty. But in the present case the tax is not imposed upon its property, objects, or agencies. The plaintiff is merely a contractor who enters into business to make either a profit or a loss, and is not exempted from provincial taxation." Five years later the issue was raised again in *Vignon v. Municipalidad de Rosario,* 23 S. C. N. 560 (1881). The lower federal court held that a sales tax on products sold by the plaintiff to the federal government was unconstitutional, on the ground that if the tax were held valid it might encourage the provinces to impose such high taxes as to impede the government in the exercise of its powers. But the Supreme Court upheld the tax as not amounting to a tax on federal instrumentalities. The Court stated:

> It is a general principle of constitutional law that the provinces cannot tax or burden the instruments employed by the national government in the exercise of their constitutional powers, since otherwise the principle

[27] Bank of Bethel v. Pahquioque Bank, 14 Wall. 383 (1871); People v. Weaver, 100 U. S. 539 (1879); Mercantile Bank v. New York, 121 U. S. 138 (1887).

of national supremacy established in Article 31 would be a mere illusion. But the present case does not deal with a tax which is in conflict with the principle of national supremacy. The mere fact that the plaintiffs are suppliers of the national army does not exempt them from the provincial taxes imposed upon the merchandise supplied by them to the army, because as suppliers they are in the same situation as any other businessmen and therefore cannot be considered as agents or instrumentalities of the federal government. From the face of the record of the case it does not appear that the municipality collected the tax from the national army, but that it was collected from the plaintiff. It does not appear either from the record, nor was it alleged in the course of the trial, that the federal government had to pay a higher price for the articles bought from the plaintiffs on account of the taxes imposed by the municipality.[28]

The Court has also refused to extend immunity to inheritance taxation of government securities. In *Ex Parte Saffores de Doumecq,* 184 S. C. N. 5 (1939), the power of the province to levy an inheritance tax on estates composed in part of government securities was questioned. The Court, on the authority of *Plummer v. Coler,* 178 U. S. 115 (1900), sustained the provincial tax law, saying that the United States Supreme Court had held in a similar case that the fact that the inheritance upon which the tax was imposed was composed wholly or in part of national securities did not invalidate the tax.

The reciprocal obligation of the federal government not to tax instrumentalities of the provinces was impliedly raised in *Buenos Aires v. Cotta,* 22 S. C. N. 161 (1880).[29] The question was whether the municipality of Buenos Aires was exempted from the application of the federal customs stamp on documents pertaining to official transactions. The Court declared that the city was not so exempted, stating that the powers of Congress to tax know no limitations not expressly set forth in the Constitution. The federal statute was therefore applicable to everyone, "to the government,

[28] The Supreme Court of the United States went farther in the application of this doctrine than the Supreme Court of Argentina. For example, the former held invalid a federal tax on motorcycles sold to the police department of a municipality. Indian Motorcycle Co. v. United States, 283 U. S. 570 (1931). And in Panhandle Oil Co. v. Mississippi, 277 U. S. 218 (1928), the Court held unconstitutional a tax on gasoline sold to the federal government for the use of the Coast Guard and a veterans' hospital.

[29] Although Buenos Aires is now, as the national capital, a federal corporation, at this time it was merely the capital of the province of Buenos Aires.

to the corporations, and to private persons." [30] When the governments of the provinces believe that for any reason the products sent to them should not be dutiable, they should make a request to the federal government for such exemption.[31]

Sixty years after this decision, however, it was held in *Banco de Buenos Aires v. Gobierno Nacional,* 186 S. C. N. 125 (1940), that, as the provinces cannot tax federal instrumentalities, so the federal government cannot tax the instrumentalities of the provincial governments. The province of Buenos Aires had created a bank long before its incorporation into the federation for the purpose of fostering the economic and general welfare of the people of the province, just as Congress had created a similar institution in order to benefit the people of the nation as a whole. The bank, besides being used as an agent to secure the welfare of the people, was also used as an instrumentality in carrying out the fiscal activities of the provincial government. Congress had enacted an income tax statute, and the question was whether the federal law was applicable to the incomes from stocks and bonds issued by the bank. The provincial authorities contended that the law was unconstitutional because the bank was a provincial instrumentality, and the Supreme Court sustained the contention on the authority of *Indian Motorcycle Co. v. United States.*[32] The Court stated:

> The instruments through which the national government exercises its powers, are exempt from taxation by the states and the instruments which the provinces employ to exercise the powers reserved by the Constitution to them are likewise exempt from national taxation, by virtue of the principle of implicit independence of the nation and the state

[30] The Supreme Court of the United States, in University of Illinois v. United States, 289 U. S. 48 (1933), refused to apply the doctrine of immunity to an article imported by the state of Illinois for the use of its state university. The Court held that Congress, in the exercise of the power to regulate commerce, may determine to what extent the state and its instrumentalities shall be relieved of the duties imposed by Congress upon articles imported by them.

[31] The national income tax laws exempt from taxation the securities issued by provincial and municipal governments provided they are exempted from taxation by the provincial governments, but the salaries of provincial and municipal officials are not exempted from federal taxation. *Recopilación de leyes usuales,* Buenos Aires, 1934, II, 273.

[32] On this point, the Court also cited: McCulloch v. Maryland, 4 Wheat. 316 (1819); Texas v. White, 7 Wall. 700 (1869); Collector v. Day, 11 Wall. 113 (1871); Johnson v. Maryland, 254 U. S. 51 (1920); Gillespie v. Oklahoma, 257 U. S. 501 (1922); Burnett v. Colorado Oil and Gas Co., 285 U. S. 393 (1932) and Willcuts v. Brunn, 282 U. S. 216 (1931).

governments within their respective spheres of constitutional power. It is only in this way that the provisions of the Constitution which tend to maintain the existence of both national and state governments can be effectively realized.

The Court further held, citing several decisions of the United States Supreme Court,[33] that the tax imposed on the bonds and securities was unconstitutional because it affected the functioning of the bank as a provincial instrumentality. But the Court made it clear that this immunity applied only to purely governmental, as distinguished from proprietary, instrumentalities. Relying on *South Carolina v. United States,* 199 U. S. 437 (1905), the Court stated: "The former are beyond the taxing power of the federal government; on the other hand, the latter, although subject to the control of the state governments or operated under public franchises, are subject to taxation." [34]

In the United States the doctrine of intergovernmental tax immunity has been weakened; many of the decisions upon which it was based have been impliedly, if not expressly, overruled. In *Helvering v. Gerhardt,* 304 U. S. 405 (1938), the Court upheld a federal income tax on salaries of employees of the Port Authority, a bi-state corporation created by compact between New York and New Jersey, against the objection that such a tax was imposed on a state governmental instrumentality.

The basis upon which constitutional tax immunity of a state has been supported is the protection which it affords to the continued existence of the state. To attain that end it is not ordinarily necessary to confer on the state a competitive advantage over private persons in carrying on the operations of its government. There is no such necessity here, and the resulting impairment of the federal power to tax argues against the advantage. The state and national governments must coexist. Each must be supported by taxation of those who are citizens of both. The mere fact that the economic burden of such taxes may be passed on to a state government and thus increase to some extent, here wholly conjectural, the expense of its operation, infringes no constitutional im-

33 Weston v. Charleston, 2 Pet. 449 (1829); Pollock v. Farmers' Loan and Trust Co., 157 U. S. 429 (1895); Evans v. Gore, 253 U. S. 245 (1920) and Brushaber v. Union Pacific Railway, 240 U. S. 1 (1916).

34 For a scholarly discussion of the legal and economic issues of this case, see the briefs by Dr. Emilio González and Dr. Teodoro Becú in behalf of the national government and the bank of Buenos Aires, respectively. *La Ley,* Buenos Aires, April 6, 7, and 8, 1940.

munity. Such burdens are but normal incidents of the organization within the same territory of two governments, each possessed of the taxing power. . . .

And in *Graves v. New York ex rel. O'Keefe*, 306 U. S. 466 (1939), the Court upheld a state tax on the salary of an employee of the Home Owners' Loan Corporation, an instrumentality of the national government. "So much of the burden of a nondiscriminatory general tax upon the incomes of employees of a government, through the effect of the tax on the price level of labor or materials, is but the normal incident of the organization within the same territory of two governments, each possessing the taxing power."

INTERPROVINCIAL RELATIONSHIPS

Four features will be discussed under this head: citizenship; full faith and credit; compacts; rendition of fugitives.

Citizenship

Although the Argentine system includes both provincial and national citizenship, the latter is not expressly provided for in the Constitution. Of provincial citizenship the Constitution says: "The citizens of each province shall enjoy in all the others the rights, privileges, and immunities belonging to the citizens of such other provinces" (Art. 8).[35]

In *Ex Parte Tabernera*, 119 S. C. N. 291 (1914), the Supreme Court interpreted this provision in the light of United States precedents. The petitioner, a member of the legislature of the province of Mendoza, was arrested and sentenced in the criminal courts of the federal capital. He alleged that the Court had no jurisdiction over him because, being a provincial legislator and a citizen of his province, he was entitled in the federal capital to the same immunity he enjoyed in his province, namely, immunity from arrest and prosecution during his term of office unless the legislature consented to waive the immunity. On appeal the Supreme Court upheld his conviction, stating:

[35] Cf. "The Citizens of each State shall be entitled to all Privileges and Immunities of Citizens in the several States" (U. S. Constitution, Art. IV, § 2).

In regard to Article 8 of the Constitution, which petitioner invokes, the Article does not sustain such a conclusion. This provision must be understood in the sense that the Argentine citizens recognized by Article 108 and Article 67, section 11, of the Constitution shall enjoy equal privileges and immunities in whatever place in the nation they are found. This provision of the Constitution refers to the privileges and immunities inherent in citizenship, and it cannot be said that those belonging to legislators are inherent in the title of citizenship. Section 2 of Article IV of the United States Constitution was incorporated in our Article 8, and its true meaning has been fixed by the Supreme Court of the United States in *Paul v. Virginia,* [8 Wall. 166 (1869)] in which that Court stated, "But the privileges and immunities secured to citizens of each state in the several states, by the provision in question, are those privileges and immunities which are common to citizens in the latter states under their constitutions and laws by virtue of their being citizens. Special privileges enjoyed by citizens in their own states are not secured in other states by this provision. It was not intended by the provision to give to the laws of one state any operation in other states. They can have no such operation, except by the permission, express or implied, of those states. The special privileges which they confer must therefore be enjoyed at home, unless the assent of the other states to their enjoyment therein be given."

In *Ariola v. Plácido,* 120 S. C. N. 224 (1914), the Supreme Court applied the same principle. The plaintiff had obtained a permit from a court of the province of Buenos Aires to sue in *forma pauperis.* With this permit he went to the federal capital and attempted to sue in its courts without paying the required court fees. The court denied him this right, and he appealed to the Supreme Court. There he contended that as the province of Buenos Aires had granted him the privilege to sue in *forma pauperis* he was also entitled to do the same in the Court of the capital. The Court held that this was not a privilege inherent in citizenship, but a local privilege not protected by Article 8.

Gobierno Nacional v. Leyva, 18 S. C. N. 156 (1870), presents another interesting aspect of the principle under discussion. The defendant, a citizen of a province, was sentenced in the courts of the federal capital for the crime of gambling. On appeal to the Supreme Court he contended that his conviction was void because in violation of Article 8, since in the province from which he came gambling was not illegal. The Supreme Court held that the mere fact that he could not be punished in a province for gambling, under a federal statute, did not constitute an immunity; Congress as a local legislature could enact a gambling statute for the federal capital.

The Argentine Constitution does not, unlike the Fourteenth Amendment to the Constitution of the United States,[36] define national citizenship nor does it prohibit the provinces from abridging the privileges and immunities of such citizenship. It merely provides that Congress "shall have power to enact general naturalization and citizenship statutes subject to the principle of *jus solis*" (Art. 67, § 11), and that "foreigners may be naturalized by residing two continuous years in the country, but this period may be shortened in favor of foreigners so requesting after adducing and proving the rendering of services to the Republic" (Art. 20). In 1869 Congress enacted the citizenship and naturalization statute.[37]

Morvanis v. Alem, 92 S. C. N. 55 (1901), held that a person born in the Republic is an Argentine citizen irrespective of the nationality of the father,[38] and that the acceptance by such person of employment or honors from a foreign country, without the consent of the Argentine government, deprives him of his political rights but not of his citizenship. And in *Calle v. Nathan,* 15 S. C. N. 233 (1874), the Court held that the sons of Argentine parents born while the latter were in exile during the dictatorship of Rosas were Argentine citizens under the principle of *jus solis.* The Court seems to imply that since the parents of these persons were involuntarily outside the country their sons acquired Argentine citizenship as if they had actually been born in Argentine territory.

Ex Parte Villalonga Nazar, 172 S. C. N. 220 (1935), presented

36 The Fourteenth Amendment provides: "All persons born or naturalized in the United States, and subject to the jurisdiction thereof, are citizens of the United States and of the State wherein they reside. No State shall make or enforce any law which shall abridge the privileges or immunities of citizens of the United States. . . ."

37 The statute provides that citizenship may be obtained, first, by having been born in the territory of the Republic irrespective of the nationality of the parents, with the exception of members of the diplomatic missions of foreign ministers and the members of the diplomatic missions residing in the Republic; second, that the sons of Argentine parents who, although born in foreign countries, choose to retain the citizenship of their parents are also Argentine citizens; third, that by having been born on the warships of the Republic, or on ships sailing under the Argentine flag, one may automatically attain Argentine citizenship. *Colección de leyes nacionales,* III, 98.

38 In United States v. Wong Kim Ark, 169 U. S. 649 (1898), the Supreme Court of the United States expounded a similar principle.

the question of the validity of an Act of Congress providing that the son of an Argentine citizen, born in a foreign country, may become a citizen by choosing the citizenship of his father. The petitioner, son of an Argentine father, had been born in France, and petitioned the federal court for admission to Argentine citizenship, not by the ordinary process of naturalization but by a special procedure established in Article V of the naturalization statute. The federal district attorney opposed the petition on the ground that since under the Constitution only persons born in Argentine territory could become citizens the petitioner would have to be naturalized. In other words, the district attorney alleged that under the Constitution citizenship could not be acquired under the principle of *jus sanguinis,* but only under the principle of *jus solis* or by naturalization. Upholding the constitutionality of the statute, the Court stated:

> Article 73 of the Constitution established the principle that the sons of native Argentinians who were born in foreign countries are eligible for President and vice-president of the nation, provided of course that they choose Argentine citizenship. Therefore, the provision which grants to sons of such Argentine fathers the right to become citizens by birth is not unconstitutional because, although it is true that Article 73 was enacted in 1853, and that it took into consideration especially the descendants of the Argentine fathers who were exiled during the tyranny of Rosas, nevertheless it is true that such an article has a general and permanent character without making any exceptions based on conditions existing after 1853.[39]

Citizenship by naturalization may also be acquired by foreigners who have rendered certain services to the Republic, regardless of the number of years of residence in the nation, such as having served honorably as an employee of the nation or of a province either within the territory of the nation or in foreign countries, or in the army or navy or in any warlike service on behalf of the Republic. The Supreme Court has held that the mere fact of rendering military services to the nation does not make the foreigner a citizen. Citizenship must be requested, and it is ob-

[39] But in Ex Parte Bidart, 91 S. C. N. 108 (1902), the question was raised whether the son of a naturalized citizen born abroad became a citizen automatically or whether he must be naturalized. The Court held that he must be naturalized.

tained as an act of grace according to the provisions of law.[40] The other services which make a foreigner eligible for citizenship irrespective of the time of residence are: to have established a new industry or useful invention; to be the builder or manager of a railroad in the provinces; to be a member of the colonies already established or those that were to be established in the national territories; to have married an Argentine woman in any of the provinces; to be an inhabitant of the frontier section of the national territories; to be a teacher in any of the industrial or professional fields of knowledge.[41]

The question whether a woman could be naturalized was decided in the affirmative in *Ex Parte Mayor Salinas,* 147 S. C. N. 252 (1926). Naturalization was denied by the lower federal court on the ground that the concept of citizenship includes the exercise of political rights and that under the Constitution and laws a woman had no right to vote. But the Supreme Court reversed, holding that the exercise of the right of suffrage was not inherent in citizenship and that a person could be a citizen without being an elector.

According to Argentine statutes and decisions, a naturalized person may lose his citizenship for several reasons. One is for not enrolling in the army. *Gobierno Nacional v. Chaleif,* 164 S. C. N. 407 (1932). Another is for fraud in obtaining naturalization. Thus in *Ex Parte Rosenblat,* 171 S. C. N. 103 (1935), the federal district attorney petitioned the sectional federal judge to cancel the naturalization certificate on the ground that when the petitioner was naturalized he had communist ideas and after naturalization he was a leader of the Communist Party in Argentina. The defendant admitted that since he was eighteen years of age he had sympathized with the Communist Party but alleged he had not

[40] Rovira v. Municipalidad de Buenos Aires, 12 S. C. N. 376 (1872).

[41] Citizenship by naturalization may be obtained by foreigners who have resided in the nation for two continuous years and who have manifested the intention of becoming citizens by filing a petition before a federal sectional court. Ex Parte Arango, 183 S. C. N. 241 (1939). The naturalization statute also provides that the son of a naturalized citizen who is under age at the time of his father's naturalization and who was born in a foreign country may obtain his naturalization papers by enrolling in the National Guard. A further provision is that the son of a naturalized citizen who is in a foreign country after his father's naturalization may obtain citizenship by enrolling in the National Guard.

become a member of the party until after he had acquired citizenship. The district attorney contended that the naturalization certificate was deceitfully obtained since the oath he swore to uphold the Constitution and the communist ideas held by him were incompatible. The lower court cancelled the certificate. On appeal, the Supreme Court affirmed, stating:

There is a contradiction between the oath taken by the defendant and communist doctrines. A person who is thinking of the revolutionary dissolution of the institutions of this country and at the same time wishes to be a citizen of it cannot sincerely promise to maintain and preserve these institutions. If the defendant had testified that he was a philosophical anarchist, or that he did not believe in the government as it is at present organized, because the true country of the workers is Soviet Russia, or that he believed only in a government of classes, it is evident that the court would have denied him citizenship. Under such conditions the privilege of citizenship could not have been granted because an alien who holds these ideas is incapable of taking and putting into effect the oath required by the statute.

Referring to the decisions of United States courts on this point, the Court stated:

The jurisprudence of the courts of the United States, although interpreting a broader law than ours, has come to the same conclusion as we have arrived at in this case. In the case of *United States v. Stupiello,* 260 Fed. 483 (1919), the naturalization certificate of an anarchist was cancelled because anarchistic ideas were opposed to the basic principles of the government of the United States and therefore a person who held such ideas could not deserve to become a citizen of the United States. In the case of *United States v. Tapolceauzi,* 40 Fed. (2d) 255 (1930), the naturalization certificate of the defendant was cancelled on the same grounds. Finally, in the case of *United States v. Swelgin,* 254 Fed. 884 (1918), the Court upheld the cancellation of the certificate of a member of a revolutionary labor organization called the Industrial Workers of the World.

Associate Justices Sagarna and Linares dissented. Justice Sagarna held that the decision of the lower court should be reversed: first, because when the defendant took the oath of naturalization there was no law, decree, or court decision requiring a declaration of political, social, or economic beliefs; and second, that neither in the oath taken by the defendant nor in any other document was he requested to state his political, social, or economic views. Citing the dissenting opinion of Chief Justice Hughes in *United States v. Macintosh*, 283 U. S. 605 (1931), Justice Sagarna said that the legislature, not the courts, can impose the requirement that petitions for naturalization should state the economic, political, and social views of the petitioners. The Justice also said that the principles expounded in the United States cases are not applicable in Argentina for these reasons: First, the naturalization and immigration policy of Argentina had not been and cannot be the same as that of the United States because Argentina, unlike the United States, does not have an excess of population nor are there racial prejudices and intolerance there as in the United States. Second, the United States practice of cancelling the naturalization certificates of persons who are Socialists or Communists cannot be applied in Argentina because in that country there are many naturalized citizens who represent the Socialist and Communist parties in the national and provincial legislatures as well as in municipal councils.

A naturalized citizen may expressly or impliedly renounce his citizenship. *Ex Parte Mari Mas*, 181 S. C. N. 175 (1938), and *Ex Parte Dos Santos*, 182 S. C. N. 289 (1938), are typical examples. The petitioners, who had been Spanish and Portuguese citizens, respectively, were naturalized citizens of Argentina. They had gone to the consuls of their former countries and obtained passports for return to their native countries. The federal district attorney requested a federal sectional judge to cancel their naturalization on the ground that they had impliedly renounced their Argentine citizenship by taking these passports. The court upheld the federal attorney and the defendants appealed to the Supreme Court. This Court upheld the lower court on the ground mentioned above and on the additional ground that the naturalization statute does not admit double citizenship.

Although the Argentine laws do not expressly provide for expatriation, the Supreme Court in *Ex Parte Barutta*, 128 S. C. N. 259 (1918), held that such a right is impliedly recognized by Article 20 of the Constitution, which permits aliens to adopt Argentine citizenship, and also by the naturalization statute in that it prohibits the exercise of political rights by Argentine citizens who have been naturalized in a foreign country.

Full Faith and Credit

The Argentine Constitution, following that of the United States,[42] provides that "full faith and credit shall be given in each province to the public acts and judicial proceedings of all other provinces, and Congress shall have the power to provide by general law how such acts and proceedings shall be proved and what legal effects they shall have" (Art. 7).[43] But under the full faith and credit clause penal judgments rendered by the courts of a province or a foreign state cannot be enforced in the courts of another province. In *Pitaluga v. Compañía de Seguros,* 98 S. C. N. 185 (1903), the Court held that a judgment for the payment of costs imposed in a criminal prosecution in a foreign state cannot be enforced in the courts of the nation because such a judgment is of a criminal nature, not enforceable under the principles of private international law which are recognized by Article 7 of the Constitution.

The question whether a judgment obtained in a foreign country can be enforced in Argentine courts was answered in the affirmative by the Supreme Court in *Gómez v. Baudriz,* 7 S. C. N. 282 (1869). The plaintiff sued the defendant in Montevideo, Uruguay, for breach of contract and received a judgment there. Being unable to execute it in that country he petitioned a federal court of Buenos Aires for its enforcement. The defendant, a resident of the federal capital, contended that it could not be enforced in the courts of Argentina because there was no law authorizing such enforcement. The lower court, as well as the Supreme Court, held that such a judgment was enforceable in the federal and provincial courts. The Court stated that Article 7 of the Argentine Constitution is based on Article 4 of the United States Constitution,

[42] "Full Faith and Credit shall be given in each State to the public Acts, Records, and judicial Proceedings of every other State. And the Congress may by general Laws prescribe the Manner in which such Acts, Records and Proceedings shall be proved, and the Effect thereof" (U. S. Constitution, Art. IV, § 1).

[43] On August 12, 1863, the Argentine Congress enacted the first statute for the enforcement of the full faith and credit clause. This statute, as amended on September 18, 1907, provides that the acts and laws of the provincial legislatures and the decrees of the governors of the provinces, as well as the decisions, proceedings, and depositions of the provincial courts, shall receive full faith and credit in all the courts within the territory of the nation when duly authenticated. *Recopilación de leyes usuales,* I, 525.

which has not been an obstacle in the United States to the enforcement of foreign judgments.[44]

The principle that under the full faith and credit clause a judgment rendered by a court without jurisdiction cannot be enforced in the courts of another province has been followed by the Supreme Court in a number of cases. In *Arias v. Nores,* 141 S. C. N. 146 (1924), the plaintiff's father, who was domiciled in the city of Córdoba in the province of the same name, died in the province of Santiago del Estero. One Nicanor Salvatierra, a relative of the plaintiff, petitioned a local court of Santiago del Estero to be appointed tutor of the plaintiff and to be authorized to sell certain lands. All these transactions took place in proceedings in which the deceased's will was probated. Plaintiff's tutor sold property belonging to the estate under the authorization of the court of Santiago del Estero. The plaintiff then sued the defendant buyer to recover the property, alleging that the authorization of the sale was illegal because the court of Santiago del Estero had no jurisdiction, since the deceased was domiciled in the province of Córdoba and only the courts of that province had jurisdiction to probate his will and determine what should be done with his property. Judgment for the plaintiff in the lower court was affirmed by the Supreme Court on the ground that full faith and credit could not be given to the judgment since it was rendered without jurisdiction over the person or subject matter.[45] The Court also stated that the court in which the judgment is brought for enforcement can investigate it and determine if the court which rendered it had jurisdiction.[46]

Compacts

The Argentine Constitution authorizes the provinces to enter into compacts with each other for several purposes. While the

[44] The court cited passages from the works of Felix, Wheaton, Kent, and Story.

[45] The court cited passages from Willoughby's *Constitutional Law;* Williamson v. Berry, 8 How. 495 (1850); Rose v. Himely, 4 Cranch 241 (1808); Webster v. Reid, 11 How. 437 (1851); and Guaranty Trust v. Green Springs, 139 U. S. 137 (1891).

[46] In the following cases the Court has interpreted the full faith and credit clause in the light of decisions of the United States Supreme Court: Sociedad Luz y Fuerza v. Mendoza, 135 S. C. N. 329 (1921); Luján v. Consejo Nacional de Educación, 120 S. C. N. 304 (1917); Barraquero v. Maccopi, 136 S. C. N. 339 (1922); Necchi de Rodríguez v. Curi, 149 S. C. N. 5 (1927).

United States Constitution impliedly grants such a power to the states,[47] the Argentine Constitution expressly grants it as follows: "The provinces may enter into treaties, with the object of administering justice, for economic interests and for works of general utility" (Art. 107). The United States Constitution requires that the states must obtain the consent of Congress; the Argentine Constitution merely declares that such compacts may be signed by the provinces with the knowledge of the federal government. In the Convention of 1853 a provision similar to that in the United States Constitution, that the consent of Congress should be obtained, was rejected as an encroachment on the autonomous powers of the provinces.[48] The constitutions of the different provinces have provisions authorizing the executive power to enter into compacts.

Although the Argentine Constitution provides that the compacts between the provinces do not need the consent of Congress, but merely that Congress must have knowledge of them, this does not mean that in practice Congress does not approve or disapprove them. Since 1857 it has been the practice for Congress to pass on the compacts entered into by the provinces. On May 13, 1856, the provinces of Tucumán, Salta, Jujuy, and Santiago del Estero concluded a treaty, creating a high court of five judges to have jurisdiction in cases in which these provinces were involved. It also provided that the cases decided by this court should be appealable to the Supreme Court. This treaty was approved by Congress on September 29, 1857. A leading authority on Argentine constitutional law has said that although the Constitution states that Congress shall take notice of these compacts, and that they do not necessarily have to be approved by Congress, yet undoubtedly Congress can approve or disapprove them.[49]

47 "No State shall, without the Consent of Congress . . . enter into any Agreement or Compact with another State . . ." (U. S. Constitution, Art. 1, § 10). In Virginia v. Tennessee, 148 U. S. 503 (1893), the Supreme Court of the United States held that the compacts or agreements which the States cannot enter without the consent of Congress are those which tend to increase the political power of the States, and which may encroach upon or interfere with, the just supremacy of the United States. The Court further held that the consent of Congress may be granted either expressly or impliedly.

48 *Asambleas constituyentes argentinas*, IV, 534–35.

49 J. V. González, *Manual de la constitución argentina*, p. 699.

Rendition of Fugitives

The Constitution of the United States imposes upon the states the obligation of delivering fugitives from justice to the states from which they have fled.[50] The Argentine Constitution imposes a similar obligation upon the provinces (Art. 8, § 2). This provision does not, unlike that of the Constitution of the United States, give any participation to the governor of the province in extradition proceedings, nor is such participation granted by the statute enacted by Congress to enforce the provision.[51]

The Supreme Court of the United States has held that the obligation of a state to deliver a fugitive is moral rather than legal, and hence that a federal court cannot compel compliance by mandamus.[52] The Argentine Supreme Court has held the contrary. Thus, in *Juez de Córdoba v. Juez de la Capital Federal,* 141 S. C. N. 420 (1924), in which the judge of the federal capital refused to honor a petition of extradition from a judge of Córdoba because the latter had once refused to honor a similar request, the Supreme Court decided that the first judge was obliged to comply with the request, on the ground that the Constitution does not establish a purely conventional reciprocal obligation subject to observance or nonobservance by one of the parties, but rather a mandatory obligation which imports a limitation upon the provincial sovereignties and which is imposed in order to achieve the superior interest of justice and public safety. And in *Ex Parte Juez de San Nicolás,* 181 S. C. N. 337 (1938), the Court stated that the statute enacted to enforce the provisions of the Constitution

[50] "A Person charged in any State with Treason, Felony, or other Crime, who shall flee from Justice and be found in another State, shall on Demand of the executive Authority of the State from which he fled, be delivered up, to be removed to the State having Jurisdiction of the Crime" (U. S. Constitution, Art. IV, § 2).

[51] The Argentine extradition statute has the following provisions: First, that the federal sectional judges or the judges of the federal capital and the national territories who were prosecuting or had convicted a prisoner who had fled to another section may request the judge of the section to which the prisoner has fled to extradite him. A copy of the order of imprisonment must accompany the petition if the person whose extradition is requested has not been convicted. Second, that the judge to whom the request is directed must immediately order the arrest of the person whose extradition is requested; and when the identity of the prisoner is proved, the judge must send him back to the requesting magistrate. *Código de procedimientos en lo criminal . . . de la capital,* Art. 675, § 1, 2, and Art. 676.

[52] Kentucky v. Dennison, 24 How. 66 (1861).

should be interpreted in a broad and comprehensive manner, not only in cases of persons convicted but also in the case of a person who had been under arrest and had fled from justice.[53]

[53] When a criminal has committed a series of crimes of different degrees in different provinces on different dates, he must be tried first in the province where he committed the most serious offence. Ex Parte González, 152 S. C. N. 62 (1928); Ex Parte Buhler, 156 S. C. N. 414 (1930).

V: POWERS OF THE NATIONAL GOVERNMENT

THE Argentine Constitution provides that the Republic shall have a representative federal form of government (Art. 1). By federal government is meant a system of constitutional organization in which the powers of sovereignty are divided between the national and the local governmental units. In *Banco de Córdoba v. Caja de Jubilaciones y Pensiones de Empleados Bancarios*, 147 S. C. N. 239 (1926), in which a province was denied the power to establish a bank with branches outside the territorial boundaries, the Court explained the nature of the federal system as follows:

According to the political system adopted by our Constitution, the powers of sovereignty are divided between the national and the provincial governments; the powers of the first are supreme and absolute and extend to all the territory of the Republic, that is to say, even within the territory belonging to the provinces; the powers of the latter have the same characteristics but can be exercised only within the territorial limits of the provinces. The powers of the national government and of the provinces, although they coexist and are exercised within the same territorial limits, nevertheless are exercised separately and independently of each other within their respective spheres of governmental action.

In Argentina, as in the United States, the national government can exercise three different types of powers, namely, those expressly delegated in the Constitution, those implied from the enumerated powers, and the inherent powers of sovereignty. The Supreme Court has held that the delegated powers are limited but supreme within the sphere of governmental action granted to the national government. Thus, in *Ex Parte Jefatura de Policía de Concordia*, 139 S. C. N. 259 (1923), which sustained the power of Congress to create a mortgage bank with all necessary powers to carry on its functions, the Court expounded the theory of delegated powers:

Although it is true that when the framers of the Constitution created the central government they proposed to grant to it a limited sphere of action in regard to the persons and things subject to its jurisdiction, they understood that within this limited sphere the national government was supreme and that it was necessary that this should be so in order that the powers granted could be effectively exercised. The makers of the Constitution also understood that in order to enable the national government to exercise such powers it was indispensable to authorize it to elect the means which according to its own judgment would be the most effective for the exercise of those powers granted, provided that these were not incompatible with the limitations imposed by the Constitution.

The framers of the Argentine Constitution, following the Constitution of the United States,[1] incorporated a necessary and proper clause upon which the implied powers are based: "Congress shall have power to enact all the laws and regulations that may be necessary to put in exercise the powers referred to, and all the others granted by the present Constitution to the Government of the Argentine Nation" (Art. 67, § 28). The Supreme Court of Argentina discusses implied powers in the light of principles and precedents established by the Supreme Court of the United States. In *Ferrocarril Central Argentino v. Santa Fe*, 68 S. C. N. 227 (1897), the power of Congress to exempt private railroads from provincial taxation was upheld on a theory similar to that expounded in cases decided by the Supreme Court of the United States.[2]

As Congress has under section 6 of Article 67 of the Constitution the power to grant the privileges and subsidies which it considers to be necessary without restricting expressly the limitations of that power, and as it also has the power to make laws and regulations that may be convenient and necessary to put into effect the powers granted by the Constitution, Congress can exempt from provincial taxation the rail-

[1] "The Congress shall have Power . . . To make all Laws which shall be necessary and proper for carrying into Execution the foregoing Powers, and all other Powers vested by this Constitution in the Government of the United States, or in any Department or Officer thereof" (U. S. Constitution, Art. I, § 8).

[2] The Court approved the citations made by the plaintiff corporation of McCulloch v. Maryland, 4 Wheat. 316 (1819), and Pomeroy, *An Introduction to the Constitutional Law of the United States,* to support the view that Congress had the implied power to exempt the railroad company from taxation as an incident of the power to grant the franchise to the company.

roads which have been created by the laws of Congress as a proper exercise of the powers expressly granted to it by the Constitution.[3]

But in *Compañía General de Ferrocarriles v. Busto de Silva,* 108 S. C. N. 240 (1908), it was stated that the implied-power doctrine does not enable Congress to exercise powers not granted to it by the Constitution. The Court thus explained the extent and limitation of the necessary and proper clause of the Constitution:

> The meaning of this clause is that Congress has all the incidental powers necessary and proper to put into effect all the powers which have been granted to it by the Constitution. This does not extend nor limit the power expressly granted nor does it give Congress any new power not already granted by the Constitution, but it is a simple declaration to solve any doubt in any given circumstance as to the power of Congress in order to prevent the government from being deprived of the means to perpetuate its existence, as happened under the Articles of Confederation. Congress is the exclusive judge as to the necessity and the means to be selected in the execution of the powers granted by the Constitution, provided the means selected are not expressly prohibited by the Constitution.[4]

The United States principle that Congress has an inherent power of national or international sovereignty besides the express and implied powers[5] has been accepted by the Argentine Supreme

[3] In the following cases the Court has applied a similar doctrine: Fiscal v. Señorans, 6 S. C. N. 67 (1868); Banco Nacional v. Villanueva, 18 S. C. N. 102 (1876); Buenos Aires v. Banco Nacional, 18 S. C. N. 340 (1876); Santa Fe v. Hue, 4 S. C. N. 311 (1867); Ferrocarril Central Argentino v. Rosario, 104 S. C. N. 73 (1906).

[4] In Suárez v. Peña y Borda, 121 S. C. N. 198 (1915), holding that Congress could not vest in the federal courts jurisdiction not authorized by the Constitution, the Court stated that the power granted by Article 67 is not indeterminate but was designed only to put into effect the powers granted by the Constitution to the national government.

[5] The United States Supreme Court has applied this doctrine of inherent power in the following cases: a case dealing with the power of Congress to acquire and govern territories, American Insurance Co. v. Canter, 1 Peters 511 (1828); a case involving the power of Congress to protect the Indian tribes, United States v. Kagama, 118 U. S. 375 (1886); a case dealing with the power to exclude and admit aliens, Fong Yue Ting v. United States, 149 U. S. 698 (1893). In United States v. Curtiss-Wright Corp., 299 U. S. 304 (1936), which sustained a law of Congress vesting in the President the discretionary power to determine when an embargo of arms should be established and what kinds of arms should be subject to the same, the Court held that Congressional legislation which is to be made effective in the international field must often accord to the President a degree of discretion and freedom which will not be admissible when domestic affairs are involved. And speaking of the inherent power of sovereignty of the national government in inter-

Court. In *Soldati v. Banco Muñoz Rodríguez y Cía.,* 52 S. C. N. 413 (1893), it was held that the power of Congress to coin money and fix the value thereof is derived not only from the enumerated powers but also from the general power of sovereignty.[6] The Court also held in *Ex Parte Veek,* 132 S. C. N. 321 (1920), that under inherent power Congress can admit or exclude aliens from Argentine territory.[7] The Court has also held that under this power Congress can confiscate the property of alien enemies, *Nación v. Eguzquiza y Ayala,* 4 S. C. N. 75 (1867).

REGULATORY POWERS

The Fathers of the Argentine Constitution granted to Congress practically the same powers which the Constitution of the United States grants to Congress. But the members of the Santa Fe Convention also granted to the Argentine Congress, for historical, political, economic, and ideological reasons, many other powers which are not expressly granted to the Congress of the United States.[8] The Argentine Congress has twenty-eight expressly dele-

---

national affairs the Court stated: "It results that the investment of the federal government with the powers of external sovereignty did not depend upon the affirmative grants of the Constitution. The power to declare and wage war, to conclude peace, to make treaties, to maintain diplomatic relations with other sovereignties, if they had never been mentioned in the Constitution, would have vested in the federal government as necessary concomitants of sovereignty."

[6] The United States Supreme Court has also held that the power of Congress to coin money and fix the value thereof is based on the power of sovereignty as well as on the currency power delegated to Congress. Legal Tender Cases, 12 Wall. 457 (1871); Norman v. Baltimore and Ohio Railroad Co., 294 U. S. 240 (1935).

[7] The Court cited Fong Yue Ting v. United States, 149 U. S. 698 (1893), and Chae Chan Ping v. United States, 130 U. S. 581 (1889).

[8] These powers are: to tax exports (Art. 67, § 1); to establish a national bank (Art. 67, § 5); to approve or disapprove the expenditures of the national government (Art. 67, § 7); to grant subsidies to those provinces which cannot cover their ordinary expenses (Art. 67, § 8); to enact code and general civil legislation (Art. 67, § 11); to arrange definitely the limits of the territories of the nation and to govern them (Art. 67, § 14); to guarantee the security of the frontiers, maintain peaceful relations with the Indians, and to promote their conversion to Catholicism (Art. 67, § 15); to promote programs of general and university instruction, to promote industry, immigration, construction of railroads and navigable channels, colonization of national lands, introduction of new industries, the importation of domestic and foreign capital, the exploration of the interior rivers—all, by laws enacted to accomplish these things and by the granting of temporary concessions and privileges and rewards (Art. 67, § 16); to create and abolish public offices, fix their duties, grant pensions, honors and general amnesty (Art. 67, § 19); to approve or reject treaties with the Vatican, and to exercise the national regulatory power over the church (Art. 67,

gated powers, while the Constitution of the United States grants to Congress only eighteen. The powers of the Argentine Congress may be grouped as follows: (1) to regulate commerce; (2) to enact code legislation; (3) fiscal powers; (4) treaty-making power; (5) miscellaneous powers.

Interprovincial and Foreign Commerce

One of the most important powers delegated to Congress is that of regulating maritime and land commerce with foreign nations and between the provinces.[9] (Art. 67, § 12.) In addition, the Constitution contains provisions which tend to complement and enlarge the commerce power of Congress,[10] giving to it a more extensive power over foreign and interprovincial commerce than that given to the United States Congress. The Argentine Supreme Court, when interpreting the nature, extent, and limitations of the commerce power of Congress, has done so in the light of the decisions of the Supreme Court of the United States, and has justi-

§ 19); to admit new religious orders in the nation (Art. 67, § 20); to permit the entrance of foreign troops into Argentine territory, and to allow national troops to go out of the country (Art. 67, § 25); to declare a state of siege in one or several districts of the nation in case of interior commotion, and to approve or establish a state of siege, declared by the President during the recess of Congress (Art. 67, § 26).

[9] The United States Constitution provides that Congress shall have power "To regulate Commerce with foreign Nations, and among the several States, and with the Indian Tribes." Art. I, § 8.

[10] These are: that within the Republic all articles of domestic production or manufacture, as well as goods and merchandise of all kinds that have been cleared at the custom houses, shall be exempt from taxation (Art. 10); that Congress shall have power to regulate the navigation of the interior rivers, to establish such ports as are necessary, and to create and abolish custom houses, with the exception of those which existed in each province at the time of their incorporation (Art. 67, § 9); that Congress shall have the power to provide for all that conduces to the prosperity of the country, to the advancement and well-being of all the provinces, and to the progress of education, prescribing plans for general and university instruction, promoting industry, immigration, the building of railroads and navigable canals, the colonization of national lands, the introduction and establishment of new industries, the importation of foreign capital, and the exploration of interior rivers by laws protecting their banks, by temporary concessions of privilege, and by the offer of rewards (Art. 67, § 16); that Congress shall have power to enact civil, criminal, commercial and mining codes (Art. 67, § 11); that the navigation of all the interior rivers of the nation shall be free to all craft, subject only to the laws issued by the national authorities (Art. 26); that articles of domestic or foreign production or manufacture, animals of all kinds passing from one province to another, as well as the carts, boats, or beasts used for their transportation, shall be exempt from duties of passage, and no duty can be levied on them beforehand, whatever their nature, for the mere act of passing through the territory (Art. 11).

fied the application of these decisions on the ground that the commerce clauses of both Constitutions are concordant and designed for the same purpose.

For example, in *Antony v. Santa Fe,* 125 S. C. N. 333 (1917), which invalidated a provincial statute imposing a higher sales tax on products brought from other provinces than on those made in the defendant province, the Court stated that the power of Congress to regulate commerce is concordant with the commerce clause of the United States Constitution, under which the courts have recognized that it was conferred upon Congress to secure uniformity of regulation of commerce against the differences which may have been established by local legislation, and that it protects property transported from foreign countries or from other provinces against the interference of local legislation until this property has been incorporated into the general mass of property within the country.[11] Furthermore, the Court stated that this power protects such property even after it has entered the country against any burden based on the fact that the property comes from outside.

And in *United River Plate Telephone Co. v. Buenos Aires,* 154 S. C. N. 104 (1929), in which the Court upheld a provincial property tax on a telephone company engaged in interprovincial commerce, the Court defined interprovincial and foreign commerce as follows:

> The term "commerce" used in the American Constitution is the same as that used in Section 12 of Article 67 of our Constitution, and both terms have been interpreted to include not only the transportation of goods but also the carrying of persons from one state to another, as well as the transmission of ideas, orders, and agreements by telephone, telegraph, and other means of communication. The power to regulate commerce, as it has been previously defined, grants to Congress the power to prescribe the regulations to which interstate commerce is subject, and therefore Congress has as complete a power as that exercised by the legislative body of a unitarian system of government. The power of Congress to regulate the means of communication between the states is so extensive and absolute that Congress has the duty of taking care that intercourse between the states and the transmission of communications,

[11] Citing two United States Cases: Welton v. Missouri, 91 U. S. 275 (1876); Walling v. Michigan, 116 U. S. 446 (1886).

either by mail, horse, or telephone, or by any other means, shall not be obstructed or impaired by any of the states through the enactment of unnecessary legislation.[12]

The power of Congress to regulate interprovincial and foreign commerce includes the power to regulate the navigation of the interior rivers and to authorize the construction of structures to improve or to limit the navigation of waterways. This power is illustrated in *Coudanne v. Ferrocarril de Buenos Aires,* 78 S. C. N. 100 (1899). The defendant railroad had built a bridge over a stream belonging to the plaintiff under the authorization of a law of Congress. The plaintiff sued defendant to compel it to raise the bridge in order not to interfere with navigation. The lower court, affirmed by the Supreme Court, dismissed the complaint on the ground that, as Congress had the power to regulate the navigation of rivers, it had also the power to authorize the defendant to build the bridge over the plaintiff's stream. On this point the Court, citing several decisions of the United States Supreme Court,[13] stated:

> There are abundant decisions in the United States to the effect that Congress, and even the individual states when Congress has not legislated on this matter, has the power to regulate the navigation of the rivers and therefore it can impose limitations on their navigability as an incident of the power to regulate commerce and by virtue of the power of eminent domain which the nation has over the navigable waters of the Republic.

The Court, following the Daniel Ball Case, 10 Wall. 557 (1871), defined a navigable river as one which is navigable in fact either in itself or which because of its connections with other waterways forms a continuous channel and may be used for foreign or interstate commerce.[14]

Under the power to regulate commerce as well as under other powers Congress has authority to enact statutes incorporating

[12] Citing Western Union Telegraph Co. v. Pendleton, 122 U. S. 347 (1887).

[13] Miller v. Mayor of New York, 105 U. S. 385 (1883); Pennsylvania v. Wheeling Bridge Co., 18 How. 421 (1856); Gilman v. Philadelphia, 3 Wall. 713 (1866).

[14] The power of the United States Congress to regulate navigable waters is not expressly granted, as it is in the Constitution of Argentina, but it is included in the power to regulate commerce. Leovy v. United States, 177 U. S. 621 (1900).

railroads, vesting in them the power of eminent domain, and exempting them from provincial taxation. In *Compañía General de Ferrocarriles v. Busto de Silva,* 108 S. C. N. 240 (1908), the powers of Congress to vest in a railroad corporation the power of eminent domain to acquire property was upheld as derived, first from Article 67, § 16, second from the power to regulate commerce, and third from the power to create corporations necessary for the public welfare and to enable them to attain the objectives for which they are created.[15]

The power of Congress to exempt congressionally created railroad corporations from provincial taxation was upheld in *Ferrocarril Central Argentino v. Santa Fe,* 68 S. C. N. 227 (1897). The province contended that Congress had no power to interfere with the taxing power of the provinces since only the government which imposes the tax has the right to determine who shall be exempted from it; further, that if Congress could exempt the railroads from taxation it could eventually destroy the taxing power of the provinces. The Court rejected the defendant's contention, stating:

> Although it is true that we have adopted a system of government which we found functioning and that its precedents and jurisprudence may serve as a model for ours, yet it is also true that in all those respects in which we have departed from such a model, our institutions are original and they have no other precedents and jurisprudence than those established by our own tribunals. The constitutional question which has been submitted to this Court in the present case is one of the points in which we differ from our model, the Constitution of the United States. In that Constitution there is no provision analogous to Article 67, section 16, of our Constitution. Under this provision Congress has the power and duty to promote the prosperity of the country and the progress of the provinces, and to promote the building of railroads by temporary concessions of privilege and by the offer of subsidies. When the Constitution granted this power to Congress it imposed no other limitations upon it except that these concessions should be for a limited period of

[15] The Court cited Kohl v. United States, 91 U. S. 367 (1876); Cherokee Nation v. Southern Kansas Railroad Co., 135 U. S. 641 (1890); and Chappell v. United States, 160 U. S. 499 (1896), to support the exercise by Congress of the power of eminent domain and the authority of Congress to vest this power in corporations created by it. The Court also cited Texas and Pacific Railroad Co. v. Kirk and Murphy, 115 U. S. 1 (1885), and Pembina Mining Co. v. Pennsylvania, 125 U. S. 181 (1888), to sustain the principle that Congress has implied power to create corporations.

time, but it did not specify anything in regard to the nature or character of the concessions.[16]

The Argentine Congress has authority to regulate the instrumentalities engaged in interprovincial and foreign commerce. In *Ferrocarril Oeste de Buenos Aires v. Buenos Aires*, 179 S. C. N. 363 (1937), the plaintiff petitioned the Supreme Court to enjoin the defendant railroad from building lines into the territory of other railroads for the purpose of unfairly competing with them. The Court, although it dismissed the case for lack of jurisdiction, stated:

> The national jurisdiction over railroads is derived from sections 12 and 16 of Article 67 of the Constitution, since these are principal instruments of commerce. In the famous decision of the United States Supreme Court rendered in the case of *Gibbons v. Ogden*, 9 Wheat. 1 (1824), by Chief Justice Marshall, it was held that interstate intercourse determines the power of Congress to regulate it as well as the instrumentalities through which it is effected. For this reason Article 107, and Article 67, section 16, of the Constitution must be interpreted in the light of Article 67, section 12, which is similar to Article I, section 8, clause 3, of the Constitution of the United States.

One of the most important phases of the power of Congress to regulate the instrumentalities of interprovincial commerce is that of fixing rates. In *Gómez v. Ferrocarril Central de Córdoba*, 146 S. C. N. 207 (1926), the defendant contended that it could by contract establish rates without submitting them to the approval of the national executive or the General Railroad Board, as provided by statute. The federal chamber of appeals, in a scholarly opinion which was later affirmed by the Supreme Court, upheld[17] the power of the national government to fix the rates of public service companies engaged in interprovincial commerce as an incident of the commerce power.

Another aspect of the power of Congress to regulate public

[16] The Congress of the United States may authorize the construction of railroads and terminal facilities and may exempt such facilities from state taxation. California v. Central Railroad Co., 127 U. S. 1 (1888); Thomson v. Union Pacific Railroad Co., 9 Wall. 579 (1870).

[17] Citing Interstate Commerce Commission v. Baltimore Railroad Co., 145 U. S. 263 (1892); Texas Railroad Co. v. Interstate Commerce Commission, 162 U. S. 197 (1896); Interstate Commerce Commission v. Cincinnati Railroad Co., 167 U. S. 479 (1897); and License Tax Cases, 5 Wall. 462 (1867).

service corporations engaged in interprovincial commerce is that of compelling them, through appropriate legal proceedings, to render the services which their franchises require. In *Ferrocarril Oeste de Buenos Aires v. Gobierno Nacional,* 174 S. C. N. 168 (1935), the defendant railroad was fined for having failed to render Pullman service in certain places along its lines as required by the regulations of the General Railroad Board. The railroad attacked the constitutionality of the regulations, alleging that to compel it to render Pullman service as required by such regulations and under the prevailing tariff rates deprived it of property without due process of law, since it could not obtain a just and reasonable return. The Supreme Court, affirming the decision of the chamber of appeals, and relying principally on United States cases, held against the railroad on the theory that in determining whether tariff rates are so unreasonable as to deprive it of property without due process of law the entire body of rates, and not merely part of it, must be confiscatory. That is to say, if, taking into consideration the whole body of rates, the company obtains a reasonable return, it cannot complain just because some of the rates charged are so low as not to allow it to obtain reasonable returns from that particular phase of its business.

But although interprovincial carriers are subject to public regulation, there are some limitations on these regulatory powers. In *Ferrocarril Central Argentino v. Dirección General de Ferrocarriles,* 140 S. C. N. 344 (1923), the plaintiff railroad was fined for not establishing a station in a certain town when ordered to do so by the General Railroad Board. The company contended that the imposition of the fine and the order to build a station were illegal because they constituted an impairment of its franchise and because there was no statute expressly authorizing the General Railroad Board to compel the company to build the station. The chamber of appeals stated that since the question was presented for the first time before an Argentine court it would turn to the judicial precedents established by the courts of the United States, first, because the principles of Argentine constitutional law are based on those of the United States, and second, because the amendments to the National Railroad Law were based on the Interstate Commerce Act enacted by the Congress of the United

States. Then the court, relying mainly on decisions of the federal and state courts of the United States, held against the company. On appeal the Supreme Court reversed the lower court's decision on the ground that executive or administrative officials cannot exercise such power as this in the absence of express legislative authorization, and that no such authorization had been given.

The power of Congress to regulate operations in interprovincial and foreign commerce has been upheld in several cases. For example, in *In re Guemes,* 107 S. C. N. 281 (1907), the Court sustained a law punishing acts inimical to the safety of railroad traffic and vesting jurisdiction in the federal courts in such cases; in *Asesores de Menores v. Ferrocarril del Oeste,* 128 S. C. N. 114 (1918), the Court upheld an employer's liability act for the protection of workers engaged in interprovincial commerce; and in *Bellocq v. Ferrocarril del Sud,* 68 S. C. N. 238 (1897), the Court sustained the power of Congress to impose civil liability on interprovincial railroads for delay in the transportation of commodities.

In the exercise of the commerce power Congress is limited, as in the exercise of other powers, by the constitutional provisions established for the protection of the individual.[18] But besides these limitations the Constitution has established two specific limitations, namely, that Congress shall not give any preference to the ports of one province over those of another, and that vessels bound to or from one province shall not be obliged to enter, clear, or pay duties in another (Art. 12). This clause, which was incorporated in the Constitution to prevent Congress from discriminating against the provinces on economic matters relating to the regulations of interprovincial and foreign commerce, was derived from the Constitution of the United States [19] because the historical, economic, and geographical circumstances which led to the inclusion of the clause in the United States Constitution were similar to those in Argentina when the Constitution was drafted.[20]

[18] Ferrocarril Central Córdoba v. Ferrocarriles del Estado, 139 S. C. N. 349 (1923).

[19] "No Preference shall be given by any Regulation of Commerce or Revenue to the Ports of one State over those of another; nor shall Vessels bound to, or from one State, be obliged to enter, clear, or pay Duties in another" (U. S. Constitution, Art. I, § 9).

[20] J. V. González, *Manual de la constitución argentina,* pp. 419–20.

Codes

An outstanding feature of the Argentine system which makes it different from that of the United States is the provision in the Constitution which authorizes Congress to enact civil, commercial, penal, and mining codes (Art. 67, § 11). These codes provide the substantive law applicable in both federal and provincial courts. However, the procedure followed in the federal courts is determined by the codes of civil procedure enacted by Congress, whereas in the provincial courts the procedure followed is determined by the codes of procedure enacted by the provincial legislatures.

In the conventions of 1853 and 1860 this power granted to Congress was attacked on the ground that in a federal system the individual states which compose the federation and not the national government should have the power to enact these codes. To support this proposition it was pointed out that in the United States the several states can legislate on matters relating to criminal, civil, commercial, and mining law.[21] But weighty reasons were presented in favor of the measure adopted in the conventions: First, that since colonial times there was unity of legislation in Argentina, because the Spanish law was applied to the entire nation. Second, that, as a reform was needed in the laws, it was better that one legislative body should enact the codes than that confusion should result by the different provinces being permitted to enact them. Third, that the United States method of reserving power to the states was not applicable to Argentina because the states had their own laws when they formed the federation, while in Argentina the Spanish civil law was applied to all the provinces of the Viceroyalty of La Plata.[22]

The power of Congress to enact codes has been the subject of many criticisms. First, it has been argued that the unity of legislation in substantive law established by the Constitution is not desirable unless there is also a unity in procedural legislation. It is alleged that since procedural laws constitute the safeguard of individual citizens, the individual citizen will not receive any bene-

[21] *Asambleas constituyentes argentinas,* IV, 528–29, 850.
[22] *Ibid.,* pp. 781–82.

fits from the uniformity in substantive law if the procedural law employed to enforce the substantive rights is defective, slow and not impartially applied. In the second place, it is alleged that, contrary to the idea of legislation uniform throughout the nation, the law may need reform in some places while not in others.[23] Finally, it may be added that, theoretically and also practically in many cases, the benefits of uniformity of legislation are not achieved when it is considered that the different courts give different interpretations to the codes, especially so since the Supreme Court has held that the decisions of the courts of the provinces when interpreting the national codes are not reviewable by the Supreme Court unless a constitutional question is involved.[24] Thus, the provisions of a code may have one meaning in one province and another meaning in another, so the intended uniformity of legislation may be destroyed through the process of judicial interpretation, although the text of the codes is the same in all the provinces.[25] But in any case, from the point of view of uniformity of legislation, the Argentine system goes far beyond that of the United States. What in Argentina has been done by constitutional provisions, in the United States has been attempted through extra-constitutional means such as the movement for the adoption of uniform statutes by the different states.

Complying with the constitutional mandate, Congress has enacted a series of codes which contain a complete body of substantive law to regulate the relations of the Argentine people. The Code of Commerce was enacted in 1862, the Civil Code in 1871, the Mining Code in 1887, and the Penal Code in 1862.[26] The Supreme Court has held that the power of Congress to enact these codes also vests in Congress the power to determine what they shall contain.[27] For this reason it is possible for Congress to take away from provincial jurisdiction matters which, if Congress had not legislated on them, could have been dealt with by the provin-

[23] A. de Vedia, *La constitución argentina*, pp. 264–65.

[24] Pintos v. Compañía Anónima Tramways, 11 S. C. N. 120 (1871).

[25] This situation may be remedied by giving appellate jurisdiction to the Supreme Court to settle questions of interpretation of the national codes, without regard to the requirement that a constitutional question be involved. It has also been suggested that a special court of appeals be set up to deal with these questions.

[26] *Códigos de la República argentina*, Buenos Aires, 1939.

[27] Ex Parte Herrero, XLII J. A. 961 (1933).

cial legislatures.[28] This has been the case with the codes, except for the Penal Code. In the Penal Code only felonies are included, the misdemeanors being left to the provincial jurisdictions to be dealt with as the provincial legislatures may determine.[29]

Although the Constitution provides that the provinces shall enforce the codes enacted by Congress and that they have the power to apply their codes of procedure in their enforcement, yet the Supreme Court has upheld certain procedural devices contained in the federal codes. Thus the provision of the Civil Code that contracts involving more than 200 pesos have to be in writing in order to be enforceable has been sustained; the Court declared that the code provision refers to the form of the contract and not to the form of the trial, implying that it is substantive and not procedural.[30] The Court has also upheld the constitutionality of a provision of the Agricultural Pledge Law which establishes a special procedure for the enforcement of agricultural contracts, stating that such a provision is essentially enabling legislation to secure the enforcement of the rights guaranteed by the substantive provisions of the statute.[31] The Court also sustained a provision of the federal National Employers' Liability Act that the compensation belonging to the heirs of a deceased employee shall be deposited in the national board of pensions. The Court stated that even if the provision was of a formal nature, Congress had power to prescribe the special formalities necessary to enforce the rights created by the code.[32]

The practical importance of the power of the Argentine Congress to enact code legislation is that it, unlike the Congress of the United States, is permitted to exercise a direct, national police power without relying on other delegated powers such as the commerce clause and the power of taxation. Under the Constitution of the United States the extent of the power of Congress to exercise a national control depends on whether or not the Supreme Court believes that the legislation is a reasonable exercise of a delegated power. For example, that Court declared unconstitu-

28 Mendez v. Corrientes, 1 S. C. N. 40 (1864).

29 J. P. Ramos, *Curso de derecho penal,* IV (Buenos Aires, 1928), 55.

30 Pintos v. Compañía Anónima Tramways, 11 S. C. N. 120 (1871).

31 Correa v. Barrios, 238 S. C. N. 154 (1923).

32 Pérez v. Ferrocarril del Sud, 143 S. C. N. 294 (1926).

tional, as interfering with matters reserved to the states, an Act of Congress which prohibited the transportation in interstate commerce of goods manufactured in a factory where children were employed.[33] On similar grounds another law was invalidated which imposed a tax upon the net income of any person employing children.[34]

In the exercise of the power to enact codes, Congress has passed: a national employers' liability act; [35] a statute authorizing the fixing of rents and regulating the leasing of houses; [36] a national moratorium statute, suspending temporarily the foreclosure of mortgages; [37] and a law giving to employees of commercial and industrial establishments a right of action against employers for wrongful discharge.[38]

FISCAL POWERS

The most important fiscal powers of the Argentine Congress are the power of taxation, the power to establish a national bank, and the power to coin money and regulate the value thereof and of foreign coin.

One of the most serious problems the framers of the Argentine Constitution had to face was how to endow the national government with sufficient taxing power to support the newly created constitutional system. In this particular respect the men of the conventions of 1853 and 1860 followed the footsteps of the men of the Convention of Philadelphia by making the national government economically independent of the provincial governments and by delegating to the Argentine Congress practically the same powers of taxation as are given to the Congress of the United States. The Argentine Constitution, like that of the United States, vests in Congress the power to levy indirect and direct taxes.

33 Hammer v. Dagenhart, 247 U. S. 251 (1918). This case was reversed in United States v. Darby Lumber Co., 312 U. S. 100 (1941), when the Court held that the provisions of the Fair Labor Standards Act prohibiting the shipment in interstate commerce of goods produced for interstate commerce by employees whose wages and hours of employment do not conform to the standard prescribed under the act is a valid exercise of the power of Congress over interstate commerce.

34 Child Labor Tax Case, 259 U. S. 20 (1922).

35 Defensa General v. Ferrocarril de Santa Fe, 137 S. C. N. 80 (1922).

36 Ercolano v. Lanteri, 136 S. C. N. 161 (1922).

37 Yaben v. Laballen, 172 S. C. N. 291 (1935).

38 Saltamartin v. Compañía Tramways La Nacional, 172 S. C. N. 291 (1931).

The power to levy indirect taxes is derived from two articles of the Constitution. One provides that Congress shall have power to legislate in regard to customs houses, and to establish import duties which, as well as the appraisements on which they are based, shall be uniform throughout the nation.[39] This article also provides that Congress shall have power to levy duties on exports (Art. 67, § 1). The Supreme Court of the United States has held that the uniformity required by the Constitution refers to uniformity in the geographical sense [40] and the Argentine Court has similarly interpreted the article of the Argentine Constitution which requires uniformity in taxation.[41] But the United States and the Argentine constitutions differ in regard to the taxation of exports, because while the latter expressly authorizes, the former expressly prohibits, such taxes.[42]

The other article from which the power is derived to levy indirect taxes provides that Congress may impose taxes on the people equitably and proportionally (Art. 4). In *Fisco Nacional v. Berhó*, 121 S. C. N. 264 (1915), the defendant attacked the constitutionality of a national excise tax on the manufacture of alcohol, contending that such a tax was not authorized by Article 4 of the Constitution. The Supreme Court upheld the tax, stating:

> The Constitution, when enumerating in Article 4 the sources of the national treasury, includes among these sources the taxes which Congress may equitably and proportionally impose in relation to the population. And although grave doubt has been raised in repeated and prolonged parliamentary debates about the meaning and extent of this clause, it cannot be questioned that under it Congress is authorized to impose taxes under exceptional circumstances upon objects and valuables subject in general to the taxing power of the provinces without determining or enumerating them. As excise taxes are not prohibited by the Constitution, as in the case of other taxes, it is not within the jurisdiction of the federal courts, which were created to hear concrete

[39] The United States Constitution provides that the Congress shall have power to lay and collect taxes, duties, imposts and excises, to pay the debts and provide for the common defense and general welfare of the United States; *but all duties, imposts and excises shall be uniform throughout the United States* (Art. I, § 8).

[40] Knowlton v. Moore, 178 U. S. 41 (1900); Steward Machine Co. v. Davis, 301 U. S. 548 (1937).

[41] Iglesias v. Buenos Aires, 105 S. C. N. 273 (1906).

[42] "No Tax or Duty Shall be laid on Articles exported from any State" (U. S. Constitution, Art. I, § 9).

judicial cases or controversies, to enter into the examination of the extensive and complex state of the revenues of the nation and of the nature of the national expenditures, as this is a function which belongs to the legislative department, which has before it all the facts necessary for the performance of its functions. Therefore the courts have no power under Article 100 of the Constitution to determine if the law whose constitutionality is questioned in this case has or has not been enacted under the exceptional circumstances which may authorize Congress to exercise the taxing power as provided in the Constitution.

The power of Congress to regulate business in the exercise of the power to levy indirect taxes was upheld in *Huergo v. Gobierno Nacional,* 115 S. C. N. 421 (1912). The statute in question prohibited the use of utensils or apparatus used in the manufacture of alcohol in places where gin was made, and also prohibited the making of alcoholic liquors in distilleries where alcohol was manufactured. The plaintiff's distillery was closed for violating the statute, and he sued the government for damages, alleging that he had been deprived of property without due process of law and of the right to carry on a legitimate industry. The Court sustained the statute on several grounds. First, that Congress has extensive powers to regulate the manufacture of alcohol and to adopt rigorous measures in order to prevent fraud in the payment of the taxes imposed on this manufacture.[43] Second, that in the United States, where the constitutional rights of property and the right to carry on a legitimate business are similar to those guaranteed by the Argentine Constitution, state legislatures have the power not only to regulate the manufacture of alcohol, but also to prohibit the manufacture and sale of liquors.[44]

Both the Argentine and the United States constitutions delegate the power to impose direct taxes with certain limitations, although there are fundamental differences in regard to the limitations. Thus, while the Constitution of the United States provides that no capitation or direct tax shall be imposed except in proportion to the census or enumeration,[45] the Argentine Constitution declares the following limitations: the taxes must be estab-

[43] The Court cited United States v. Simmons, 96 U. S. 360 (1878).

[44] Mugler v. Kansas, 123 U. S. 623 (1887); Crowley v. Christensen, 137 U. S. 86 (1890).

[45] U. S. Constitution, Art. I, § 9.

lished for a definite period of time, must be proportionally equal throughout the territory of the nation,[46] and must be levied whenever the defense of the country, the common safety, or the general public good may require it (Art. 67, § 2). These limitations demonstrate that it is an extraordinary power, which Congress should exercise only in exceptional circumstances. For this reason direct taxes have seldom been imposed by Congress, and the field of direct taxation has been left to the provincial legislatures, which have used it as their chief source of revenue.[47] The question whether the Court may review the discretion of Congress when exercising this power seems to have been answered in the negative in *Fisco Nacional v. Berhó,* already discussed (p. 130).

Spending

The Argentine and the United States supreme courts have held practically similar views in regard to the use Congress may make of money raised by taxation. Both have held that it may be used for other purposes than merely paying the necessary expenses of government. In the United States the question arose in relation to the interpretation of the clause which provides that Congress shall have power to lay and collect taxes, duties, imposts, and excises to pay debts and provide for the general welfare. Concerning the meaning of the clause "provide for the general welfare of the United States" Madison and Hamilton held different views. The first contended that under this clause Congress could spend money raised by taxation only to carry into execution the other powers which were granted to Congress. Hamilton, on the other hand, contended that the clause authorizes Congress to spend for other purposes than those within the expressly granted powers. Hamilton's views were accepted by the Supreme Court in *United States v. Butler,* 297 U. S. 1 (1936), and applied in *Helvering v. Davis,* 301 U. S. 619 (1937). In the latter the Court upheld the constitutionality of a federal tax imposed on employers and employees for the purpose of establishing an old age pension system. The Court,

[46] In Díaz Vélez v. Buenos Aires, 151 S. C. N. 359 (1928), the Court, when interpreting the clause "proportionally equal throughout the nation," held that this has the same meaning as Article 16, which provides that equality shall be the basis of taxation and of the public burdens.

[47] J. González Calderón, *Derecho constitucional argentino,* III, 95–96.

speaking of the power of Congress to levy the tax for the purpose provided in the statute, stated:

The conception of the spending power advocated by Hamilton and strongly reinforced by Story has prevailed over that of Madison, which has not been lacking in adherents. Yet difficulties are left when the power is conceded. The line must still be drawn between one welfare and another, between particular and general. Where this shall be placed cannot be known through a formula in advance of the event. There is a middle ground or certainly a penumbra in which discretion is at large. The discretion, however, is not confided to the courts. The discretion belongs to Congress, unless the choice is clearly wrong, a display of arbitrary power, not an exercise of judgment. . . . Nor is the concept of the general welfare static. Needs that were narrow or parochial a century ago may be interwoven in our day with the well-being of the nation. What is critical or urgent changes with the times.[48]

As to what constitutes general welfare for the purpose of determining the scope of the spending power, the Argentine Court has expressed views like those of the United States Supreme Court. In *Viñedas y Bodegas Arizú v. Mendoza,* 157 S. C. N. 359 (1930), although the Court declared unconstitutional a provincial tax for the purpose of establishing an old age pension system, on the ground that it violated the equal protection clause, nevertheless it declared that the legislature could levy a tax and spend the money for the purpose provided in the statute, since taking care of the old, the poor, and the unemployed comes within the scope of the general welfare.[49] On the power of the nation to spend for promoting the general welfare, the Court stated:

It is of course impossible to establish a uniform rule by which to distinguish between its public and private use. It is very difficult for a law enacted for the general welfare not to contain some elements which may contribute to individual welfare in the same way that it is difficult for a law created for individual welfare not to embody also certain elements which may contribute to public welfare. For this reason the criterion

[48] The power of Congress to levy taxes and spend the money under the general welfare clause in order to establish unemployment insurance and to enable municipalities to establish electric plants was upheld in Steward Machine Co. v. Davis, 301 U. S. 548 (1937), and Alabama Power Co. v. Ickes, 302 U. S. 461 (1938).

[49] Although this case deals with the power of the provinces to spend money raised by taxation for the general welfare, the principle of law governing the taxing power of the legislature or the Congress is equally applicable to both the national and provincial governments. Doncel de Cook v. San Juan, 155 S. C. N. 290 (1929).

for defining what is private or public welfare is circumstantial and depends on the examination of the particular facts of each case. The word public, when used in relation to the taxing power (says James Gray when citing a decision rendered by Justice Cooley), must not be interpreted or applied in a narrow or antiliberal sense, or with a meaning that would prevent the legislature from taking a broad view about the public interests and necessities so that these may be protected through the exercise of the taxing power. The limits of the power of the state in this particular respect cannot be defined, and such power must be interpreted in conformity with the enlightened view of the statesmen who consider that the taxing power may be exercised not only to pay the absolutely indispensable expenditures of government but also to protect the general welfare of society and the future happiness of the people. The construction of public buildings, the payment of public officers and of the public debts, are not the only objects for which public moneys may be spent. On the contrary, reasons of natural equity, gratitude, and beneficence are not out of place when the public welfare is in question and should be taken into consideration in the exercise of the taxing power.

One of the most important fiscal powers delegated to Congress is that to establish and regulate a national bank in the capital and branches in the provinces, with power to issue bills of credit (Art. 67, § 5). Although a similar provision is not found in the Constitution of the United States, knowledge of the political, economic, and juridical controversies which took place in the United States in connection with the establishment of the Bank of the United States influenced the makers of the Argentine Constitution to incorporate this specific provision in their instrument.

That this is so is reflected in the statement of the Supreme Court in *Banco Nacional v. Villanueva,* 18 S. C. N. 102 (1876), where the constitutionality of the law creating the bank was first brought into question.[50] In this case the National Bank sued the defendant in the federal courts to recover a debt. The defendant objected to the jurisdiction of the court on the ground that the

[50] The Court, after reviewing the history of the Bank of the United States, said: "Our constituents, knowing the importance of such an institution for the public administration and for the public in general, wished to have a similar institution at the disposal of the government. Thus, in order to prevent the obstacles to the establishment of such an institution in the United States existing because of the silence of the Constitution in regard to the constitutional power of Congress to create the National Bank, our constituents expressly granted such a power to Congress in Article 67, section 5, of the Constitution."

bank was not the bank contemplated by the Constitution, but a private institution, in as much as the shares and the control of the same were not totally in the hands of the national government. But the Court sustained the law and stated that even if private individuals owned shares of the bank and participated in the control of the same these facts did not make the bank a private institution; and that the bank had all the essential characteristics of a national bank.

Currency

The framers of the Argentine Constitution adopted the currency powers almost literally from the Constitution of the United States.[51] The Argentine Constitution provides that Congress shall have the power to coin money and to regulate the value thereof and of foreign coins (Art. 67, § 10). The power of Congress under this clause is a very extensive one and is not limited to providing a currency on a metallic basis alone. Thus *Posse Hermanos v. Fregoni,* 36 S. C. N. 167 (1889), sustained the power of Congress to provide that obligations contracted on a gold basis could be discharged through the payment of paper money authorized to circulate as legal currency. This power was said to be extensive enough to enable Congress to create one or more types of money for the country, to emit bank and credit bills and put them into circulation, to give these bills the character of legal tender, and to suspend payment in cash.

Notwithstanding the decision just cited, the general problem was raised again four years later in *Soldati v. Banco Muñoz Rodríguez y Cía.,* 52 S. C. N. 413 (1893), on review of a lower federal court holding that the statute of Congress was unconstitutional. Several grounds were assigned by the lower court: first, that the law impaired prior contractual obligations; second, that it deprived the plaintiff of property rights without due process of law; third, that the power of Congress to coin money and fix the value thereof merely authorized Congress to determine the weight and quality of fine gold which the coin should contain but did not authorize Congress to assign a determinate value to the coin since

[51] "The Congress shall have Power To coin Money, regulate the Value thereof, and of foreign Coin . . ." (U. S. Constitution, Art. I, § 8).

such value is superior and existed before the enactment of the law; fourth, that according to decisions of the United States Supreme Court, when an obligation is contracted on a gold basis the debtor cannot discharge it except by payment in the kind of money provided in the contract.[52] The Supreme Court, however, held that the power of Congress to enact the law in question emanated not only from the general power of sovereignty but also from the special powers granted by the Constitution.[53]

The power of Congress to regulate the value of foreign coin and to make this legal currency in the country was upheld in *Duguid y Cía. v. Muñoz,* 22 S. C. N. 450 (1880). In this case the defendant wished to pay an obligation with Bolivian money which had been declared legal currency by an act of Congress, but the plaintiff refused to accept such payment. It was held that payment could be effected as the defendant desired, since Congress could nationalize foreign coin by making it legal currency in the country. Another fiscal power which the framers of the Argentine Constitution adopted from the United States Constitution [54] is that which authorizes Congress to punish the counterfeiting of se-

[52] The lower court cited Bronson v. Rodes, 7 Wall. 229 (1868), and Butler v. Horwitz, 7 Wall. 258 (1868).

[53] In 1862 the Congress of the United States enacted two statutes providing that treasury notes should be legal tender in payment of all debts public and private. In the Legal Tender Cases, 12 Wall. 457 (1871), the Court held the statutes valid, stating that Congress had the power to give to other things than the precious metals the value of money; that any contract for the payment of money is necessarily subject to the constitutional power of the government over the currency, and the obligations are presumed to be made with reference to that power; that the Fifth Amendment applies only to the taking of property directly and not to consequential injuries resulting from the exercise of a lawful power.

After the enactment of a Joint Resolution in 1933 abrogating the gold clauses in public and private contracts, and the change in the gold content of the dollar, the validity of these changes was litigated. In Norman v. Baltimore and Ohio Railroad Co., 294 U. S. 240 (1935), the Court upheld the power of Congress to devalue the currency by reducing the gold content of the dollar on the same theory as that used in the Legal Tender Cases. But in Perry v. United States, 294 U. S. 330 (1935), the Court made a distinction between public and private contracts as affected by this Congressional move. Punctilious fulfillment of obligations induced by the pledging of the credit of the government is essential to the maintenance of the public credit, and the government could not ignore its own solemn pledge to pay a certain return for money loaned to it. At the same time, the Court denied recovery to the plaintiff because he had failed to prove that he had suffered damages by the action of the government.

[54] "The Congress shall have Power To provide for the punishment of counterfeiting the Securities and current Coin of the United States" (U. S. Constitution, Art. I, § 8).

curities and of current coin of the nation (Art. 67, § 11).[55] Interpreting this provision of the Constitution, the Court held that counterfeiting can be punished in the federal courts only when the money is authorized to circulate in the country; when it is not so authorized the crime of counterfeiting may be prosecuted in the provincial courts.[56]

Although Congress has the power to regulate the value of foreign coin, the provincial governments under certain circumstances may exercise a like power without encroaching on the powers of Congress. This point is illustrated in *Caffarena v. Banco Argentino de Rosario,* 10 S. C. N. 427 (1870). The province of Santa Fe enacted a statute providing that within thirty days thereafter the banks of the province should redeem their bank notes in gold. The plaintiff presented to the defendant a bank note payable in Bolivian coin or in legal currency at the discretion of the bank and requested payment in gold according to the statute; the defendant bank refused so to pay. In subsequent litigation the bank contended that the statute was unconstitutional for three reasons: first, because it constituted an invasion of the power of Congress to regulate the value of foreign coin; second, because it impaired the obligation of prior contracts; third, because it deprived the bank of property rights guaranteed by the Constitution. The lower federal court sustained these contentions. On appeal the Supreme Court upheld the statute.[57] As to the first contention, the Court held that the exclusive power of Congress to regulate the value of foreign coin extends only to admitting the foreign coin and making it a legal currency within the nation and that a province can enact legislation excluding or limiting the circulation of foreign coin which has not been recognized as legal currency by Congress. The Court further held that the provincial statute, instead of usurping a power vested in Congress, had rather helped the enforcement of federal law which did not recognize the Bolivian coin as legal currency, since the statute tended to exclude or limit the circulation of the Bolivian coin in the nation. As to the second

[55] The national Penal Code punishes the counterfeiting of national money, bank bills, and also all types of public documents (Art. 282–98). Gobierno Nacional v. Guerci, 10 S. C. N. 440 (1871).

[56] *Gobierno Nacional v. Poncelli,* 23 S. C. N. 81 (1880).

[57] This case was decided on September 21, 1871, and the Legal Tender Cases were decided by the United States Supreme Court on May 1 of the same year.

ground, the Court answered that as the Argentine Constitution, unlike that of the United States, does not prohibit the provinces from enacting laws impairing the obligation of contracts, the province had the power to enact the statute even if it affected contractual obligations entered into before the enactment of the statute. And as to the third contention, the Court advanced the theory that the law did not deprive the bank of any property rights guaranteed by the Constitution, since no person can acquire irrevocable rights against laws of public order such as a law regulating and fixing the value of money and bank notes.[58]

But although the provinces can regulate the value of foreign coin when this has not been nationalized by Congress, the Argentine Constitution, like that of the United States, prohibits the provincial governments from coining money. In *Galleti v. San Juan*, 148 S. C. N. 65 (1926), the Court stated:

> It is true that the provinces have, under the power reserved to them by the Constitution, the authority to promote their economic and moral well-being, and can therefore issue securities under certain conditions for the purpose mentioned above. But under the powers reserved by the Constitution the provinces are not permitted to issue securities payable to the bearer with the external form of bank notes and which the government that issued the same offers and accepts as money and which as such are put into circulation as a means of exchange. The issuing of such securities amounts to the emission of money, thus affecting the unity and uniformity of the monetary system of the nation, which under the Constitution is subject exclusively to the control and regulation of the national Congress.

The Constitution of the United States prohibits the states from issuing bills of credit, but such a prohibition is not found in the Argentine Constitution. For this reason the provinces can issue bills of exchange or securities based on the public credit of the provinces,[59] provided these securities do not have the characteristics which might make them legal tender. The case of *Otero v. Córdoba*, 57 S. C. N. 337 (1884), presents an interesting problem. The defendant province owed a debt to the plaintiff based on a government security which under the terms of the instrument had to be paid in national currency. When the debt was due, the

[58] The United States Constitution provides that "No State shall . . . make any Thing but gold and silver Coin a Tender in Payment of Debts . . ." (Art. I, § 10). But such a provision is not found in the Argentine Constitution.

[59] Medina v. Santa Fe, 95 S. C. N. 282 (1902).

province tendered other securities, but the plaintiff rejected the offer and insisted upon payment in national money as provided for not only in the instrument but also in the Civil Code. Plaintiff sued the province for breach of contract and the Court held in his favor. The Court said:

As Congress has the power to enact the Civil Code, the provinces cannot alter it once it has been enacted. This explains the fact that under our Constitution the provinces do not have the power to legislate on common law matters as is the case under the Constitution of the United States. This difference between the two constitutions explains the reason why our Constitution does not prohibit the provinces from legislating on certain common law matters, as is permitted under the Constitution of the United States, which forbids the states from offering anything but gold and silver for the payment of their debts and also from impairing the obligation of contracts. As in the United States the states and not the national government have the power to enact common law legislation, the former limitations are necessary, while in our system they are not because the national government and not the provinces exercises the power to legislate on common law matters.

TREATIES

While the Constitution of the United States vests only in the Senate the power to approve or reject treaties made by the President with foreign nations,[60] the Argentine Constitution vests such power in both houses of Congress (Art. 67, § 19).[61] This Constitution imposes no other limitation on the treaty-making power of Congress except that the treaties must be in conformity with the principles of public law established in the Constitution (Art. 27).[62] Treaties are approved or rejected by Congress by an absolute majority of each house.[63]

The principle expounded by the Supreme Court of the United States that a treaty is not a greater obligation than a law of Congress, and that therefore a law can modify or repeal a treaty and vice versa, has been followed by the Argentine Supreme Court in *Alonso v. Haras los Cardos,* 186 S. C. N. 258 (1940). In this case

60 U. S. Constitution, Art. II, § 2.

61 The Argentine Constitution in Article 108 and the Constitution of the United States in Article I, § 3, prohibit the provinces and the states respectively from making treaties.

62 A similar provision is not found in the Constitution of the United States.

63 *Rules of the Chamber of Deputies,* Buenos Aires, 1938, Art. 161; *Rules of the Senate,* Buenos Aires, 1940, Art. 161.

one of the issues was whether an international labor convention approved by Congress dealing with employers' liability in agricultural employment had modified a national statute of a narrower scope than the convention. The Court held in the negative and, on the authority of a decision of the United States Supreme Court,[64] said that a treaty may repeal a statute or a statute a treaty, but the purpose of such a repeal must clearly appear in the text and in the records of legislative intent in enacting the statute or approving the treaty.

García v. Buenos Aires, 139 S. C. N. 42 (1923), also illustrates the point under consideration. Plaintiff, a resident of Spain, had a son in Argentina who was killed in an accident while working on a railroad. The employer deposited a sum of money which was the compensation due to the plaintiff for his son's death under the federal compensation law. The plaintiff demanded the compensation from the province of Buenos Aires, which was in charge of the administration of the law, but the provincial authorities refused to surrender it because the law provided that if the heirs of the deceased were not living in Argentina when the accident occurred they were not entitled to any compensation. The plaintiff alleged that according to the provision of a treaty entered into between Spain and Argentina he was entitled to the compensation. The Court held in favor of the plaintiff on the ground that the treaty had repealed the statute.

MILITARY POWERS

The Argentine Congress is vested exclusively with war and military powers.[65] These powers are: to authorize the executive to declare war and make peace, to grant letters of marque and reprisal and make rules concerning captures, to fix the strength of the land and naval forces in times of peace and war, and to make rules and regulations for the government of the same. Under the power to fix the strength of the army and the navy Congress has

[64] United States v. Lee Yen Tai, 185 U. S. 213 (1902).

[65] The Argentine Constitution provides that the provinces shall not declare or make war upon one another (Art. 109); and Article 108 provides that no province shall arm ships of war, nor raise troops except in case of invasion, or in such imminent danger as will not admit of delay, rendering afterwards an account to the federal government.

enacted statutes providing for compulsory military training, and the Supreme Court has upheld their constitutionality.[66]

The Court has also sustained the power of Congress to establish military tribunals under the power to make rules and regulations for the government of the military and naval forces, against the contention that they were in conflict with Article 16 of the Constitution, which prohibits the granting of special privileges in criminal trials to certain classes of persons. Thus, *Ex Parte Mortola,* 147 S. C. N. 45 (1926), upheld a statute creating a military court on the ground that Congress had such power under Article 67, § 23. Citing as precedent *Dynes v. Hoover,* 20 How. 65 (1857), and *Johnson v. Sayre,* 158 U. S. 109 (1895), the Court stated:

> In view of these considerations in the judicial decisions of this court, concordant with those decisions of the courts of the American Union based upon the interpretation of constitutional provisions which have served as a model to ours, the constitutionality of the military courts cannot be denied, since their creation is impliedly authorized by sections 23 and 24 of Article 67 of the Constitution and other clauses of the Constitution creating the judicial power.

And in *Nación v. Hernández,* 149 S. C. N. 175 (1928), in which the Court upheld the power of Congress to provide that judgments rendered by military courts shall be final and not subject to review by the Supreme Court unless the courts acted without jurisdiction, it was stated:

> The Supreme Court of the United States has declared that the military courts have ample authority to decide in last instance all the cases in which they have jurisdiction and their procedure cannot be reviewed by the federal courts except for determining whether the federal courts have jurisdiction over the person or subject matter involved in the controversies decided by them.[67]

An important military power delegated to Congress and taken almost literally from two clauses of the United States Constitu-

[66] Ex Parte Álvarez, 181 S. C. N. 281 (1939). In the Selective Draft Law Cases, 245 U. S. 366 (1918), the United States Supreme Court upheld the power of Congress to enact compulsory military service statutes on the theory that such a power is derived from the powers to declare war, raise and support armies, and make rules for the government and regulation of the land and naval forces.

[67] Citing Kurtz v. Moffitt, 115 U. S. 487 (1885); Runkle v. United States, 122 U. S. 543 (1887); Swaim v. United States, 165 U. S. 553 (1897); Carter v. McClaughry, 183 U. S. 365 (1902).

tion [68] is that of calling, arming, organizing, and disciplining the provincial militia. The Constitution provides that Congress shall have power to call the militia in all or some of the provinces whenever the execution of the laws of the nation may so require and whenever necessary to suppress rebellion or repel invasion. It also provides that Congress shall have the power to organize, arm, and discipline the militia and to govern such part of them as may be employed in the service of the nation, leaving to the provinces respectively the appointment of officers and the responsibility of establishing the military discipline prescribed by Congress (Art. 67, § 24). The Supreme Court has interpreted this provision of the Constitution in the light of decisions of the United States Supreme Court. Thus, in *García v. Aguilar,* 21 S. C. N. 134 (1879), the Court, citing *Houston v. Moore,* 5 Wheat. 1 (1820), held that the provinces had power to discipline a member of the national guard when not called up by the national government.

Other powers granted by the Constitution to Congress are, first, to permit the entrance of foreign troops into and the departure of the national forces outside the territory of the nation (Art. 67, § 25), and second, to declare a state of siege in one or more districts of the nation in case of interior commotion, and to continue or suspend a state of siege declared by the executive during a recess of Congress (Art. 67, § 26). The Constitution of the United States provides that the writ of habeas corpus shall not be suspended except when in case of rebellion or invasion the public safety requires it. But this provision is not exactly equivalent to one providing for a state of siege, since the latter is a measure of wider scope in as much as its declaration suspends all constitutional guarantees, including the writ of habeas corpus.[69] Although the Constitution of the United States does not expressly provide that the suspension of the writ of habeas corpus is a prerogative of Congress rather than of the executive, nevertheless it has been held that the exercise of such a power belongs to Congress and

[68] The United States Constitution, Art. I, § 8, cl. 15, provides that Congress shall have the power to call the militia to execute the laws of the Union, suppress insurrections and repel invasions; and cl. 16 provides that Congress shall have power to organize, arm, and discipline the militia, and to govern such part of them as may be employed in the service of the United States, reserving to the states respectively the appointment of the officers, and the authority of training the militia according to the discipline prescribed by Congress.

[69] Ex Parte Alem, 54 S. C. N. 432 (1893).

not to the President.[70] During the Civil War President Lincoln suspended the writ of habeas corpus, insisting that this power could also be exercised by the executive, but Congress, in order to remove any doubt about the legality of the President's action, passed various acts which indirectly gave validity to it.[71] In Argentina the problem is solved in the Constitution in a more satisfactory manner by its provision that Congress is the department of government which has the power to declare the state of siege or to continue or suspend the state of siege declared by the executive during the recess of Congress.

BANKRUPTCY

The Argentine Congress is empowered by the Constitution to enact general bankruptcy legislation (Art. 67, § 11).[72] Under the authority of this provision Congress enacted a comprehensive bankruptcy statute, embodied in Book IV of the Code of Commerce. In doing so Congress has followed the tradition of the civil law according to which bankruptcy legislation forms an integral part of the Code of Commerce. In *Ex Parte Vidal,* 129 S. C. N. 181 (1911), the Court upheld such action by Congress, instead of having this legislation remain as a special statute.

In *Hernández v. Castells,* 135 S. C. N. 122 (1921), the Court discussed the extent of the bankruptcy powers of Congress. In this case the bankrupt, who was not a merchant, petitioned the Court to be discharged of his debts after being declared a bankrupt according to the provisions of the statute. A creditor attacked the constitutionality of the statute on the ground that the bankruptcy clause authorizes only legislation applicable to merchants. The Court, after stating that the provision of the Argentine Constitution is based on that in the Constitution of the United States, upheld the statute:

> The power of Congress to legislate on bankruptcy cannot be considered to be limited to bankruptcy proceedings involving merchants only. On the contrary, the amplitude of the power vested in Congress and the precedent and doctrine established by the United States Supreme Court

[70] Ex Parte Merryman, 17 Fed. Cases No. 9487 (1861).

[71] Edward S. Corwin, *The President, Office and Powers*, New York, 1940, p. 187.

[72] The United States Constitution provides that "The Congress shall have Power . . . To establish a uniform law on the subject of Bankruptcies throughout the United States" (Art. I, § 8).

in the case of *Hanover National Bank v. Moyses*, 186 U. S. 181 (1902), demonstrate that the purpose of the authors of the Constitution was to authorize Congress to enact bankruptcy legislation to meet the exceptional circumstances presented by a bankruptcy or insolvency case whether the parties involved were merchants or not.

POSTAL POWERS

The Argentine Constitution vests in Congress the power to establish post offices and post roads (Art. 67, § 13),[73] and in 1875 Congress established a post office system throughout the nation. It is a state monopoly. The law creating the system authorizes the provincial governments to establish post offices where no national post offices exist, but they cannot continue to operate after the federal government establishes national post offices. Congress has also created a national telegraph system, which is operated by the post office department. The telephone system, on the other hand, is operated by private corporations.

The use of the mail is not a constitutional right but rather a privilege which can be regulated by Congress. In *Ex Parte Bertotto*, 168 S. C. N. 15 (1933), the petitioner's newspaper had been excluded from the mails because it contained a seditious article. He contended that the action of the postal authorities violated the right of freedom of the press guaranteed by the Constitution, but the Court sustained the legality of the action of the postal authorities on two grounds. First, the right of particular persons to use the postal service is not absolute and therefore it cannot be used for ends contrary to the essential principles of the political organization, public morals, and good customs of the Republic; and second, there was no violation of the right of freedom of the press because the petitioner's newspaper contained an article which constituted a crime, making the newspaper unmailable matter under the postal laws.[74]

[73] The Constitution of the United States provides that "The Congress shall have Power . . . To establish Post Offices and Post Roads" (Art. I, § 8).

[74] The Supreme Court of the United States has applied similar principles in several cases. In In re Rapier, 143 U. S. 110 (1892), the Court upheld the power of Congress to prohibit the sending through the mails of letters containing lottery tickets. In Horner v. United States, 143 U. S. 207 (1892), such a prohibition was held not to be an interference with the freedom of the press. And finally, in Schenck v. United States, 249 U. S. 47 (1919), the Court held constitutional a law of Congress prohibiting the sending through the mail of matter published in violation of the espionage laws.

VI: POWERS OF THE PROVINCES

THE Argentine Constitution reserves to the provinces important powers of local self-government. It provides that the provinces reserve all the powers which are not delegated to the national government and which had not been reserved by special treaties at the time of their incorporation into the federation (Art. 104).[1] In *Mendoza v. San Juan,* 3 S. C. N. 131 (1865), in which a provincial tax on exports was declared invalid on the ground that the power of such taxation was delegated to Congress, the Court stated the principles governing the reserved powers of the provinces:

> The provinces have all the powers not delegated to the federal government. The acts of the provincial legislatures can be invalidated only under the following circumstances: when the Constitution in express terms delegates a power exclusively to Congress; when the exercise of the power is expressly prohibited to the provinces; and when there is an absolute incompatibility in the exercise of these powers by the provinces and the national government.

In *Orien v. Costa,* 3 S. C. N. 468 (1866), where the power of a provincial legislature to authorize a municipality to regulate market places and grant exclusive franchises for selling in the same was sustained, the Court stated:

> The legislatures of the provinces have the constitutional power to authorize municipalities to regulate local commerce, because although it is true that Congress can pass a similar statute when regulating foreign and interprovincial commerce or industry the legislatures of the provinces have the same power in regard to local industry, commerce, health, and general welfare, as provided in Article 104 of the Constitution under which the provinces have all the powers not delegated to the federal government. Also, under Article 105 of the Constitution, the provinces have the power to establish their own institutions. And finally, by

[1] The Tenth Amendment of the United States Constitution reads: "The Powers not delegated to the United States by the Constitution, nor prohibited by it to the States, are reserved to the States respectively, or to the People."

Article 107 the provinces are authorized to promote industry, commerce, immigration, etc.

The Court added that the doctrine was supported by authorities like Kent and Wheaton, and also by the decision in *Sturges v. Crowninshield*, 4 Wheat. 122 (1819).

In *Mendoza v. San Juan*, mentioned above, the Court stated that the provinces cannot exercise a power if such exercise is incompatible with the exercise of the same power delegated to Congress, and in *Ferrocarril Central del Sud v. Municipalidad de Juárez*, 183 S. C. N. 190 (1939), the Court explains the meaning of this limitation. The issue in this case was whether Congress, in the exercise of the powers which authorized it to foster the prosperity of the country by promoting the building of railroads and granting temporary privileges, could exempt such railroads from the payment of municipal taxes. The defendant municipality contended that the exemption was unconstitutional because under Article 104 the provinces reserve all the powers not delegated and that there was no express delegation on this subject. But the Court upheld the exemption and declared the municipal tax invalid on the theory that as Congress had the delegated power to foster the construction of railroads it had also the implied power to exempt them from provincial taxation as a means to encourage the building of railroads; the provinces could not exercise a power which would obstruct the powers delegated to Congress.

CONCURRENT POWERS

Under the Argentine Constitution there are certain powers which can be exercised by the provincial and national governments at the same time, or which may be exercised by the provinces in cases where the national government has not acted. These are termed concurrent powers. There are two types, transitory and permanent.

Transitory Concurrent Powers

The Constitution deals expressly with concurrent powers of a transitory nature which the provinces may exercise because the national government, although having the power to legislate on the subject matter, has not done so. Thus, it provides that until Congress enacts a national election law the provincial laws shall regulate the election of national officers (Art. 41), and that until Congress enacts civil, mining, criminal, and commercial codes, the codes of the provinces shall be the law of the land (Art. 108). The Supreme Court has held that, in view of the fact that Congress has not legislated on the subject, the provincial courts have jurisdiction over maritime contracts for the unloading of merchandise in the ports, *Figari v. Palma,* 13 S. C. N. 233 (1872).

In *Buenos Aires v. Ferrocarril Central Argentino,* 94 S. C. N. 396 (1902), the province of Buenos Aires prosecuted the defendant, a railroad engaged in interprovincial commerce, for violation of the provincial law in that it failed to present to the provincial authorities the plans for the change of a station and for the construction of a stockyard. The defendant railroad was fined for the violation, and it appealed to the Supreme Court. That Court held that the provincial law could not be applied to the defendant, saying that the province had no power to impose fines for the violation of a provincial statute after Congress had enacted a statute regulating the affairs of interprovincial roads. The decision of the Court seems to imply that if there had been no law of Congress covering the subject the provincial regulation would have been upheld.

Permanent Concurrent Powers

The other types of concurrent powers which the provinces may exercise are those of a permanent nature. In *Griet Hermanos v. Tucumán,* 137 S. C. N. 212 (1922), the national government had enacted, in 1919, a tariff act which imposed a duty on imported sugar in order to protect the sugar industries of the province of Tucumán. In 1921 the province of Buenos Aires enacted a statute imposing a tax on the manufacture of sugar on the basis of the number of kilograms of sugar produced, the tax differing according to whether or not the sugar was refined. The plaintiff attacked the statute on the ground that it was in conflict with the law of Congress, the contention being that while Congress attempted to protect the sugar industry the provincial law would destroy this protection by taxing the industry. The power to tax may mean the power to destroy, said the plaintiff, citing Marshall's dictum in *McCulloch v. Maryland,* 4 Wheat. 316 (1819).

The Court sustained the provincial statute on the ground that there was no conflict between it and the national law. The governments had enacted their statutes under different powers for different purposes.

The power which each state has to levy taxes on corporations and on real and personal property and franchises, and the power to fix taxes according to the value of property and the volume of business, when these taxes are not discriminatory and when they are not imposed on imports or exports from other states or foreign countries, cannot be regarded as being in conflict with any constitutional power of Congress.[2]

Respecting the nature of concurrent power in taxation matters as being equally applicable to other governmental matters, the Court added:

The principle of concurrent powers of the states and of the central government has been expanded and upheld by well-known Argentine and United States commentators on constitutional law. They have demonstrated that there is perfect compatibility in the exercise of such powers by the national and local governments, and that there is no conflict between the exercise of these powers and the principle of the supremacy of the national law, since this supremacy prevails only when the laws of Congress are constitutional, and therefore this principle cannot be applied when a law of Congress encroaches upon the powers which the Constitution has reserved to the states.[3]

Banco de Córdoba v. Caja de Jubilaciones y Pensiones de Empleados Bancarios, 147 S. C. N. 239 (1926), presents another important aspect of the doctrine of concurrent powers. The question was whether a province could create a bank with branches in other provinces and in the federal capital. The branch in the federal capital was ordered to come under the provisions of the national employer's pension act, but the province contended that the statute was not applicable to its bank because it would constitute an encroachment on the autonomy of the province. The Court denied the contention, and held that although the province could validly create a bank, in spite of the fact that Congress had power to create a national bank, yet the provincial power must be subject to the

[2] Citing the Delaware Railroad Tax Case, 18 Wall. 20 (1874).

[3] In Sociedad Anónima Bodegas y Viñedos San Carlos v. San Juan, 185 S. C. N. 209 (1939), the Court, citing Willoughby, *Constitutional Law of the United States,* III, 192, held constitutional a federal tax law against the objection that it was unconstitutional because the provinces had imposed a similar tax on the same property.

limitation that the bank could operate only within the territorial limits of the province, citing *Bonaparte v. Tax Court*, 104 U. S. 592 (1882).

The Argentine Constitution contains other provisions recognizing the principle of permanent concurrent powers. Both the provincial and the national governments are empowered to construct railroads and navigable channels (Art. 107; Art. 67).[4] The Supreme Court has held that the provinces can construct railroads provided they do not go outside their territorial jurisdiction. The Court has also held that the power to expropriate lands for the building of works of general public utility is not an exclusive power of Congress but may be exercised by the provinces as well.[5]

POWERS OF THE PROVINCES AS AFFECTED BY THE DELEGATION OF POWERS TO THE NATIONAL GOVERNMENT

The powers of the Argentine provinces are, as is true also in the United States, affected by the delegation of powers to the national government. That is, the provinces cannot exercise their reserved powers when to do so would obstruct or burden the powers delegated to the national government. Two general phases of this limitation, as touching the so-called police power and the power of taxation, will be examined separately.

Police Power

Although the Argentine provinces do not have as extensive a police power as have the states of the United States because the Argentine Congress, unlike that of the United States, has the power to enact the civil, criminal, commercial, and mining codes, yet the Supreme Court has recognized the police power of the provinces in many local matters.

The Supreme Court defined the police power of the provinces for the first time in *Empresa de Toros v. Buenos Aires*, 7 S. C. N.

[4] Other concurrent powers are the administration of justice, civil and criminal, promotion of industry, immigration, colonization of lands, establishment of new industries, importation of foreign capital, exploration of rivers, education, declaration of a state of siege, and the granting of privileges to persons and corporations.

[5] Arguello v. Buenos Aires, 97 S. C. N. 408 (1903). The Court held in Murua v. Salta, 104 S. C. N. 247 (1900), citing United States precedents, that the provinces can exercise the power of eminent domain in behalf of the national government.

450 (1869), which involved an attack on the constitutionality of a statute prohibiting the establishment of bull-fighting arenas, on the ground that it violated Article 14 guaranteeing the free exercise of industry and trade. The Court upheld the statute, and said:

It is a fact and also a principle of constitutional law that the police power of the provinces is in charge of provincial legislatures and municipal councils. The police power is one of the powers which the Constitution has reserved to the provinces and may be defined as the power to provide for the security, health and morality of its inhabitants, and in the exercise of this power the local governments may enact laws and regulations for the purpose of accomplishing these ends. The national judiciary is incompetent to compel a province which has prohibited bull fights to permit the construction of a bull-fight arena under the pretext that bull fights are commercial or industrial enterprises when the province has decided that bull fights are spectacles against morality, culture, and public decency.

In *Ex Parte Manuel González Maceda,* 154 S. C. N. 6 (1929), the petitioner requested a federal court to enjoin the municipal authorities of Buenos Aires from interfering with his right to use the public streets to hold a public meeting, but the lower court denied the request. This judgment was affirmed by the Supreme Court on the ground that in the exercise of the police power the municipality could prevent the petitioner from using the public streets for a political meeting. Citing United States commentators the Court stated that it was a general principle in the Argentine system, similar to that of the United States, that the police power belongs to the provinces and that the national government exercises such power within the provinces only when it has been expressly granted or is a resultant of other powers so granted.

In the exercise of this power the provinces can impose reasonable regulations on the practice of the learned professions. Thus, in *Ex Parte Ivanissevich,* 117 S. C. N. 432 (1913), the petitioner attacked the constitutionality of a law of the province of Mendoza which required a bond of fifteen thousand pesos as a condition for the practice of engineering; the statute was sustained. The Court referred to the work of the late Professor Freund, *The Police Power,* and stated:

It cannot be considered that a right has been altered by the mere fact that a law has been enacted to regulate its exercise when such regulations impose reasonable conditions or are of such a character that they do not amount to a destruction or an impairment of such right. Thus, applying to the present case the institutions which have served as a model to ours, United States doctrine and jurisprudence has maintained that regulations enacted in the exercise of the police power must be reasonable, and the rule to determine the reasonableness of the regulation is whether it prohibits, destroys, or confiscates the property or the right which the law attempts to regulate.

Buenos Aires v. Díaz, 101 S. C. N. 126 (1905), upheld a statute of the province prohibiting gambling, against the contention that it was in conflict with the national penal code. The Court found no such conflict and held that the statute was a reasonable exercise of the police power reserved to the provincial governments.

The provinces may also, in appropriate circumstances, destroy private property without paying compensation therefor. In *Podestá v. Buenos Aires,* 31 S. C. N. 273 (1887), the Court dismissed a suit for damages against the defendant province because its officers had ordered the destruction of certain salting places (i. e., places where beef was salted) near cities and towns and required that they be taken away from urban centers.

But the provinces cannot enact minimum wage legislation; that power has been delegated to the national government. *Viñedas y Bodegas Arizú v. Mendoza,* 156 S. C. N. 20 (1929), declared a provincial statute of this sort unconstitutional. The Court said:

When the Constitution vested in Congress the power to enact a Civil Code it was the intention of the framers to vest in Congress the power to legislate on matters relating to the organization of the family, real property, inheritance, obligations, and contractual relations, that is, all the matters which come under the term, "common law." The Civil Code deals with personal service contracts in Chapter VIII of Book II, section 3, defining them as consensual and saying that such contracts exist when one or more persons obligate themselves to another and receive a compensation for their services. The minimum wage law enacted by the province of Mendoza not only modifies the institution of personal service contracts as established in the article previously referred to but also is in conflict with the freedom and capacity of the individual to contract, a legal norm established for all the Republic and consecrated in Article 1197 of the Civil Code.

The same principle was applied as between the police power of the province and the national power to enact trademark legislation. In *Peters Hermanos v. Buenos Aires,* 155 S. C. N. 112 (1929), the constitutionality of a provincial statute was questioned on the ground that it conflicted with an Act of Congress. To the plaintiff the national government had granted the right to sell beverages with the trademark "Ajenjina," a name used to distinguish beverages not of a medical nature, whether they contained alcohol or not. The plaintiff attempted to register the trademark with the provincial authorities; but registration was refused on the ground that the provincial statute did not permit the use of misleading words in trademarks and also because the sale of *ajenjina* wormwood, used in absinthe, was prohibited in the province. The Court declared the provincial statute invalid on the ground that although the provinces can prohibit the sale of products which they consider dangerous to health or morality they cannot prohibit the registration of trade marks duly authorized by the laws of Congress.[6]

Like the states of the United States the Argentine provinces cannot exercise the police power so as to interfere with, obstruct, or burden the power of Congress to regulate interprovincial and foreign commerce. A leading case on this point is *Rosauer v. Mendoza,* 179 S. C. N. 69 (1937). The defendant province enacted a statute prohibiting the introduction of living plants unless they were taken to the provincial nursery, where they had to remain one year under observation. The statute also provided that only those varieties of plants which the provincial authorities deemed necessary and convenient would be admitted into the province. The provincial authorities justified the statute as a police regulation to protect agriculture. It was attacked as in violation of the power of Congress to regulate interprovincial commerce and also as in conflict with a law of Congress enacted for the protection of agriculture. The Court held the statute invalid on the first ground, saying that the introduction of plants from one province to another is a typical act of interprovincial commerce, subject to the

[6] The Supreme Court of the United States held invalid, in United States v. De Witt, 9 Wall. 41 (1869), a federal law which prohibited the sale of naphtha for illuminating purposes if it was inflammable at a temperature of 110 degrees Fahrenheit, on the ground that such a law constituted a police regulation which under the Constitution is reserved to the states.

regulation of Congress. The Court further held that the provincial statute was not a legitimate exercise of the police power, but tended to establish an economic war which was irreconcilable with the freedom of interprovincial commerce guaranteed by the Constitution.[7] Again and on like ground, in *Lostalo v. Buenos Aires,* 170 S. C. N. 71 (1933), the Court declared unconstitutional a provincial statute which obstructed the power of Congress to regulate interprovincial commerce. The defendant province enacted a statute which required all human or veterinary medicines to be registered in the province, and required a fee for such registration. As in the former case, the province justified the enactment of the law as a police measure to protect the health of its inhabitants and of livestock. But the Court declared the statute void, saying that, although the provinces can pass statutes prohibiting the making and sale of articles injurious to health and morality, yet such laws must not obstruct or impair the power of the national government to regulate interprovincial and foreign commerce.[8] As to the fee, the Court held that it was not levied as a means to enforce the police regulations, since only thirty percent of it was expended for the execution of the statute.[9]

The Court has declared unconstitutional regulations of the provinces dealing with the sanitary inspection of imported and exported products. In *Swift de la Plata v. Tucumán,* 168 S. C. N. 268 (1933), the defendant municipality imposed a fee upon the plaintiff's imported meat to cover the charge of veterinary inspection. The Court declared the tax illegal, and said that as it must be presumed that the meat had been inspected in the place from which it originally came the tax was not for police purposes but rather a revenue measure, which constituted an unconstitu-

[7] In Oregon-Washington Co. v. Washington, 270 U. S. 87 (1926), the United States Supreme Court held invalid a state statute prohibiting the importation of alfalfa hay and meal found to contain the alfalfa weevil as in conflict with the act of Congress giving the Secretary of Agriculture full control over the subject matter.

[8] In Bourjois v. Chapman, 301 U. S. 183 (1937), the Supreme Court of the United States upheld a statute of one state requiring the registration of cosmetics manufactured in another state.

[9] In determining whether a fee is really designed for police purposes, and not for revenue, the Supreme Court of the United States also has taken into consideration the extent to which the fee is expended in administration of the measure. Foote & Co. v. Stanley, 232 U. S. 494 (1914).

tional burden on interprovincial commerce and the free circulation of goods among the provinces. And in *Cerruti v. Municipalidad de San Nicolás*, 132 S. C. N. 205 (1920), the Court on similar grounds declared unconstitutional a tax imposed as an inspection fee on fruits exported from the province.

In *Compañía Azucarera Concepción v. Tucumán*, 173 S. C. N. 429 (1935), the defendant province, which produced three-fourths of the sugar consumed in the nation, enacted a statute for the control of the sugar industry within the province. The statute prohibited the sugar mills from grinding their own sugar cane beyond the limits imposed by provincial authorities; compelled them to grind the sugar cane belonging to independent sugar growers, whose quota was fixed by provincial authorities, and to pay to these producers the highest price obtained in the market; provided that the sugar mills could not offer for sale in the local market an amount of sugar beyond that authorized by the local authorities. The Court declared the statute invalid because, although the control of the sugar industry was local regulation, the limitation upon the amount of sugar that could be offered for sale was an obstruction of interprovincial commerce. The Court further held that the regulation was in conflict with the power of Congress to enact a code of commerce and with the tariff law enacted by Congress to protect the sugar industry.

TAXATION

The power of taxation reserved to the Argentine provinces is as extensive as the taxing power of the states of the United States. The provinces can exercise this power on the same persons, property, possessions, and franchises as those subject to federal taxation. In *Iglesias v. Buenos Aires*, 105 S. C. N. 273 (1906), the Court upheld a provincial tax on agricultural products, saying: "The imposition of taxes, the selection of the objects for taxation, and the procedure for imposing the same, are matters within the exclusive jurisdiction of the province, whose power in this particular respect has been reserved by the Constitution. This power of taxation extends to persons, property, possessions, franchises, professions, or any other rights which may be subject to taxation."

The provinces must confine their taxing laws to persons or

property within their jurisdiction.[10] In *Badenia v. Salta,* 179 S. C. N. 86 (1937), the plaintiff company was incorporated in and had most of its capital invested in the city of Buenos Aires, but it had a farm in the defendant province. The province imposed a tax on the company for doing business there, taking as a basis for taxation not the entire capital of the corporation but the capital invested in the province. The company contended that the tax was unconstitutional because it amounted to a tax on capital and business outside the province. But the Court, relying on decisions of the United States Supreme Court,[11] held the statute valid.

Although the Argentine Congress may legislate on the law of inheritance, as within its power to enact civil codes, this does not prohibit the provinces from levying inheritance taxes. The leading case on this problem is *Migoni v. Mendoza,* 100 S. C. N. 157 (1904). It was contended that since the question of inheritance was regulated in the Civil Code the provinces had no power to regulate hereditary transactions through the imposition of taxes. The Court upheld the statute, and, citing Story's *Commentaries,* stated: "According to the most favorable constitutional doctrine concerning the extension of the national powers, the provinces can, in the exercise of their legitimate legislative power, enact the same legislation as Congress, provided the subject matter of the legislation has not been expressly or impliedly vested in Congress alone."

The taxing power of the provinces is limited by the delegation to the national government of power to regulate interprovincial and foreign commerce. But the Argentine Constitution has several other provisions which not only limit the taxing power of the provinces in so far as its exercise may affect this commerce but also tend to clarify the extent of the power of Congress. These provisions are: that the provinces shall not lay any duty on tonnage (Art. 108); that throughout the territory of the nation there shall be no customs houses except the national ones, in which shall be enforced the tariff duties imposed by Congress (Art. 9); that all articles of domestic production or manufacture, as well as goods and merchandise of all kinds cleared at the customs houses, shall

[10] Banco de Córdoba v. Caja de Jubilaciones y Pensiones, 147 S. C. N. 239 (1926).

[11] Cudahy Packing Co. v. Hinkle, 278 U. S. 460 (1929); Looney v. Crane Co., 245 U. S. 178 (1917); Alpha Portland Cement Co. v. Massachusetts, 268 U. S. 203 (1925); Baltic Mining Co. v. Massachusetts, 231 U. S. 68 (1914).

be exempted from duties (Art. 10); that the articles of national and foreign production or manufacture, as well as livestock of all kinds, and the vehicles, vessels, or beasts in or on which they are transported through one province to another, shall be free from transit duties, and no other duty, whatever its denomination, shall be imposed upon them for passing through (Art. 11); and that Congress shall have power to establish import and export duties (Art. 67).

The Supreme Court has held that the provinces cannot levy the following forms of taxes: tonnage duties; taxes on exports and imports; discriminatory taxes on interprovincial commerce; and taxes on the transactions and instrumentalities of interprovincial and foreign commerce. Although the Argentine Constitution prohibits the provinces, as the Constitution of the United States prohibits the states,[12] from levying tonnage duties, the Argentine Court has held such taxes unconstitutional not on the basis of this specific prohibition but on the fact that the Constitution has delegated to Congress the power to regulate navigation and maritime commerce. Thus in *Casares v. Sivori*, 11 S. C. N. 257 (1872), the Court declared invalid a duty of twenty-five cents per ton imposed on ships entering the port of Buenos Aires.[13]

Although the Argentine Constitution does not in express terms prohibit the provinces from taxing exports and imports as the Constitution of the United States does,[14] such a prohibition has been impliedly recognized. In an early case, *Mendoza v. San Juan*, 3 S. C. N. 131 (1865), the Court declared unconstitutional a provincial tax on exports on the ground that only Congress has power to lay such taxes. And in *Las Palmas Produce Co. v. Buenos Aires*, 100 S. C. N. 364 (1904), the Court found such a limitation in Article 9 and in Article 67, section 12, of the Constitution. The defendant province had imposed an ad valorem tax on exports.

[12] "No State shall, without the Consent of the Congress, lay any Duty of Tonnage" (U. S. Constitution, Art. I, § 10).

[13] The Supreme Court of the United States declared invalid a New York statute imposing a fee of one and a half cents a ton, according to registered tonnage, upon vessels used in the port of New York. *Inman Steamship Co. v. Tinker*, 94 U. S. 238 (1877).

[14] "No State shall, without the Consent of Congress, lay any Imposts or Duties on Imports or Exports, except what may be absolutely necessary for executing its inspection Laws" (U. S. Constitution, Art. I, § 10).

The plaintiff, an exporter of animal products, was taxed as provided by the statute and attacked its constitutionality. The Court held that the tax constituted a burden on interprovincial and foreign commerce which only Congress could impose.[15]

The terms "exports" and "imports" as used in the Constitution of the United States mean goods in foreign commerce, and not those transferred from one state to another.[16] The Supreme Court of Argentina has taken a wider view. In *Freitas y Gurgio v. Corrientes,* 101 S. C. N. 8 (1904), the plaintiff attacked a tax imposed on goods about to be transported to another province. The defendant province contended that the terms "exports" and "imports" correspond only to acts of foreign commerce and not to interprovincial commerce, and that therefore the tax was not unconstitutional. But the Court stated that, although it is true that the terms "importation" and "exportation" generally refer to international commerce, it is not less true that interprovincial commerce is subject to the regulation of Congress and must be kept free from provincial taxation.

Invoking the decision rendered in the case of *Woodruff v. Parham,* to sustain its position that the provincial statute was unconstitutional, the Court stated that, although the Constitution of the United States does not expressly prohibit taxes on goods exported and imported from one state to another, such a prohibition is found in the commerce clause; and that the commerce clause of the Argentine Constitution is the equivalent of the commerce clause of the United States Constitution. The Court also stated that the distinction in the United States between taxes on interstate and on foreign commerce is based on the fact that the Constitution of the United States imposes an absolute prohibition on the states against taxing imports and exports. It was added that the same principle may be applied under the Argentine Constitution, since Articles 9 and 10, which have no equivalent in the Constitution of the United States, have impliedly placed domestic products and foreign products cleared in the exterior customs houses on the same footing.

[15] The Court cited two United States decisions, May and Co. v. New Orleans, 178 U. S. 496 (1900); Brown v. Houston, 114 U. S. 622 (1885).

[16] Woodruff v. Parham, 8 Wall. 123 (1869).

A tax which burdens the exportation of goods is as unconstitutional as a tax on the articles themselves. In *Mazzocone v. Mendoza,* 135 S. C. N. 272 (1921), the defendant province imposed a license tax on the exportation of certain wine, and prohibited exportation unless it was paid. The Court held the statute void, even though disguised as a license tax. But the fact that certain goods may be destined for exportation does not prohibit the provinces from levying a tax on them. In *Arias v. Entre Ríos,* 20 S. C. N. 304 (1878), the constitutionality of a tax was questioned, where the tax was imposed on animal hides eventually to be exported. The Court held the tax valid, since it was not imposed on the hides when they were to be exported and since it did not discriminate between hides for domestic use and those intended for exportation. It also stated that the mere fact that goods may be destined for exportation does not prevent the provinces from taxing them, unless the tax is imposed only when they are actually to be exported.

The Argentine and the United States constitutions do not absolutely prohibit the provinces and states respectively from taxing products or goods because of the mere fact that they have been imported from other states or provinces. In *Tirasso v. Buenos Aires,* 174 S. C. N. 192 (1935), the defendant province passed a statute which provided that merchants not registered in the province must pay a tax on products imported when these were to be introduced in the province, and that the goods must be declared to the provincial authorities for the purpose of taxation before they could be taken from the port or railroad station. The Court, after deciding that the statute was unconstitutional because it conflicted with the power of Congress to regulate interprovincial commerce, discussed the power of the provinces to tax goods imported from other provinces or foreign countries. The power of the Argentine Congress to regulate interprovincial and foreign commerce is equivalent to the power of the Congress of the United States under the commerce clause, under which the courts of that country have acknowledged that this power was conferred upon Congress to secure uniformity of commercial regulation. This power, held the Court, protects property which is transferred from foreign countries or other states against local taxation until the goods have been incorporated into the general property of the state; but the provinces can tax goods imported from other provinces or foreign countries the very moment they are mixed with the general mass of property within the province, since then it cannot be said that the tax is levied on their importation.[17]

For the purpose of determining when the goods imported have become mixed with the general property so that they may be subject to local taxation, the Argentine Court has established several tests. First, the goods are not yet intermingled when they are in transit from one province to another; when they have recently arrived within the province; and when they belong to institutions or agencies created by Congress.[18] Second, when the goods imported are sold at wholesale and have not been destined for retail transactions. Thus, in *Ovejero Hermanos v. Tiseyro y Pirola,* 30 S. C. N. 332 (1886), the Court declared invalid a tax imposed on sugar introduced into one province from another, where the tax was levied on the first sale at wholesale.

A third test is the familiar "original package" doctrine. This test, first enunciated by Chief Justice Marshall in *Brown v. Maryland,* 12 Wheat. 419 (1827), in which it was applied to protect goods imported from a foreign country into a state, was applied by the Argentine Supreme Court in *Benci v. Medina,* 26 S. C. N. 94 (1883), where a tax on wine in the original containers was held unconstitutional.[19] The Court stated that as long as the wine remained in the original container in which it was imported it could not be taxed without violating the commerce clause of the Constitution.[20]

17 For these propositions the Court cited a number of United States decisions: Guy v. Baltimore, 100 U. S. 434 (1880); Webber v. Virginia, 103 U. S. 334 (1881); Walling v. Michigan, 116 U. S. 446 (1886); Darnell and Son Co. v. Memphis, 208 U. S. 113 (1908); Robbins v. Shelby County, 120 U. S. 489 (1887).

18 Geddes Hermanos v. Buenos Aires, 95 S. C. N. 327 (1902).

19 This doctrine is applicable in Argentina to goods imported both from other provinces and from foreign countries, since under Article 10 domestic goods are equally protected with foreign goods against provincial taxation. Justo v. Córdoba, 178 S. C. N. 308 (1937).

20 The Court cited with approval the following passage from Brown v. Maryland, 12 Wheat. 419 (1827): "It is sufficient for the present to say, generally, that when the importer has so acted upon the thing imported that it has become incorporated and mixed up with the mass of property in the country, it has, perhaps, lost its distinctive character as an import, and has become subject to the taxing power of the State; but while remaining the property of the importer, in his warehouse, in the original

But the Argentine Court has maintained that the original package doctrine is not an inflexible and final rule, and that it is subject to different qualifications according to the case. In *Justo v. Córdoba,* 178 S. C. N. 308 (1937), the defendant province levied a license tax on the sale of table wine bottled in containers of a certain size; the payment of the tax had to be made by the buying of internal revenue stamps which were required to be placed on the containers forty-eight hours after the goods were taken from the railroad depots. The plaintiff alleged that the tax was void because it was levied on the goods before they became mixed with the general property of the province, while they remained in the original containers. But the Court held the statute valid, and, citing Chief Justice Taft's opinion in *Sonneborn Bros. v. Cureton,* 262 U. S. 506 (1923), stated: "The taxes levied by a state on goods imported from other states after these have arrived at their final destination within the state, are constitutional, if they do not discriminate against imported goods because of their origin."

A fourth test is whether the products imported have been offered for sale. In *Chiossone v. San Luis,* 163 S. C. N. 285 (1931), the defendant province imposed a license tax on stores and other places dedicated to the buying and selling by merchants and brokers of goods on commission. To this province the plaintiff sent sugar to be deposited for the purpose of sale. Orders for the sugar were received only in the main office of the plaintiff in the province of Tucumán. The local agent of the plaintiff, in the defendant province, sold the sugar only upon instruction from the main office. The plaintiff contended that the tax was invalid because it constituted a burden on interprovincial commerce. The Court held that wherever goods are offered for sale, whether in the original package or not, they are no longer in interprovincial commerce, and the fact that the goods were actually brought into the province and offered for sale there was paramount over the interprovincial nature of the selling transactions; the tax was valid. Citing United States cases [21] and Willoughby, *The Constitutional*

---

form or package in which it was imported, a tax upon it is too plainly a duty on imports to escape the prohibition in the Constitution."

[21] Brown v. Houston, 114 U. S. 622 (1885); Coe v. Errol, 116 U. S. 517 (1886); Susquehanna Coal Co. v. City of South Amboy, 228 U. S. 665 (1913).

Law of the United States, the Court developed the distinction, made by the courts of the United States, between drummers and peddlers. Drummers, who deal in merchandise located outside the state in which the transactions are made, are engaged in interstate commerce, and the state cannot tax them or their businesses. But peddlers, who although they may reside in another state, carry the goods with them into the taxing state, may be subjected to a license tax in order not to discriminate against local merchants with whom they are on equal competitive footing.

Even after the goods imported have become incorporated in the general property in the provinces, no provincial tax may be imposed which discriminates against them on the basis of their extraprovincial origin. Thus in *Antony v. Santa Fe,* 125 S. C. N. 333 (1917), the defendant province imposed a higher license tax on stores which sold beer imported from other provinces than on those which sold only beer of the taxing province. The Court declared the statute unconstitutional, saying: "In view of these authorities [22] and other decisions it must be taken for granted that no province can, according to the Constitution, impose upon the products of other provinces a higher burden than that imposed upon local products or the persons who sell them." [23]

The provinces cannot tax the instrumentalities and transactions of interprovincial and foreign commerce. In *South American Stores v. Buenos Aires,* 149 S. C. N. 137 (1927), the plaintiff's place of business was in the federal capital and he employed several trucks which delivered goods, purchased in the federal capital, to customers living in the province of Buenos Aires. The defendant province enacted a statute levying a license tax of 400 pesos on each truck used for delivering goods and required the plaintiff to pay the tax. The plaintiff contended that his business was interstate commerce and that the tax was a burden on this commerce. The Court upheld the plaintiff's contentions, stating:

> The interpretation of the Constitution, declares the Supreme Court of the United States, leads to the conclusion that no state has the power

[22] Darnell and Son Co. v. Memphis, 208 U. S. 113 (1908); Cooley, *Treatise on the Law of Taxation,* 3rd ed., p. 150.

[23] In Romero v. Tucumán, 159 S. C. N. 23 (1930), the Court held that if the goods imported have suffered some transformation they become part of the general property in the province, and are therefore subject to provincial taxation.

to tax interstate or foreign commerce transactions, whether the tax is imposed on the transportation or on the business or occupations engaged in such commerce. The reason for this prohibition is that such a tax would be a burden on interstate or foreign commerce, which under the Constitution can be regulated only by Congress and not by the states.[24]

But the Argentine provinces, like the states of the United States, can, within their jurisdiction, tax the property of those corporations engaged in interprovincial or foreign commerce. In *United River Plate Telephone Co. v. Buenos Aires,* 154 S. C. N. 104 (1929), the plaintiff, a corporation engaged in interprovincial commerce, attacked the constitutionality of a provincial tax upon its property. The Court upheld the statute, stating that although the provinces cannot tax the transportation of goods in interprovincial commerce nor the incomes derived from such transportation, yet the property of the corporation, either domestic or foreign, located within the province can be subjected to taxation even if the corporation is engaged in interprovincial or foreign commerce.

In *La Immobiliaria S. A. Cía. de Seguros v. Provincia de Corrientes,* 179 S. C. N. 42 (1937), the defendant province imposed a tax on marine insurance contracts, and the Court held it invalid on the ground that it constituted a burden on interprovincial commerce.[25] The Court stated that insurance is a contract auxiliary of maritime commerce, and a necessary and integral part of interprovincial commerce, which under the Constitution is subject to the control of the national government.

[24] Citing Leloup v. Port of Mobile, 127 U. S. 640 (1888).
[25] Citing Postal Telegraph Co. v. Adams, 155 U. S. 688 (1895).

Part Three: PROTECTION OF THE INDIVIDUAL

VII: CRIMINAL PROCEDURE

AN OUTSTANDING feature of the constitutional development of Argentina is that each of its constitutions has contained a bill of rights for the protection of the individual against governmental action. Some of the more general aspects of these protections may be noted before we turn to those having to do specifically with persons accused of crime. The Constitution of 1853 established a number of constitutional rights for the protection of citizens and other persons who form part of the body politic.

There are three striking differences between the bill of rights of Argentina and that of the United States: First, the Argentine Constitution contains the bill of rights in the first chapter; the Constitution of the United States does not include the bill of rights in the original document but carries it in the form of amendments. Second, while in the United States Constitution no rights are expressly granted to aliens,[1] in the Argentine Constitution such rights are expressly vested in Article 20 as follows: "Foreigners enjoy in the territory of the nation all the civil rights of the citizens, they can engage in commerce and industry and practice their professions, own real property, purchase and sell it, navigate the rivers and the coast of the nation, freely practice their religion, make wills and marry in accordance with the laws, and cannot be compelled to become citizens nor pay discriminatory taxes."

Third, the bill of rights in the United States constitutes a limi-

[1] In the United States aliens are protected through judicial interpretations, particularly of the due process clauses as applicable to persons. Wong Wing v. United States, 163 U. S. 228 (1896); Yu Cong Eng v. Trinidad, 271 U. S. 500 (1926).

tation on the powers of the national government alone [2] whereas in Argentina it limits the powers of both the nation and the provinces. *Hileret y Rodriguez v. Tucumán*, 98 S. C. N. 20 (1903), and *Pereyra Iraola v. Buenos Aires*, 138 S. C. N. 161 (1923). In the former the plaintiff attacked a tax statute of the defendant province on the ground that it violated property rights guaranteed by the Constitution. The province, citing the United States doctrine, contended that this provision limited only the powers of the national government and not the powers of the provincial governments. The Argentine Court denied the applicability of that doctrine and stated: "It is an error to maintain that the constitutional rights and guarantees incorporated in the first part of the Constitution should be interpreted in the light of alien theories and precedents which are not in harmony with the immediate sources of our fundamental law, because these rights limit not only the powers of the national government but also those of the provincial governments as well." In the second case a similar result was reached, the Court rejecting the application of the principle of the Slaughter House Cases, 16 Wall. 36 (1873), in which the Supreme Court of the United States declared that there are certain rights inherent in state citizenship and other rights inherent in national citizenship protected respectively by state and federal constitutions. "In the Argentine Republic this doctrine [of the Slaughter House Cases] cannot be applied because all civil liberties have been protected by the national Constitution and in this respect, as in many others, our Constitution is superior to the American. Since the Argentine Constitution was drafted in 1853 it has protected all the civil rights, and among them the right of property against encroachment on the part of the national as well as of the provincial government." [3]

CONSTITUTIONAL PROTECTIONS

The Argentine Constitution, like that of the United States, either expressly or impliedly throws certain protections around

[2] Some of these rights are considered so fundamental in their nature that they are held to be included in the concept of due process of law and thus made applicable to the states by virtue of the Fourteenth Amendment. Powell v. Alabama, 287 U. S. 45 (1932).

[3] The Court cited J. W. Burgess, *Political Science and Comparative Constitutional Law*, criticizing the decision of the Slaughter House Cases.

persons accused of crime, e. g., protection against illegal arrest or detention (habeas corpus), right of bail, protection against unreasonable search and seizure, protection against ex post facto laws, protection of trial by jury in the district where the crime was committed, protection against self-incrimination, right of defense (due process of law), protection against cruel and unusual punishment, protection against confiscation of property as a punishment for crime, protection against legislative definition of treason. The following protections, not found in the Constitution of the United States, are expressly guaranteed by the Argentine Constitution to persons accused of crimes: trial by regular judges, prohibition of capital punishment in political crimes, prohibition of special privileges in criminal trials, and humane treatment in prisons and jails.[4]

Habeas Corpus

The supreme guarantee of personal liberty, the writ of habeas corpus, although not expressly guaranteed, has been incorporated in the Argentine Constitution by judicial construction.[5] Since the Constitution provides that no one can be arrested except by a written order from a competent authority, the Supreme Court has held that a person who is arrested in violation of this provision has the right to be freed through a writ of habeas corpus. In sustaining this view the Court has stated:

> According to the Constitution and to the laws of the nation no one can be arrested except by a written order from a competent authority, and no one can be arrested for the doing of acts which are not punishable by a law enacted before the commission of the act. It is also provided in the Constitution and statutes of this country that any person who is deprived of his liberty for any reason whatsoever can petition a court by himself or through his friends to investigate the causes of his detention, and in case he is illegally deprived of his liberty the Court has the duty to free him immediately by a writ of habeas corpus.[6]

[4] On the other hand the following protections with regard to criminal prosecutions are found in the United States Constitution but not in the Argentine: A speedy and public trial, compulsory process for obtaining witnesses, protection against excessive fines, indictment by grand jury, and protection against double jeopardy.

[5] The United States Constitution provides: "The privilege of the writ of habeas corpus shall not be suspended, unless when in cases of rebellion or invasion the public safety may require it." Art. 1, § 9.

[6] Ex Parte Tripulantes de la *Pilcomayo,* 43 S. C. N. 321 (1891).

The first habeas corpus legislation enacted in Argentina was passed in 1863, vesting the federal judiciary with jurisdiction in matters relating to the federal administration of justice. This law, which is based largely on the United States Judiciary Act of 1789, provides for habeas corpus in the following words:

> When any person is detained or imprisoned by a national or provincial authority, or under the color of an order issued by a national authority, or when a provincial authority imprisons any member of Congress or any person acting in behalf of the national government, the Supreme Court or the sectional judges may, at the request of the prisoner, or his friends or relatives, investigate the causes of his imprisonment, and in case his imprisonment has not been ordered by a competent authority the petitioner shall be freed immediately.

The writ of habeas corpus has also been incorporated, but with a wider scope, in the Code of Criminal Procedure of the federal capital and the national territories.[7] The most important provisions of this code are the following: The writ of habeas corpus, or *auto de amparo,* lies, first, against an order of a public official which tends to restrict the liberty of a person, and second, against a provincial authority who has imprisoned a member of Congress or any person acting in behalf of the national government. The writ does not lie against the detention, arrest, or imprisonment of a person by a superior judicial official when the order of imprisonment or detention has been issued by the judges of the correctional court of the federal capital, nor does it lie when the order of detention or imprisonment has been issued by either of the houses of Congress.

The Supreme Court has interpreted the nature, extent, procedure, and limitations of the writ in a long series of cases, only a few of which will be discussed in this chapter. Although the Constitution seems to imply that the writ of habeas corpus protects only the liberty of persons illegally arrested for alleged crimes, the Court has nevertheless indicated that it extends also to persons deprived of their liberty for other reasons than violating the criminal laws.[8]

In deciding whether the writ of habeas corpus will be granted,

[7] *Códigos de la República argentina,* Buenos Aires (1938), p. 1469.

[8] Ex Parte Duba de Moravich, 139 S. C. N. 154 (1923).

the Supreme Court has established certain general principles. Thus, although the Court will not determine whether or not a crime has been committed,[9] it will determine if there is any justification for the arrest of the petitioner.[10] In order to determine whether the authority who has ordered the arrest of the petitioner is a competent one, the Argentine courts, like the American courts, will examine whether he had jurisdiction over the person and subject matter of the controversy.[11]

Although it is a general rule that by habeas corpus proceedings the courts will not review the President's discretion in declaring a state of siege, such a declaration being a political act,[12] yet, if he has violated any provision of the Constitution, the Court will review his act even during the state of siege. Thus in *Ex Parte Alem,* 54 S. C. N. 453 (1893), where the President had arrested a national senator during a state of siege, the Supreme Court issued a writ of habeas corpus on the ground that the Constitution prohibited the arrest of a national legislator during his term of office without the permission of the Chamber to which he belongs. And in *Ex Parte Alvear,* 167 S. C. N. 267 (1933), where the President had arrested the petitioner during a state of siege and the petitioner asked the President's permission to leave the country, as provided in the Constitution, and the President refused the permission, the Court granted the writ.

Nor will the courts review by habeas corpus proceedings the President's act of deporting undesirable aliens[13] unless he has acted without authority, in which event the writ will issue. In *Ex Parte Macía y Gassol,* 151 S. C. N. 211 (1928), the petitioners, Spanish immigrants, entered the country without presenting certificates of good conduct issued by the police authorities of Spain, and subsequently the executive ordered them deported on the ground that they had entered the country illegally. A federal court granted habeas corpus and the Supreme Court affirmed, holding that the President had no authority to deport the petitioners, because the regulation requiring certificates of good conduct was

[9] Ex Parte Mancini, 65 S. C. N. 369 (1896).
[10] Ex Parte Rodríguez, 10 S. C. N. 55 (1871).
[11] Ex Parte Corbatta, 181 S. C. N. 249 (1938).
[12] Ex Parte Pueyrredón, 170 S. C. N. 246 (1934).
[13] Ex Parte Deportados en el Transporte Chaco, 164 S. C. N. 344 (1932).

not in force when the petitioners entered Argentina but was issued by the President thereafter.

In *Ex Parte Zlatnik*, 182 S. C. N. 45 (1938), the petitioner, an immigrant, was not permitted to enter the country on the ground that she was suffering from trachoma, a disease which under the law prevented her entrance into Argentina. On a petition denying that she was suffering from such disease a writ of habeas corpus was issued. On appeal the Supreme Court upheld the decision.[14]

Concerning the summary character of the writ of habeas corpus and the matters which may be considered by the courts, the Court has said:

> As the habeas corpus proceeding is summary in character because its main object is to obtain the immediate release of a person who is alleged to be illegally deprived of his liberty, in a habeas corpus trial all the facts and circumstances which may throw light on the reasons why the petitioner was arrested or imprisoned must be considered. Also because of the summary character of the proceeding, all procedural steps which are of a dilatory nature and which are embodied in ordinary common law cases must be set aside and only procedural rules which give discretion to the judge and which are compatible with the privileged nature of the writ should be applied in the courts of the trial.[15]

The Supreme Court has refused to grant a writ of habeas corpus in the following types of cases: (1) when the petitioner has been arrested by military authorities for an act committed in violation of the military laws;[16] (2) when the arrest has been ordered by a competent judge;[17] (3) when the person arrested was a sailor who refused to comply with a valid contract and was taken to the ship to work under the terms of such contract;[18] (4) when the petitioner was a bankrupt who had been arrested by order of the Commerce Court;[19] (5) when the petitioner has been called to military service under the general compulsory military laws;[20]

[14] In Ex Parte Miguel, 117 S. C. N. 165 (1913), the Supreme Court through a writ of habeas corpus prevented the deportation of an alien on similar grounds.

[15] In re Montaña, 9 S. C. N. 388 (1870).

[16] Ex Parte Gard, 14 S. C. N. 406 (1890).

[17] Ex Parte Mancini, 65 S. C. N. 369 (1896).

[18] Ex Parte Jolly, 70 S. C. N. 213 (1897).

[19] Ex Parte Riera, 21 S. C. N. 312 (1897).

[20] Ex Parte González, 82 S. C. N. 241 (1899).

(6) when the petitioners were Indians transported by a contractor to work for him and they were detained by a government official in order to give them an opportunity to determine whether they willingly entered into the contract with the contractor; [21] (7) when the petitioner was a member of the crew of a foreign ship arrested for a crime committed on the high seas; [22] (8) when the petitioner is constantly followed by the police in order to determine his domicile and the possible change of the same, for the purpose of investigating a crime.[23]

There is a fundamental difference between the use made of the writ of habeas corpus in Argentina and in the United States. In Argentina it is used simply to protect individual liberty when a person is arrested or when he might be subject to a deprivation of his liberty. In the United States, on the other hand, it may be used also for the purpose of obtaining bail when the authorities refuse to fix bail, or fix an amount which is excessive. In Argentina there are special procedural devices to remedy the evils of the administration of justice which in the United States are remedied by the writ of habeas corpus.[24]

The Code of Criminal Procedure has extended the scope of habeas corpus to cases where the liberty of a person might be subject to illegal restriction although no actual restraint has been attempted. In other words, it is not necessary under the Code that there be a physical restraint, arrest, or imprisonment in order that the writ may lie.[25] Because the Code has a wider scope than the earlier law and uses the words *auto de amparo,* many efforts have been made to induce the Argentine Supreme Court to give to the provisions of Article 18 of the Constitution the effect of the *auto de amparo,* a procedural device which has been adopted by many South American countries and which appears to involve a combination of the English and American writs of habeas corpus and injunction.[26]

[21] Ex Parte Podestá, 81 S. C. N. 246 (1899).
[22] Ex Parte Franzese, 62 S. C. N. 601 (1895).
[23] Ex Parte Pérez, 79 S. C. N. 135 (1899).
[24] M. A. Montes de Oca, *Lecciones de derecho constitucional,* I, 441, 442.
[25] Ex Parte Berreta, XLIV J. A. 9 (1933).
[26] For an interesting discussion of *auto de amparo* and the difference between it and the writ of habeas corpus, see R. Reyes, *La defensa constitucional,* Madrid,

Ex Parte Bertotto, 168 S. C. N. 15 (1933), illustrates the effort to secure an interpretation of the habeas corpus provisions of the Code of Criminal Procedure of the federal capital in the light of the *auto de amparo* so as to protect other constitutional rights than those of personal liberty. The petitioner sought through habeas corpus to compel the postmaster of the city of Rosario to accept and send through the mail a newspaper which the petitioner had published and which the postmaster had refused to accept in the mails on the ground that it contained articles inciting to the commission of crime. The lower federal court dismissed the petition and on appeal to the Supreme Court the judgment was affirmed: the writ of habeas corpus is designed to protect persons from illegal arrest, detention, or imprisonment, but not in other constitutional rights.

> Neither in the letter nor in the spirit, nor in the constitutional tradition of the writ of habeas corpus, do we have any basis to extend this right for the protection of the right of property, commerce, industry, teaching, or circulation of newspapers through the mail, against the violations or abuses by particular officers of the exercise of these rights. The law and jurisprudence of this country contain judicial and administrative remedies against the abuse or violation of the right which in this petition is alleged to have been violated.[27]

Bail

The Argentine Constitution, unlike the Constitution of the United States,[28] does not expressly provide for the right of bail either before or after conviction of a criminal offense. But by a process of interpretation of Articles 18 and 33 of the Constitution the Supreme Court has created such a right for certain types of offenders. In *Ex Parte Llanos,* 102 S. C. N. 219 (1905), a provision

1934; I. L. Vallarta, *El juicio de amparo y el writ of habeas corpus,* Mexico, 1881; D. E. Rabasa, *El juicio constitucional,* Mexico, 1930; J. M. Duret, *Derecho constitucional mejicano,* Mexico, 1931; Carlos Sánchez Viamonte, *El habeas corpus,* Buenos Aires, 1927.

27 In Ex Parte Malvar, 169 S. C. N. 103 (1933) and Compañía Sud-Americana de Servicios Públicos v. Comisión de Fomento de Gálvez, 174 S. C. N. 178 (1935), the Supreme Court refused to extend the protection of the writ of habeas corpus to other rights than exemption from illegal arrest, detention, or imprisonment.

28 The Eighth Amendment of the United States Constitution provides that "excessive bail shall not be required, nor excessive fines imposed, nor cruel and unusual punishment inflicted."

of the Constitution of the province of Santiago del Estero which denied the right of bail to persons accused of crimes not punishable with corporal punishment was held to conflict with these articles, the Court stating:

Although the Constitution does not expressly grant the right of bail, such a right has been derived by this Court from the final clause of Article 18 of the national Constitution according to which the jails of the nation must be kept clean and healthy, and for the security and not for the punishment of the prisoners confined therein. . . . This provision, according to the decisions of this Court, guarantees the right of bail to persons who have not committed crimes punishable with corporal punishment because if their provisional freedom under bail is denied they would be retained in jail although their detention may not be justified as a necessary measure of safety. Therefore, according to this principle the right of bail is a constitutional guarantee and not a privilege granted by the law of criminal procedure. The preventive or temporary imprisonment of the accused is simply to assure that he will not escape from punishment if convicted. But such a security can be achieved in some cases through the requirements of bail, a method which is compatible with the principles of personal liberty and with the presumption of the innocence of the accused, inasmuch as he has not yet been convicted. The right of bail is also based on our Constitution because it emanates from the republican form of government and from the liberal spirit of our Constitution.

Search and Seizure

The Argentine Constitution protects persons against unreasonable searches and seizures and against the use in criminal trials of evidence obtained in violation of these constitutional rights. The Constitution provides that the home is inviolable, as well as letters and private papers, and that a law is to determine in what cases and under what circumstances their search and occupation will be permitted.[29]

[29] The codes of criminal procedure applicable to the federal capital, the national territories, and the federal courts, as well as the codes of criminal procedure of the provinces, contain provisions for making searches and seizures. The code of criminal procedure applicable to the federal courts provides that the judges of instruction and state attorneys can make investigations in the residence or domicile of persons accused of crimes or in other places where there is reasonable proof that the offender is found or that in these places useful objects may be found which may lead to the proof of the commission of a criminal offense. The statute has several provisions to protect persons from unreasonable or unlawful searches and seizures. It provides, first, that searches in domiciles can be made only between sunrise and sunset; second,

A leading case on the extent and nature of this constitutional and statutory protection is *Ministerio Fiscal v. Charles Brothers*, 46 S. C. N. 36 (1891). Defendants were charged with the crimes of contraband and forgery, and in the preliminary hearing they objected to the introduction in evidence of objects and papers which they claimed the authorities had unlawfully obtained from their domicile. The judge denied the motion and the defendants appealed. The Supreme Court reversed, holding that the objects were unlawfully obtained and could not be introduced as evidence:

> Whether the documents obtained were authentic or false they cannot serve as basis for the criminal prosecution nor be introduced as evidence against the defendant, because the search of these documents was unlawful and illegal and therefore in violation of the constitutional and statutory provisions prohibiting unlawful searches and seizures.

Again in *Founes v. Administración de Aduanas*, 135 S. C. N. 57 (1921), the Court enforced the constitutional protection. The plaintiff received from France a certified package containing jewelry. The postal and customs authorities opened the package without any legal authorization and confiscated the jewels as contraband. The lower court held against the plaintiff and he appealed to the Supreme Court, alleging that the confiscation of the jewels was illegal because in violation of Article 18 of the Constitution. In the Supreme Court the attorney general presented a brief sustaining the decision of the lower court and, citing *Boyd v. United States*, 116 U. S. 616 (1886), stated:

> In the famous case of *Boyd v. United States* the Supreme Court of the United States, in interpreting provisions analogous to those found in our Constitution relating to searches and seizures, held that the search and seizure of stolen or confiscated goods or goods hidden for the purpose of evading the payment of duties is different from the search and seizure of private books and papers of a person with the object of obtaining evidence that may serve as a basis for the prosecution of that person. In the first case, the government has a right to the possession of the property; in the second case, the government does not have such

that persons in charge of the domicile must be notified of the search, and if this person is not found in the home any other person who is of age found in the domicile must be notified of the search; and third, that the person making the search must make an affidavit specifying the persons and objects found. (*Códigos de la República argentina*, pp. 1523–25.)

a right. The seizure of stolen goods is authorized by the common law and the seizure of merchandise confiscated for violation of the customs laws or hidden in order to evade the payment of such duties has been authorized by the English laws during at least two centuries, and such seizures have also been authorized by our customs laws since the beginning of the nation.

The Supreme Court, following a more liberal rule than that established in the Boyd case, said that the confiscation of the jewels was void because in violation of Article 18 of the Constitution:

When this Court has interpreted the constitutional article under discussion it has held that certified correspondence is not within the jurisdiction of the customs officials and is inviolable, and it can be opened only by judicial authorization for the purpose of discovering the commission of a crime.

But in *Santa Fe v. Seganevich,* 177 S. C. N. 390 (1937), and *Gobierno Nacional v. Leiba,* 98 S. C. N. 156 (1903), the Court limited the application of the protection. The defendant in the first case was arrested on suspicion that he was violating the gambling laws and from his person was seized, in the presence of the judge of instruction, a number of lottery tickets, possession of which was held to be a crime.[30] He was convicted, and he appealed, alleging that his conviction was illegal because the evidence was illegally obtained. Sustaining the conviction, the Court stated that "the inviolability of certified correspondence and private papers from unreasonable searches and seizures has not been established in an absolute form. Like all individual rights, this right is subject to the regulation of the laws and can be restricted or limited as the circumstances require for the sake of general welfare or public order." In the second case the attack was on a law of Congress applicable to the federal district which authorized the chief of police to search houses in which lottery tickets not authorized by law were sold, provided there was reasonable belief that the gambling laws were being violated. The Court upheld the statute on the ground that the arrest was reasonable under the circumstances.

The power of the government to investigate the books of corporations, and a possible conflict in the exercise of this power

[30] The law of the province authorized an arrest on reasonable suspicion that a person was violating the gambling laws of the province.

with Article 18 of the Constitution, is fully discussed by the Supreme Court in *Compañía Swift de La Plata v. Gobierno Nacional,* 171 S. C. N. 348 (1934). Congress had enacted a statute which provided that any person engaged in the slaughter-house business or in the selling and buying of cattle, sheep, pork, etc., should register with the Ministry of Agriculture. The statute also provided that all persons subject to it should keep accounts as provided by regulations and give reports to the Minister of Agriculture upon request, and that their books should be subject to inspection. The plaintiff company was fined for not supplying the information. It attacked the constitutionality of the statute on the ground that it violated Article 18 of the Constitution, in as much as the company was a private one whose documents could not be examined at the will of the government unless under a charge that the company was committing a criminal offense. The Supreme Court, citing several decisions of the United States Supreme Court,[31] said that the cattle industry had become affected with a public interest to such an extent that it is subject to governmental control of the kind provided in the statute under consideration and that such a statute does not violate Article 18 of the Constitution.[32]

Ex Post Facto Laws

Another constitutional protection in criminal prosecutions is that no person shall be punished for the violation of a law enacted after the commission of the offense (Art. 18). The Argentine Court has interpreted this clause in the light of the judicial precedents interpreting the ex post facto provision of the Constitution of the United States. Thus, in *Ex Parte Ordoqui,* 151 S. C. N. 103 (1928), in which the petitioner attacked a provincial statute giving retroactive effect to a tax law, the Court held that such a law was not ex post facto:

> Neither the national nor the American Constitution prohibits the provinces from enacting retroactive laws but only prohibits them from

[31] Stafford v. Wallace, 258 U. S. 495 (1922); Munn v. Illinois, 94 U. S. 113 (1877); Wolff Packing Co. v. Court of Industrial Relations, 262 U. S. 522 (1923); New State Ice Co. v. Liebmann, 285 U. S. 262 (1932).

[32] In Gobierno Nacional v. García, 184 S. C. N. 417 (1939), a similar principle was applied in a case not dealing with a corporation but with a private individual.

enacting ex post facto legislation. The Argentine courts, as well as the American, have repeatedly held that the phrase "ex post facto laws" refers exclusively to the prohibition of enacting retroactive laws of a penal nature and not of a civil or administrative nature.[33]

But in *Administración de Impuestos Internos v. Nebreda,* 169 S. C. N. 309 (1933), in which the defendant was fined under a decree of April 8, 1932, for a fraudulent act committed before the issuing of the decree, the Court declared the decree unconstitutional:

It is not essential for a law to be ex post facto that the act which it punishes shall be of a criminal nature. If the law subjects a person to a fine for an act which when committed involved no criminal responsibility, such an act would be ex post facto in spite of the fact that it does not declare that the acts committed before its passing were criminal in nature.[34]

The Court has declared that the following types of laws are not ex post facto: (1) Laws dealing with the jurisdiction, competence, and procedure of the courts although enacted after the commission of the crime. About them the Court has said: "The object of these laws is to make the application of the penal law more equitable and exact. There is no vested right in behalf of persons accused of crime that they shall be tried before a certain judge and under certain procedural formalities, provided they are not in violation of Article 18 of the national Constitution." [35] (2) A law which vests jurisdiction in a court which before the defendant committed the crime had no power to try him.[36] (3) Laws which although passed after the commission of the crime impose a lesser penalty than that in the statute when the crime was committed.[37] (4) Laws which change the procedure to prove the crime committed even if enacted after the commission of the crime.[38] (5) A law repealing another which granted the defendant the right to challenge the judge.[39]

[33] The Court cited two United States decisions, League v. Texas, 184 U. S. 156 (1902), and Brown v. Keene, 8 Peters 112 (1834).

[34] The Court cited Fletcher v. Peck, 6 Cranch 87 (1810), and Cummings v. Missouri, 4 Wall. 277 (1867), and Cooley, *Treatise on Constitutional Limitations.*

[35] Still v. Goldsoll, 114 S. C. N. 89 (1910).

[36] Ex Parte Chumbita, 17 S. C. N. 22 (1875).

[37] Gobierno Nacional v. Córdoba, 101 S. C. N. 298 (1905).

[38] Spotorno v. Departamento Nacional del Trabajo, 181 S. C. N. 288 (1938).

[39] United River Plate Telephone Co. v. La Capital, 127 S. C. N. 18 (1917).

Trial by Natural Judges

An interesting constitutional right guaranteed in criminal trials closely related to the ex post facto provision, but one which goes far beyond the United States concepts of ex post facto legislation, is that no person can be criminally tried or punished by special committees nor taken away from the judges designated by law before the crime was committed (Art. 18). This guarantee was incorporated in the Constitution of 1853 in order to prevent and correct abuses existing before that date where the executive power had created special judges to try offenders who for different reasons they wanted to get rid of. By "natural judges" is meant those who have been appointed under the laws of the nation with competent jurisdiction, while "special commissions" are those which the legislative or the executive department appoint to try special cases and persons without following the laws and regulations established by the Constitution and the laws relating to the administration of justice.[40]

What the Constitution has attempted by means of this prohibition is to make it impossible that persons accused of crime shall be prejudiced by being taken away from the jurisdiction of judges who have been legally appointed before the commission of the crime, and be subjected to the jurisdiction of judges who may be selected or appointed for the specific purpose of condemning the defendant.[41] But a mere change in the subject matter of the jurisdiction of the Court with the result that judges other than those already appointed when the crime was committed might try the case does not come under this prohibition.[42]

Trial by Jury and Place of Trial

The right of trial by jury in criminal prosecutions is guaranteed in the Argentine Constitution although not in the unequivocal terms of the Constitution of the United States.[43] The Argentine Constitution provides that all ordinary criminal trials except

[40] J. González Calderón, *Derecho constitucional argentino,* II, 158.

[41] Vega v. Martínez, 123 S. C. N. 82 (1916); Suárez v. Alvarez, 154 S. C. N. 101 (1929).

[42] Passo v. Freyre, 27 S. C. N. 170 (1884).

[43] The Sixth Amendment of the United States Constitution provides: "In all criminal prosecutions, the accused shall enjoy the right to a speedy and public trial, by an impartial jury of the state and district wherein the crime shall have been committed, which district shall have been previously ascertained by law. . . ."

cases of impeachment shall be by jury as soon as this institution is established in the Republic (Art. 102). These trials shall be held in the province where the crimes shall have been committed, but when committed against international law and outside the jurisdiction of the nation, Congress, by special law, shall determine where the trial shall be held.[44]

Congress has never enacted a law establishing trial by jury, and the question whether it was under a duty to do so was settled in *Loveira v. Mulhall,* 115 S. C. N. 92 (1911). The defendant, being accused in the federal capital of the crime of slander, objected to the jurisdiction of the court on the ground that he could not be tried except by jury. The Court, however, overruled his contention and held that Congress was not compelled to proceed immediately to establish the institution of trial by jury.[45]

The clause of the Constitution which states that the accused must be tried in the province where the crime was committed was enforced by the Court in *Fiscal v. Lastra,* 151 S. C. N. 67 (1928). In this case the defendant committed the crime of attempt to duel in the city of Mercedes, in the province of Buenos Aires, but he was prosecuted in the courts of the federal capital, a different jurisdiction. The Court held that the trial should be held in the city of Mercedes: "It is a principle of procedural law incorporated in Article 102 of the national Constitution that the place where the crime is committed determines the jurisdiction of the court which shall have the power to try the offender and that the jurisdiction of the court cannot be waived by the offender under the provisions of Article 17 of the Code of Criminal Procedure."

Self-Incrimination

The constitutional guarantee that a person shall not be compelled to be a witness against himself is established not only in the Argentine Constitution (Art. 18) but also in the Codes of Criminal

[44] In Article 24 and Article 67, § 11, it is provided that Congress shall establish the institution of trial by jury. The right of trial by jury in press offenses is granted in the following provincial constitutions: Buenos Aires, Art. 11; Córdoba, Art. 38; Catamarca, Art. 9; Entre Ríos, Art. 12. The province of Jujuy is the only province in which the right of trial by jury is granted in all criminal trials (Art. 35).

[45] The Supreme Court of the United States has held that under the Sixth Amendment the right of trial by jury in the federal courts accrues to an accused the moment he is put on trial. Callahan v. Wilson, 127 U. S. 540 (1880); Capital Traction Co. v. Hof, 174 U. S. 1 (1899).

Procedure.[46] The nature and extent of this guarantee are discussed in *Ex Parte Méndez,* 130 S. C. N. 166 (1919), and *Carete v. Martínez Montero,* 1 S. C. N. 350 (1864). In the Méndez case, the defendant was charged with a criminal offense and was requested by the prosecuting attorney to testify under oath. Under the Code of Criminal Procedure the defendant was bound to testify or else be punished for contempt of court. The defendant objected that he could not be compelled to testify. The Supreme Court held that for the defendant to be compelled to testify against himself by giving testimony under oath and under the threat of punishment for contempt would violate Article 18 of the Constitution. In the Carete case, the Court said that the mere calling of a person to testify does not import a violation of the right of exemption from self-incrimination; in order that there be a violation of this right the person must be compelled to testify and give incriminating testimony against himself.

Due Process of Law

Though the Argentine Constitution contains no due process clause as such, the fundamental concepts of due process of law in their procedural aspects, as enunciated in the United States Constitution[47] and in the decisions of the United States Supreme Court, have been substantially adopted in the Argentine Constitution and by the decisions of the Supreme Court. These concepts are embodied in two clauses of Article 18 which provide that no inhabitant of the nation shall be punished without a previous trial and that the right of defense shall be inviolable. In various cases the Supreme Court has declared the essential requisites of a previous trial and the inviolability of the right of defense.

A previous trial within the meaning of Article 18 is a judicial trial, that is, no person can be criminally punished in Argentina unless tried by a court of justice. Thus, in *Jensen v. Mendoza,* 136 S. C. N. 200 (1922), in which the plaintiff attacked a decree of

[46] *Códigos de la República argentina,* p. 1480.

[47] The Fifth Amendment of the United States Constitution provides: "No person shall be . . . deprived of life, liberty, or property without due process of law. . . ." And the Fourteenth Amendment declares: "No state shall deprive any person of life, liberty, or property without due process of law; nor deny to any person within its jurisdiction the equal protection of the laws."

the governor of the province imposing a fine upon him for an alleged violation of the laws regulating the manufacture of wine, the Court held that the decree was void on the ground that the plaintiff had been punished without a previous trial. "It cannot be admitted that the legislature of Mendoza has delegated to the executive the power to impose penal sanctions as a means of enforcing the laws enacted by it." [48] And in *Ex Parte Duba de Moravich*, 139 S. C. N. 154 (1923), in which the petitioner claimed that she had been sent to an insane asylum without any judicial trial, on the opinion of two physicians who certified that she was suffering from moral insanity, the Court ordered her release on habeas corpus.

The Court has further held that the substantial forms of a previous trial which must be strictly followed are: accusation, defense, evidence presented for and against the accused, and a judgment rendered by natural judges and not by special commissions.[49]

Regarding the accusation, the Court has held that it must not be general and vague but specific and limited to the acts charged.[50] The accusation must also be based on a specific law punishing the act alleged to have been committed by the defendant. Punishment by analogy is not permitted.[51] The Court has held that in the trial the criminal law must be construed in favor of the defendant and that all doubts must be resolved in his favor,[52] that he is presumed to be innocent until he is proved guilty, and that in order that he may be convicted it is necessary that there be clear proof that he committed the crime.[53]

In defining what constitutes the inviolability of the right of defense the Court has stated: "The inviolability of the right of de-

[48] In Ex Parte Deportados en el Transporte Chaco, 164 S. C. N. 344 (1932), in which the constitutionality of a law authorizing the president to deport undesirable aliens was attacked on the ground that the proceeding established amounted to a punishment without a previous trial, the Court, citing Turner v. Williams, 194 U. S. 279 (1904), and Wong Wing v. United States, 163 U. S. 228 (1896), held the statute constitutional on the theory that the act of deporting an alien is not judicial but administrative.

[49] Ex Parte Leivar, 119 S. C. N. 284 (1914).

[50] Ex Parte Méndez, 15 S. C. N. 40 (1864).

[51] Ex Parte Porta, 116 S. C. N. 23 (1912).

[52] Ministerio Fiscal v. Weiss, 137 S. C. N. 425 (1923).

[53] Ministerio Fiscal v. Brocate, 10 S. C. N. 338 (1871).

fense means that when a person is tried for his life, liberty, or property he must be heard before convicted, and must be tried under certain conditions which permit him to exercise the rights guaranteed to him by the Constitution and by the laws of criminal procedure relating to indictment, proof, and judgment." [54]

By a process of exclusion and inclusion the Court has determined in several cases what does and what does not constitute a violation of the right of defense. First, the Court has held that the defendant must be notified of the charges against him in order that he may have the opportunity to defend himself in the trial, but if he is notified through his counsel such notification will satisfy the constitutional requirement.[55]

Second, the Court has held that in order to constitute a legal trial it is necessary that the defendant shall have a hearing.[56] In the application of this principle the Court has held that a sentence imposed without the presence of the accused is void; [57] similarly, that the confiscation of a person's property by customs authorities without giving him a hearing is void.[58] Also void is the confiscation of a person's property as contraband when the owner does not know the Spanish language and no interpreter is appointed during the hearing.[59] But it is not necessary that the defendant have a hearing in all stages of the proceedings. Thus, where the party had a hearing in the first instance but not on appeal, the Court held that there was no violation of the Constitution since it merely requires that in some stage of the proceedings [60] the accused shall have an opportunity to defend himself.[61]

Third, the Court has held that the accused shall be effectively defended by counsel,[62] and that the right of defense shall not be limited by the judge except as provided by the law.[63] But it is not

[54] Ex Parte Chaccal Areff, 183 S. C. N. 68 (1939).
[55] Ex Parte Ernst, 125 S. C. N. 72 (1916).
[56] Lamadrid v. Busto, 129 S. C. N. 193 (1919).
[57] Gobierno Nacional v. Varas, 55 S. C. N. 52 (1894).
[58] Ex Parte Charles Hermanos, 41 S. C. N. 198 (1890).
[59] Burns v. Administración de Aduanas, 94 S. C. N. 107 (1914).
[60] Mascazzini v. Calcagno, 138 S. C. N. 75 (1923); Hauri v. Baru, 139 S. C. N. 59 (1923).
[61] In the United States it has been held that the right of appeal is not one of the essential elements of due process of law, McKane v. Durston, 153 U. S. 684 (1894).
[62] Ex Parte Vázquez, 155 S. C. N. 374 (1929).
[63] Pitranera v. Deurs, 12 S. C. N. 164 (1872).

a limitation of the right of defense that an officer charged with a military crime shall be compelled to choose as defense counsel one of the officers of the army. In such a case the Court has stated that Article 18 of the Constitution does not prohibit the government from regulating the procedure of a trial, and that the statutory provision that a defendant in a military trial shall be limited in selecting his defense counsel from among the officers of the army is valid.[64] It is not a violation of the right of defense that an accused pleads guilty in the absence of his lawyer provided there is no evidence of intimidation and coercion on the part of the prosecuting authorities,[65] or that the Court appointed one counsel to defend two accused persons.[66]

Cruel and Unusual Punishment

Another provision of the Argentine Constitution which shows the liberality of the framers of the instrument is that which abolishes all kinds of tortures and scourging as punishment for crime (Art. 18). This provision is practically similar to the Eighth Amendment of the United States Constitution which provides that no cruel and unusual punishment shall be inflicted. The provisions of both constitutions are similar, not so much because the United States Constitution had any definite influence upon the framers of the Argentine Constitution but because the penological principles which stood for the abolition of this type of punishment were so widespread over the world that they influenced the framers of both the United States and the Argentine constitutions.

Confiscation of Property as a Punishment for Crime

The Argentine Constitution prohibits the confiscation of property as a punishment for crime (Art. 17). The Argentine Supreme Court has stated:

The confiscations prohibited by the Constitution are those which are imposed as a punishment for crimes and by which a person is dispossessed of his property without due process of law or requisition by military authorities. But it does not apply to property obtained from

[64] Ex Parte Calderón, 110 S. C. N. 210 (1908).
[65] Herrera v. Aduana de la Capital, 120 S. C. N. 267 (1915).
[66] Viera v. Gilbert, 134 S. C. N. 191 (1921).

persons by the state through the exercise of the taxing power for the legitimate purposes of government.[67]

Thus in *Abella de Colombres v. Buenos Aires,* 160 S. C. N. 114 (1931), where the question was whether a fine imposed by law for not paying a tax was a confiscation of property forbidden by the Constitution, the Supreme Court stated:

> When in the tax law a fine is provided for not paying the taxes when due, this fine becomes by virtue of the same statute part of it, because ordinarily the imposition of a fine is not a tax in legal contemplation.[68]

Again in *La Eléctrica del Norte v. Tucumán,* 179 S. C. N. 54 (1937), in which the plaintiff attacked the constitutionality of fines imposed by the defendant municipality on the plaintiff company in order to compel it to fulfill the provisions of its franchise, the Court stated:

> The imposition of penal sanctions on public utilities is necessary in order to make them comply with the provisions of the franchises imposed by law and does not violate any constitutional right protected by the Constitution.

And finally, in *Croceo v. Gobierno Nacional,* XXXVIII J. A. 934 (1932), in which the plaintiff attacked the act of customs authorities in confiscating certain goods of the plaintiff alleged to be contraband, the Court stated:

> The confiscation of property forbidden by Article 17 of the Constitution refers to confiscations imposed as a punishment for crime and does not apply to a case similar to the one under consideration.

Political Crimes

The constitutional guarantee that the death penalty shall not be imposed for political crimes (Art. 18) has its roots in the political history of Argentina; it attempts to wipe out acts of tyranny on the part of public authorities who might employ the death penalty in order to get rid of their political opponents.

Political crimes are those which are committed against the established political order with the view of establishing a new sys-

[67] Faramiñón v. La Plata, 105 S. C. N. 50 (1906); Griet Hermanos v. Tucumán, 137 S. C. N. 212 (1922).

[68] The Court cited Cooley, *Treatise on the Law of Taxation,* I, 35.

tem, and the motives which impel their commission are different from the motives which lead persons to the commission of common crimes. The theory underlying the punishment of political crimes is that because the motives impelling the commission of these crimes are of a noble and not of a low nature the offenders should receive a more lenient penal treatment than common criminals. The Argentine Penal Code, following this theory, makes a distinction between political and common crimes based on the motives, and imposes different types of punishment. The political crimes are sedition and rebellion, and the punishments are generally banishment, fines, military service, or imprisonment. The common crimes committed in connection with political crimes are punished separately.[69]

Treason

Another protection of persons accused of crime is that which limits the power of Congress to define and punish the crime of treason. The Constitution provides that treason against the nation shall consist only in levying war against her or in adhering to her enemies, giving them aid and comfort, and that Congress shall by special law specify the punishment for this crime, but no attainder of treason shall work corruption of blood or forfeiture except during the life of the person attainted (Art. 103).[70]

On September 14, 1863, Congress enacted a law[71] defining the crime of treason and fixing the punishment thereof. In *Nación v. Eguzquiza y Ayala,* 4 S. C. N. 75 (1867), the Court held that aliens could not be prosecuted for treason under the law but only Argentine citizens and other persons owing allegiance to the Argentine Republic.

69 Nación v. Araceno, 6 S. C. N. 39 (1868).

70 The United States Constitution provides: "Treason against the United States, shall consist in levying War against them, or in adhering to their Enemies, giving them Aid and Comfort. No person shall be convicted of Treason unless on the Testimony of two Witnesses to the same overt Act, or on Confession in open court.

The Congress shall have Power to declare the Punishment of Treason, but no Attainder of Treason shall work Corruption of Blood, or Forfeiture except during the Life of the Person attainted" (Art. III, § 3).

71 *Colección de leyes nacionales,* II, 70. Article 214 includes among the persons liable for treason Argentine citizens and any other person who by reason of holding any employment or exercising any public function in behalf of the nation owes allegiance to the same.

It is a principle of law, and especially of criminal law, that in the classification of crimes the courts cannot go beyond the words of the statute, and that when a penal statute is interpreted the interpretation of the same must not be extended so as to prejudice the rights of the accused. The principle is recognized not only by the common law but also by the national Constitution. The Constitution is the fundamental code which regulates the relations between the departments of government and the people. The article of the Constitution defining the offense of treason, as well as the statute also defining the offense, does not make reference to foreigners or inhabitants, and therefore according to its provision only Argentine citizens and other persons owing allegiance to the Argentine nation can be punished for the offense of treason.

In *Gobierno Nacional v. Azula y Leiva,* 9 S. C. N. 108 (1870), the defendants were accused of the crime of treason because they had given material aid to the enemies of the nation, but they alleged that they were compelled to do so by force. The Court reversed the conviction of the defendants and stated:

The crime of treason against the Argentine nation is not committed, according to Article 103 of the Constitution, by the mere fact of giving material aid to the enemy occupying the territory of the nation when this aid is given under the compulsion of force and as a means of defense in order to prevent the enemy from doing greater harm to the persons giving this aid.

No Special Privileges in Criminal Trials

The principle of the equal protection of the laws as applied to criminal prosecutions is embodied in Article 16 of the Constitution, which provides that there shall be no special privileges granted to persons in regard to their trial and punishment. Under the old Spanish law members of the clergy, soldiers, and students were tried by special tribunals composed of members of their classes. In the early case of *Ex Parte Candia,* 9 S. C. N. 533 (1870), the constitutionality of military tribunals was questioned on the ground that they violated this Article, but the Court held that the purpose of the Article was to abolish the special privileges granted to the clergy and to students in criminal trials and that it did not prohibit Congress from creating military courts for the purpose of trying the members of the army.[72]

[72] In Ex Parte Mortola, 147 S. C. N. 45 (1926), the Court held that Article 16 does not prohibit the trial of soldiers or officers by military tribunals for the violation of military laws.

Purpose and Conditions of Prisons and Jails

An interesting provision of the Argentine Constitution which has relation to the rights of persons accused of crime is that the jails and prisons shall be healthy and clean and that they shall be for the purpose of security, not punishment, of the criminals confined therein; and that if any measure, under pretext of precaution, causes more harm to the prisoners than is necessary under the circumstances, the judge who authorizes such methods shall be responsible for such harm (Art. 18). This provision shows once more the humanitarian spirit and philosophy of the framers of the Argentine Constitution. According to this provision, the jails and prisons of the Republic must become places of reformation of the prisoners rather than of punishment. Argentine penal legislation in recent times has, generally speaking, been true to the wishes of the Fathers of the Constitution.

VIII: PERSONAL FREEDOM AND LIBERTY OF THE MIND

PART I of the Constitution of the Argentine Nation is entitled: "Declarations, Rights and Guarantees." No special designation of what might be called a Bill of Rights is made, but Articles 14 to 20, inclusive, afford protection to many of those liberties of the individual which after 1789 became commonplaces of the democratic creed.

FREEDOM OF THE PERSON

The Argentine Constitution, loyal to the liberal tradition and principles upon which it was founded, prohibits slavery. It provides the following: that no persons shall be held as slaves; that those persons who had been slaves before the Constitution was established shall become free; that a special law shall compensate the slaveholders; that the Constitution shall make it a crime to contract for the sale of persons and that the notary or officer authorizing such contract shall be held responsible; that all slaves shall be free by the mere fact of setting foot on the territory of the Republic (Art. 15); and that no involuntary servitude shall be imposed upon any person except by virtue of a law or a sentence based on law (Art. 17).[1]

FREEDOM OF THOUGHT

Speech and Press

Freedom of speech and freedom of the press—rights essential in the democratic state—are either expressly or impliedly recognized by the Argentine Constitution. Freedom of speech, although not expressly granted by the Argentine Constitution as it is in the

[1] The Thirteenth Amendment of the United States Constitution provides: "Neither slavery nor involuntary servitude, except as a punishment for crime whereof the party shall have been duly convicted, shall exist within the United States, or in any place subject to their jurisdiction."

Constitution of the United States,[2] is nevertheless impliedly recognized in Article 14, which guarantees freedom of the press and which provides that all inhabitants of the nation have the right to publish their ideas through the press without previous censorship; and in Article 33, which provides that the declarations, rights, and guarantees enumerated in the Constitution shall not be considered a denial of other rights and guarantees not enumerated but which arise from the principle of the sovereignty of the people and of the republican form of government. Freedom of the press is also guaranteed by Article 32, which declares that the national government shall not enact laws restricting the liberty of the press or establishing the federal jurisdiction thereon.

The first case in which the Court interpreted Article 32 was *Fiscal v. Argerich,* 1 S. C. N. 130 (1864), where the federal attorney charged the defendant with the offense of contempt and libel committed against the chief of police of the city of Buenos Aires. The information was filed in a federal sectional court and was based upon a law of Congress making it a crime to slander, insult, or threaten the authorities in the exercise of their duties. The defendant alleged, first, that the offense of which he was accused was not punishable by any federal law, the law under which he was prosecuted not applying to press offenses; and second, that if the law covered offenses committed by the press it was unconstitutional. The charge was dismissed for lack of jurisdiction. On appeal the Supreme Court affirmed the judgment on the grounds, first, that Article 32 of the Constitution embodied the principles of the First Amendment of the United States Constitution prohibiting Congress from passing any law dealing with press offenses, and, second, that the Argentine federal courts, like the United States courts, have no common law jurisdiction.[3]

The second case that went to the Supreme Court was *Fiscal v. Calvete,* 1 S. C. N. 297 (1864), in which the defendant, who published a libel against a national senator for a speech delivered on

[2] The First Amendment of the United States Constitution provides: "Congress shall make no law respecting an establishment of religion, or prohibiting the free exercise thereof; or abridging the freedom of speech, or of the press; or the right of the people peaceably to assemble, and to petition the Government for a redress of grievances."

[3] Citing United States v. Hudson, 7 Cranch 32 (1812), and United States v. Coolidge, 1 Wheat. 415 (1816).

the floor of the Senate, was prosecuted for libel and contempt. Upon conviction he appealed to the Supreme Court, contending that such conviction was a violation of Article 32 of the Constitution. The Supreme Court affirmed, holding that Article 32 only prohibited Congress from passing laws regulating the press in order to prevent the commission of common law offenses, such as libel, but that it did not forbid legislation tending to prohibit acts done in violation of the Constitution or of the authorities which the same have created.

But in *Fiscal v. Laforest,* 3 S. C. N. 371 (1866), in which the defendant was indicted in a federal court for publishing a newspaper article in which he advocated revolution, the Supreme Court upheld the decision of a lower court acquitting the defendant on the ground that since the offense committed by the defendant was through the press the federal courts had no jurisdiction. In other words, the Court went back to the case of *Fiscal v. Argerich.* After the decision of the Laforest case the Supreme Court maintained the same principle in a long list of cases in which attempts were made to have the federal courts entertain jurisdiction in all types of press offenses.[4] According to the decisions of the Supreme Court after the holding in the Calvete case, Congress could not punish any offense even if committed against the nation if it was committed through the press, nor could the federal courts assume jurisdiction of any case based on similar circumstances. The national government had to depend upon the provincial legislatures and courts to defend the national government against crimes committed through the press.

But finally, in *Fiscal v. La Provincia* (a newspaper), 167 S. C. N. 121 (1932), the Court reversed the decisions since the Calvete case and accepted the ruling of that case as the law of the land. The editor of this newspaper published an article inciting the people against the national government, a crime prohibited by the federal penal code. He was indicted in the federal court but both the federal sectional court and the chamber of appeals refused to take jurisdiction on the ground that the offense was committed

[4] Fiscal v. Moreno, 10 S. C. N. 361 (1871); Gobierno Nacional v. Jofre, 17 S. C. N. 110 (1875); Gobierno Nacional v. Acevedo, 30 S. C. N. 112 (1886); Robles v. Cornejo, 100 S. C. N. 337 (1904); Agente Fiscal v. El Telégrafo, 150 S. C. N. 310 (1928); Repetto v. Castellarín, 153 S. C. N. 195 (1928).

through the press. The prosecuting attorney appealed to the Supreme Court, which reversed the decision of the lower courts, and held that Article 32 of the Constitution did not deprive Congress of the power to punish through its courts offenses which threatened the security of the nation. After saying that the first paragraph of Article 32 was taken from the First Amendment of the United States Constitution, and citing the debates of the Constitutional Convention of 1860 in which Article 32 was fully discussed, the Court said:

> The most probable meaning of the second part of Article 32 is in effect that the makers of the Constitution of 1860 wished to reproduce in the Argentine Constitution the same constitutional provision which existed in the Constitution which served as the model for ours. In the United States, where each state has the reserved power to enact the common law codes, there is no danger that Congress, through a national penal code, can legislate over press offenses. But among us, on the other hand, this danger is real, since by an expressed constitutional provision Congress has power to enact the common law codes. That being so, the only thing that can be inferred from the last clause of Article 32 is that although the Constitution reserves to the provinces the power to punish common law offenses when committed through the press,[5] this Article does not prohibit Congress from legislating over common law offenses committed through the press if these offenses are against the existence of the national Constitution or against the authorities of the national government in the exercise of their functions.[6]

In *Ex Parte Bertotto,* 168 S. C. N. 15 (1933), the Supreme Court discussed the nature, extent, and limitations of freedom of the press. The petitioner's newspaper was barred from the mail because it contained articles inciting the people to revolution through the use of physical force. He contended that such an act on the part of the post office authorities constituted a violation of the freedom of the press. The lower court denied petitioner's contention and he appealed to the Supreme Court. This Court upheld the lower court on the ground that the petitioner's pub-

[5] In Loveira v. Mulhall, 115 S. C. N. 92 (1911), the Court held that the provisions of Article 32 do not apply to Congress when legislating for the federal capital and the national territories.

[6] The limitations imposed by Article 32 are applicable to the provinces when a person is prosecuted in a provincial court for the violation of a press offense where the accusation is based on the federal penal code and not upon a provincial penal statute. Segovia v. Orellana Herrera, 128 S. C. N. 175 (1918).

lication violated the criminal law and barring it from the mails did not constitute a violation of the freedom of the press. After saying that the editorials of the petitioner's newspaper were illegal because they preached armed revolution, the Court, on the authority of Blackstone, stated: "The freedom of the press is essential in a free state, but such freedom consists only in not being subject to previous censorship or restriction before publication, not in exempting the publisher from criminal prosecution if the publication violates the criminal law." And citing Cooley, *Constitutional Limitations*, p. 267, the Court thus defined liberty of the press: "Liberty of the press is the liberty to publish anything which the citizen thinks is convenient as well as the liberty of being protected, unless the publication is contrary to public morals or private reputation, or is in violation of the criminal law." [7]

In *Gobierno Nacional v. Antilli y Barrera*, 119 S. C. N. 231 (1914), the facts were as follows: Congress had enacted a statute making it a criminal offense to publish any article justifying the commission of a criminal act. The defendants had published an article justifying the assassination of the chief of police of Buenos Aires and praising the assassin as the executor of popular justice. They were prosecuted under the statute referred to above, and in defense contended that the statute violated freedom of the press. The Supreme Court, however, dismissed this contention and held that Article 14 of the Constitution prohibits previous censorship, but does not forbid the legislative department from punishing the publication of ideas which are contrary to public morals or safety, or which excite people to rebellion or civil war, or which affect the reputation of private persons.

Paz v. La Municipalidad de la Capital, 133 S. C. N. 31 (1920), presents the question whether the government in the exercise of the taxing power may abridge the freedom of the press. The municipality classified buildings into commercial, industrial, and residential, for the purpose of imposing a light and cleaning tax.

[7] In Fiscal v. *La Provincia*, 167 S. C. N. 121 (1932), in which a similar issue was presented, the Court, citing Willoughby, *The Constitutional Law of the United States*, 2d ed., II, 771, held that neither the provisions of the United States Constitution nor those of the Argentine Constitution exempt from criminal prosecution or civil action the author of a publication which is criminal in nature or invades private reputation.

Buildings dedicated to commercial and industrial enterprises were to pay a higher tax than private homes. The plaintiff alleged that publishing a newspaper was not a business or commercial enterprise, and that the tax was in conflict with Article 32 of the Constitution because it imposed a higher tax on the plaintiff's newspaper than on private homes by merely calling it a business or commercial enterprise. The lower court declared the tax constitutional. On appeal the Supreme Court upheld the statute:

> Article 32 of the Constitution has no other object than that of limiting the power of Congress as a national legislature to regulate the freedom of the press and to repress abuses which might be committed through the press, leaving to the provincial legislatures and local authorities the enactment of legislation regulating the press and punishing crimes committed by means of it. Therefore the freedom of the press cannot be said to have been violated by a tax imposed by Congress acting as a local legislature, especially when this tax has not been imposed on newspaper agencies only but placed upon all property within the municipality dedicated to industrial or commercial enterprises and upon homes, when the tax imposed is not confiscatory in nature.[8]

Petition and Assembly

The right of petition is expressly granted by the Argentine Constitution in Article 14, which provides that all the inhabitants of the nation have the right to make petitions to the authorities. And the right of assembly, although not expressly granted, as it is in the Constitution of the United States, has been held by the Argentine Supreme Court in *Comité Acción Radical v. Jefe de la Policía de la Capital,* 156 S. C. N. 81 (1929), to be impliedly derived from the following articles of the Constitution: Article 33, which provides that the declarations, rights and guarantees enumerated in the Constitution shall not be considered to be a denial of all other rights and guarantees not enumerated but which arise from the principle of the sovereignty of the people and of the republican form of government; Article 14, which guarantees the right of petitioning the authorities and which at the same time

[8] In Grosjean v. American Press Co., 297 U. S. 233 (1936), the Supreme Court of the United States declared unconstitutional as a violation of the freedom of the press a state license tax imposed on owners of newspapers enjoying a circulation of more than twenty thousand copies per week for the privilege of selling or charging for the advertising therein and measured by a percent of the gross receipts.

assumes the right of assembly in order that the right of petition may be collectively exercised; Article 22, which permits the right of assembly provided the people assembled do not assume the right to exercise powers in the name of the people; and Article 19, which provides that no inhabitant of the nation can be forbidden to do what is not prohibited by law.

The plaintiff in this case was denied permission by the chief of police of the federal capital to hold a political rally in one of the busiest streets of the city of Buenos Aires. The defendant did not refuse to permit the meeting in any other street nor did the plaintiff request permission to hold the rally in another place in the city. The plaintiff attacked the constitutionality of the order of the chief of police on the ground that it impaired the right of peaceful assembly. The Court held that the act of the defendant was constitutional, because it was justified under the circumstances and because he had not refused to permit the holding of the rally in some other place of the city.

> Any law or regulation prohibiting a meeting whose object is to protest against the acts of public officers, or which indefinitely postpones such meeting or limits the number of persons who may attend it; or which fixes an arbitrary length of time within which a meeting can be held, or authorizes the holding of a meeting only at a distance from the urban district where the sponsors desire it to be held, is without doubt a violation of the constitutional right of petition and assembly.[9]

Religious Freedom

Although the Argentine Constitution provides that the federal government shall support the Roman Catholic Church (Art. 42), the Constitution at the same time grants complete freedom of worship by providing that all the inhabitants of the nation shall enjoy the right of freely professing their religion (Art. 14). In *Nación v. Hueses,* 141 S. C. N. 31 (1924), the defendant was charged with violation of a statute regulating the practice of medicine, and his defense was that the statute was in violation of the freedom of worship guaranteed by the Constitution. His conviction in the lower court was affirmed by the Supreme Court:

[9] The right of peaceful assembly, the Supreme Court of the United States has held, is a right cognate to those of free speech and free press and is equally fundamental. De Jonge v. Oregon, 299 U. S. 353 (1937).

It is impossible to admit that that part of Article 14 of the Constitution which guarantees the freedom of religion can be legitimately invoked against Article 208 of the Penal Code, which is based on reasons of public hygiene and social policy, and which in no way attempts to interfere with the freedom of worship guaranteed by Article 14 of the Constitution but which on the other hand attempts to prevent the endangering, in the name of freedom of religion, of public health and public morals.[10]

Teaching, Learning, Professions

The rights of teaching and learning, of any licit industry, trade, or profession, and of associating for useful purposes are expressly granted to citizens and aliens alike by the Argentine Constitution (Art. 14). But these rights are not absolute and are subject to laws regulating their exercise. The power of Congress to regulate the rights of teaching and learning is discussed by the Supreme Court in *Ex Parte Benvenutto,* 154 S. C. N. 119 (1929). The petitioner, a graduate from the law school of the Catholic University of Buenos Aires, petitioned the chamber of appeals of the federal capital to be admitted to the bar. The Court denied the petition on the ground that the petitioner was not a graduate of one of the national universities, which under the law are the only universities that can grant professional degrees. The petitioner appealed to the Supreme Court, alleging that such a law was unconstitutional because it violated the right of teaching and learning. The Supreme Court upheld the lower court, holding that the law constituted a reasonable regulation of the right of teaching and learning. Speaking on the power of Congress to provide that the national universities shall have the exclusive power to grant professional degrees, the Court stated that the enactment of such legislation was in the interest of national culture and constituted an exercise of the power to promote general and university instruction, as authorized by the Constitution.[11]

[10] In Reynolds v. United States, 98 U. S. 145 (1879), the Supreme Court upheld the validity of a federal law prohibiting polygamy even when practiced in the name of religion.

[11] A statute of Nebraska provided that no person, individually or as a teacher, could in any private or public institution teach any subject to any person in any language other than the English language. It also provided that any language other than English could be taught as a subject only after a pupil had attained and successfully passed the eighth grade. In Meyer v. Nebraska, 262 U. S. 390 (1923), the

In *Arcelus v. Gómez,* 42 S. C. N. 274 (1891), the Court sustained the power of Congress to regulate the practice of a profession. The question was whether a law excluding women from the profession of notary public violated the right to work. The attorney general declared that under the Fourteenth Amendment of the United States Constitution women, as well as men, have the right to engage in useful and licit enterprises, and cited the fact that in the United States women practiced the liberal professions. The Court held the law constitutional. Under present legislation women in Argentina have the same rights as men in regard to the practice of the learned professions.[13]

United States Supreme Court declared it unconstitutional. A statute of Oregon requiring every guardian, parent, or other person having control or custody of a child to send him to a public school was held invalid in Pierce v. Society of Sisters, 268 U. S. 510 (1925).

[13] Ex Parte Camperchioli, 136 S. C. N. 379 (1922).

IX: ECONOMIC INTERESTS

THE Argentine Constitution has several provisions protecting property rights: that all the inhabitants of the nation shall enjoy the right of using and disposing of their property, subject to the laws regulating the same (Art. 14); that property is inviolable and that no inhabitant can be deprived of the same except by a judgment based upon law (Art. 17); [1] that the condemnation of property for public use shall be regulated by law and that previous compensation shall be paid for the property to be used (Art. 17); that all authors or inventors shall have the exclusive property of their works, inventions, or discoveries, for the length of time accorded by law (Art. 17); that taxes and other public burdens shall be equally imposed (Art. 16).

Due Process of Law

The Argentine Supreme Court has, as a general rule, interpreted the provisions of the Constitution protecting property rights in the light of the substantive and procedural concepts of due process of law enunciated by the United States Supreme Court when interpreting the Fifth and Fourteenth Amendments. For example, in *Mango v. Traba,* 144 S. C. N. 219 (1925), the question was whether Congress had power to regulate lease contracts in the absence of any emergency. Holding in the negative and citing *Campbell v. Holt,* 115 U. S. 620 (1885), the Court stated: "The word 'property' used in the Fourteenth Amendment, the Supreme Court of the United States has declared, comprehends all valuable interest which a man possesses apart from himself, his life, and his liberty." [2] And in *Empresa Ferrocarril de Entre Ríos v. La Nación,*

[1] In Ferrocarril Central Córdoba v. Ferrocarriles del Estado, 139 S. C. N. 349 (1923), it was held that a corporation was an inhabitant within the meaning of Article 17 of the Constitution.

[2] In Ercolano v. Lanteri, 136 S. C. N. 161 (1922), where the Court sustained the validity of a congressional enactment regulating rent contracts in times of emergency, Chief Justice Bermejo dissented and said that Article 17, which provides that property is inviolable, is the equivalent of the due process provisions of the Fifth and Fourteenth Amendments of the United States Constitution.

176 S. C. N. 363 (1936), involving the question whether a public franchise was a property right within the meaning of Article 17, the Court enlarged the definition by saying that the term "property" includes every right which has a recognized value in law, whether it originates from relations recognized by private law or from administrative acts, and declared that the owner of such right has a cause of action against anyone who interferes with its enjoyment.

In *Lucena v. Matadero Frigorífico Mendoza,* 173 S. C. N. 548 (1935), the Court discussed a new aspect of property rights. The province of Mendoza granted a monopoly to the defendant for the slaughtering of animals, and one of the conditions of the monopoly was that the defendant, besides receiving fees for killing animals for other persons, was entitled to the entrails of the slaughtered animals. The plaintiff attacked the constitutionality of the clause which granted to the defendant the right to acquire the entrails, on the ground that these were property of which he could not be deprived by the state without compensation. The Supreme Court upheld his contention.

In *Compañía Sud-Americana de Servicios Públicos v. Comisión de Fomento de Gálvez,* 174 S. C. N. 178 (1935), the Court discussed another aspect of the right of property. The plaintiff company was a public utility engaged in selling electricity to the city of Gálvez. It wanted to transfer a Diesel motor with a dynamo from that city to the city of Rufino, where the company had another electric plant. The Public Service Commission of the city of Gálvez objected to the transfer on the ground that it would affect the service which the company rendered to the city. The plaintiff company obtained an order prohibiting the Public Service Commission's interfering with the transfer, and the defendant appealed to the Supreme Court. This Court sustained the lower court: the defendant's action would amount to a violation of the property right of the plaintiff guaranteed by the Constitution. The Court then said that the possession of a thing confers on the owner the right to give to it the use which he thinks convenient and to transfer it from one place to another, and that the civil law has affirmed the basic principle of the national Constitution that no one can be deprived of his property without just compensation or without due process of law.

Cadaján v. Compañía Alumbrado Eléctrico de Río Gallegos, 173 S. C. N. 65 (1935), deals with the constitutionality of an ordinance of the city of Río Gallegos which provided that any person or corporation engaging in the public sale of light, water, gas, etc., is forbidden to charge for the use or lease of the meters employed in rendering such services. The plaintiff company alleged that the ordinance deprived it of property without due process of law, and the municipality justified it as an emergency measure. The Court declared it unconstitutional.

Property, as well as contracts, may be regulated when the legislature has decided that there is an emergency which justifies such regulation, because such power of Congress is authorized by Article 14 and Article 67, § 8, of the Constitution. But due to the exceptional nature of the exercise of such power and in accordance with the judicial decisions of the United States, it is indispensable that the emergency which justifies the regulation of property and contractual rights should be declared first by the legislature, and not by the officers in charge of the execution of the laws.

In *Quindimil y Cía. v. Administración de Impuestos Internos,* 173 S. C. N. 123 (1935), the question was whether Congress could authorize the destruction of foodstuffs, drinks, etc., not suitable for human consumption without violating the right of property guaranteed by the Constitution, and the Court sustained the authorization:

The doctrine and constitutional decisions of the United States have established that the destruction of products unsuitable for consumption can be authorized by the state under the exercise of the police power without violating the property rights guaranteed by the Constitution. The doctrine and jurisprudence have also held that the destruction of such property amounts to a regulation and not to an expropriation of the same, and that property acquired or created in violation of the law is per se dangerous and the state may authorize its destruction.

But in *Canale v. Mendoza,* 118 S. C. N. 278 (1913), the Court declared unconstitutional a provincial statute that all private hospitals should be established outside the boundaries of the municipalities and those already functioning should be transferred to the outskirts of the cities thirty days after notice to the owners of the institutions. Public hospitals were not included within the provisions of the statute. The plaintiff attacked the constitutionality of the statute, and the Court held it to be an unreasonable exercise of the police power:

> In regard to private hospitals and sanatoria the American courts have decided, basing their decisions on scientific conclusions, that they do not constitute per se places dangerous to the public health, especially when they do not take in persons affected with contagious diseases, and that therefore the authorities or private persons cannot demand that the hospitals be removed from the center of the cities, although they may be subjected to the necessary sanitary regulations.

And referring to the power of the Court to protect property rights against infringement by the government in the exercise of the police power, the Court stated:

> Although the courts are not called upon to examine the occasion and convenience of the legislative or administrative measures tending to protect the public health,[3] it is unquestionable that according to the Constitution and the constitutional doctrine and jurisprudence the courts have the power to decide if these legislative and administrative measures are justified and whether they violate the fundamental rights guaranteed by the Constitution.[4]

The Constitution of the United States provides that no state shall pass a law impairing the obligation of contracts, but such a provision is not found in the Argentine Constitution. However, the Argentine Supreme Court has decided that contractual rights are property rights and cannot be impaired without violating the property clauses of the Constitution. In *Horta v. Harguindeguy*, 137 S. C. N. 47 (1922), declaring unconstitutional a law of Congress regulating rent contracts as applied to contracts made before the enactment of the statute, the Court discussed at length the difference between the protection afforded to contractual relations

[3] Citing Dobbins v. Los Angeles, 195 U. S. 223 (1904); Mugler v. Kansas, 123 U. S. 623 (1887); Cooley, *Treatise on Constitutional Limitations*, p. 292.

[4] In Compañía Azucarera Concepción v. Tucumán, 173 S. C. N. 429 (1935), the Court declared unconstitutional a statute which prohibited sugar mills from grinding their own sugar cane beyond the limits imposed by the authorities, and compelled them to grind sugar cane belonging to independent sugar growers, whose number was fixed by the provincial authorities, and to pay these producers the highest price obtained in the market.

by the Argentine Constitution and that of the United States. The Court declared that although in Argentina the legislature is not prohibited in specific terms from enacting laws which may alter the obligations of contracts, yet the government cannot impair the obligations of contracts, since contractual rights are property rights secured in general terms by Article 17 of the Constitution. Explaining why the states of the United States are expressly prohibited from impairing the obligations of contracts and why such a prohibition is not necessary in Argentina, the Court stated:

> The insertion of a clause in the United States Constitution prohibiting the states from impairing the obligations of contracts was due to special circumstances, since in the original text of the Constitution there was no general principle protecting property rights such as was later established in the Fifth and Fourteenth Amendments. . . . A specific prohibition against the impairment of contracts by the states would have been unnecessary if the Constitution of the United States had contained from the beginning a provision similar to Article 17 of the Argentine Constitution, which serves the same purposes as the Fifth and Fourteenth Amendments of the United States Constitution. Therefore, although there is not a provision in the Constitution of the United States prohibiting the national government from impairing the obligation of contracts, yet the Supreme Court of the United States held in the case of *Hepburn v. Griswold*, 8 Wall. 603 (1870), and in the *Sinking Fund Cases*, 99 U. S. 727 (1879), that the Fifth Amendment prohibits the national government from impairing contractual obligations.[5]

The constitutional guarantee that contractual rights cannot be impaired extends not only to contracts between private individuals but also to those between individuals and the government. Hence, in *Bourdieu v. Municipalidad de la Capital*, 145 S. C. N. 307 (1925), holding unconstitutional a municipal ordinance which impaired a contract between the plaintiff and the defendant municipality concerning the sale of a lot in a cemetery, the Court, on the basis of precedents of the United States Supreme Court, declared what type of governmental action may impair a contract,

[5] In Carranza v. Alvarez, 137 S. C. N. 294 (1922), in which the issue was similar to that of the leading case, the Court stated: "Contractual rights are patrimonial rights and consequently property within the meaning of the Constitution. The word 'property' used in the Fourteenth Amendment, the Supreme Court of the United States has declared, comprehends all interests valuable to man outside his life and liberty."

and also what types of contracts are protected from impairment. First, "law" includes not only the laws of Congress but also the constitutions of the provinces, the laws of the provincial legislatures, and the municipal ordinances.[6] Second, "contract" includes any agreement between two or more parties whether the contract is executed or executory.[7] Third, the prohibition against the impairment of contractual obligations is general and applicable to contracts of any sort,[8] that is, contracts between private individuals, between individuals and the state, and those entered into between states themselves. Finally, with the exception of licenses revocable at will, when the government enters into a contract with individuals the state cannot annul it without complying with the constitutional principles relating to the inviolability of property.[9]

The following are examples of the application of the principles expounded by the Supreme Court in the previous case. In *Barreda v. San Juan*, XLII J. A. 593 (1933), the Court declared unconstitutional a law of the province of San Juan compelling farmers to insure their products with the government of the province and prohibiting insurance companies from making insurance contracts with farmers.

> A province cannot monopolize the insurance business in such a way as to prohibit a person from making an insurance contract with other entities than the state for the purpose of protecting the person's private interests. Such an act on the part of the province constitutes an excessive tutelage which is not justified and which, if permitted to be extended to other fields of economic activity, would destroy progress.

In *Quinteros v. Compañía de Tranvías Anglo-Argentina*, 179 S. C. N. 113 (1937), the Court declared unconstitutional a law of

[6] Citing Williams v. Bruffy, 96 U. S. 176 (1878).

[7] Citing New Jersey v. Wilson, 7 Cranch 164 (1812).

[8] In Cook v. Naveira, 138 S. C. N. 122 (1923), the Court held that the prohibition against impairing the obligation of contracts is applicable not only to written contracts but also to oral contracts.

[9] In Da Rosa v. Tucumán, 168 S. C. N. 83 (1933), the Court sustained the constitutionality of a provincial statute repealing a former law which granted to the plaintiff the right to establish a gambling place for thirty years. The Court, citing Douglas v. Kentucky, 168 U. S. 488 (1897), stated: "The Supreme Court of the United States, in a case analogous to the present one, has held that the privilege granted to a person to run a lottery is not properly speaking a contract within the meaning and spirit of the Constitution of the United States. It is simply a gratuitous license which the state may at any time, in the exercise of the police power, revoke or prohibit from functioning."

Congress, retroactive for five years, which required employers to pay employees who have been unreasonably discharged damages of not less than one-half the monthly salary for every year of service.

If it were to be recognized that Congress has the power to legislate toward the past, modifying the form and effect of existing contracts and giving retroactive effect to this law as far as five years prior to the enactment of the statute, as in this case, then Congress could also legislate retroactively so as to affect contracts executed ten, twenty, thirty years prior to the enactment of a law. This would cause disastrous results, juridically, economically, and socially, and would bring about instability and insecurity of social and economic relations.

The right of contract under both the Argentine and the United States constitutions is not absolute; it can be regulated in appropriate circumstances. Thus, in *Avico v. de la Pesa,* 172 S. C. N. 21 (1934), the Court discussed the power of the national government to enact a moratorium mortgage statute which prorogued the payment of debts for three years after its enactment, the debtor meanwhile being bound to continue paying interest on the mortgage at the rate of six percent. The plaintiff debtor instituted an action under the statute to compel the defendant to accept payment of interest as provided by the law. The defendant attacked the statute as unconstitutional because it impaired the obligation of a contract entered into before the enactment of the statute. The Court upheld the statute, basing its decision mainly on *Home Building and Loan Association v. Blaisdell,* 290 U. S. 398 (1934), upholding the Minnesota Moratorium Statute.

Our Constitution, when adopting in great part the principles of the Constitution of the United States, has given us, among others, the immense advantage of having the opportunity to use the wise interpretation given by the United States Supreme Court to those principles which we have adopted from their Constitution. The right of property guaranteed by Article 17 of our Constitution has its precedent in the amendment of the Constitution of the United States. It is therefore of great interest to study how the Supreme Court of that country has interpreted the nature, extent, and limitations of the property rights guaranteed in their Constitution in order to adapt such interpretation to our law, as the most authoritative interpretation of the principles we have incorporated in our Constitution, provided that we find such an interpretation to be a reasonable one.

The Court, after citing many other precedents of the United States Supreme Court,[10] came to the conclusion that the principles of law expounded in the Minnesota case were applicable to the case under consideration; first, because there was an emergency which justified Congress in exercising the police power to protect the vital interests of the community; second, because the law was enacted, not to give any particular advantage to debtors, but to protect the fundamental interests of society; third, the conditions under which the payment of the debts was prorogued were not unreasonable; fourth, the law was of a temporary nature.[11]

In *Otaño v. Castells,* 135 S. C. N. 122 (1921), the plaintiff attacked the constitutionality of a bankruptcy statute enacted by Congress on the ground that it impaired the obligation of contracts in as much as it was applicable to contracts made before the enactment of the statute. But the Court sustained its validity.[12]

The Argentine Supreme Court has held that a public service franchise is a contract which, unless the state reserves the power, cannot be revoked or annulled. But the Court has further held that when interpreting a franchise granted to a public service corporation the terms of the said franchise must be strictly construed against the company. In *Compañía Swift de la Plata v. Gobierno de la Nación,* 149 S. C. N. 218 (1927), the plaintiff corporation had a franchise to establish a packing house. The national government compelled the plaintiff to pay a certain fee for the use of the government's hoisting machine employed in loading and unloading

10 Wilson v. New, 243 U. S. 332 (1917); Ogden v. Saunders, 12 Wheat. 213 (1827); Sturges v. Crowninshield, 4 Wheat. 122 (1819); Walker v. Whitehead, 16 Wall. 314 (1873); Green v. Biddle, 8 Wheat. 1 (1823); McCracken v. Hayward, 2 How. 608 (1844); Stephenson v. Binford, 287 U. S. 251 (1932); Manigault v. Springs, 199 U. S. 473 (1905); Levy Leasing Co. v. Siegel, 258 U. S. 242 (1922); Munn v. Illinois, 94 U. S. 113 (1877); West River Bridge Co. v. Warren, 11 Peters 420 (1837); Nebbia v. New York, 291 U. S. 502 (1934); Brass v. North Dakota, 153 U. S. 391 (1894); German Alliance Insurance Co. v. Lewis, 233 U. S. 389 (1914).

11 In Yaben v. Laballen, 172 S. C. N. 291 (1935), in which the same statute was attacked as unconstitutional, the Court, after citing Chief Justice Hughes's opinion in Worthen Co. v. Thomas, 292 U. S. 426 (1934), again upheld the validity of the statute.

12 In Louisville Joint Stock Land Bank v. Radford, 295 U. S. 555 (1935), the United States Supreme Court held that Congress, in the exercise of the bankruptcy power, is limited by the provisions of the Fifth Amendment which prohibit Congress from depriving a person of his property without due process of law. But in Wright v. Vinton Trust Bank, 300 U. S. 440 (1937), the Court upheld a mortgage moratorium statute on the ground that it did not impair the rights of the mortgagee.

the materials necessary to carry on the packing business. The company contended that according to the terms and the spirit of the franchise it was exempted from paying such fees. But the Court held against it and citing a decision of the United States Supreme Court,[13] stated:

> The rule of construction applied in interpreting the granting of franchises by the state to private corporations is that the franchise must be restrictively interpreted against the corporation. Every reasonable doubt must be resolved in favor of the state and against the corporation. Nothing must be taken as granted or implied when the terms of a franchise are equivocal.[14]

In the field of taxation the Court has declared the following taxes unconstitutional on the ground that they impaired the property rights guaranteed by the Constitution: a provincial tax of one cent on every kilogram of grapes produced within the province for the purpose of compensating grape producers who had suffered damages as a result of hail, *Barrera v. San Juan,* 168 S. C. N. 305 (1930); a tax imposed for the purpose of establishing government insurance for the protection of certain agricultural products, *Passera v. Mendoza,* 139 S. C. N. 388 (1923); an inheritance tax which as applied amounted to fifty percent of the estate, *Bunge v. La Nación,* 186 S. C. N. 421 (1940).

The provision of the Argentine Constitution that no inhabitant of the nation can be deprived of his property except by virtue of a judgment based upon law has incorporated into the instrument the procedural concept of due process of law. According to the decisions of the Argentine Supreme Court, this provision has three significant effects. First, the judgment rendered by the Court must not be arbitrary, but must have a legal basis. This principle is illustrated in several cases. In *Rey v. Rocha,* 112 S. C. N. 384 (1909), the defendant was accused of infringing trademarks and

[13] Fertilizing Co. v. Hyde Park, 97 U. S. 659 (1878).

[14] In Macaferri v. Municipalidad de Cerrillos, 164 S. C. N. 213 (1932), in which the question was whether a public service corporation could continue to operate its plants after its franchise had expired, the Court held in the negative and, referring to New Orleans Gas Co. v. New Orleans Light Co., 115 U. S. 650 (1885), stated: "The right of the guarantee to operate a business affected with a public interest arises not from the right to work and to carry on a legitimate industry but from a regulated concession granted by the state which, although it has the character of a privileged franchise, must cease immediately when, according to the terms under which it was granted, it has expired."

of selling goods with these infringing trademarks. The Court acquitted the defendant on technical grounds but ordered the destruction of the trademark. The defendant appealed from this order, contending that it was void because not based upon law. But the Supreme Court upheld it as based upon Article 53 of the Trademark Law, which authorizes the destruction of infringing trademarks even in cases where the defendant is acquitted of the offense charged against him. In *Gobierno Nacional v. Echeguren,* 67 S. C. N. 185 (1897), the defendant, accused of illegally introducing lottery tickets into the country, had been acquitted, but the Court had ordered the destruction of such tickets. The order was upheld on the ground that the tickets were not property within the meaning of the Constitution; they were evidence of the corpus delicti, and the court had the power to order their destruction without violating the Constitution.

Again in *Castro v. Miño,* 131 S. C. N. 387 (1920), defendant appealed from an adverse decision of a court alleging that, as the court had erred in the interpretation of the law applicable to the case, it was therefore not based upon law. The Supreme Court, however, refused to review the judgment, saying that the constitutional requirement applies only to arbitrary judgments based exclusively upon the will of the judges and not to judgments based upon an erroneous interpretation of the law applicable to the case. Neither is a judgment arbitrary because it is based upon decisions of a court interpreting a statute and not upon the statute itself. This is illustrated by *Bemberg y Cía. v. Roca,* 133 S. C. N. 298 (1921).

The second meaning is that no judgment depriving a person of his property is valid unless the person affected was notified and given a hearing. In *Necchi de Rodríguez v. Curí,* 149 S. C. N. 5 (1927), the plaintiff obtained a judgment against the defendant in a provincial court and attempted to enforce it in a federal court of another province under the full faith and credit clause of the Constitution. The defendant alleged that the judgment could not be enforced because it was void for want of notice and hearing. The plaintiff won in the lower court; on appeal the Supreme Court reversed:

The guarantee of Article 17 of the Constitution under which no one can be deprived of his property except by virtue of a sentence based upon law, combined with the inviolability of the right of defense secured by the Constitution, necessarily leads to the conclusion that a judgment depriving a person of his property must not be rendered without giving a hearing to the party affected.[15] Unless this is done, there is not a proper trial in the constitutional sense, and therefore under the full faith and credit clause of the Constitution (Art. 17) a judgment rendered by a provincial court without giving the parties affected a hearing cannot be given any validity in the courts of other provinces.[16]

The third meaning given to Article 17 is that after a person has acquired a property right he cannot be deprived of it except by a judgment of a competent authority. The Court applied this principle in *Sociedades Anónimas de Petróleo v. Salta,* 164 S. C. N. 140 (1932). The plaintiff had acquired certain mining concessions from the defendant province but later the newly elected governor issued a decree revoking the said concessions, alleging that they had been granted in violation of the laws of the province. The plaintiff attacked the decree in the Supreme Court, contending that it was unconstitutional because it deprived him of property rights without a judgment of a competent authority. The Court upheld this contention and declared the decree null and void.

The Argentine Constitution, like that of the United States, provides that no private property shall be taken for public use without just compensation. But the Argentine Constitution, unlike that of the United States, provides that the owner of the property must be previously compensated before the government takes his property (Art. 17).[17]

[15] Citing Williamson v. Berry, 8 How. 495 (1850).

[16] In Quinteros v. La Nación, 181 S. C. N. 449 (1938), the Court declared unconstitutional a presidential decree depriving a former government employee of a pension without giving him a hearing.

[17] In 1869 Congress enacted a statute providing for the expropriation of private property according to the provisions of the Constitution. The main provisions of this statute are: First, any property belonging to the provinces or to particular individuals which may be necessary for national public use is subject to expropriation. Second, Congress shall declare by law the necessity for the expropriation of such property. Third, the declaration that the property is necessary for public use shall be made the basis of plans made beforehand and showing the property which is to be expropriated. Fourth, the expropriation shall not be perfected until the government has paid the value of the property, but in case of emergency the prop-

The power to expropriate private property for public use and the limitations imposed upon the exercise of this power are discussed in several cases. Both the national and the provincial governments may exercise the power,[18] but the power can be exercised only under the authority of a law, therefore public officials cannot condemn private property for a public use unless there is legislative authorization to that effect.[19] If a law has been enacted authorizing the expropriation of private property it cannot be attacked as unconstitutional on the ground that the legislature made an error in determining the public use; under the Constitution the legislative department has the discretion to determine the use for which the property is to be used.[20] The power to condemn more property than necessary for the public work to be done was denied in *Municipalidad de la Capital v. Elortondo,* already discussed (p. 77). But in *Casado v. Bombal,* 85 S. C. N. 303 (1888), the statute was held constitutional on the ground that the property owners were protected by the right of reversion created by Article 19 of the national expropriation law.[21]

The question whether the government can desist from expropriating property after the Court has rendered a judgment fixing the price of the same has been impliedly answered in the affirmative in *Fehling v. Municipalidad de la Capital,* 166 S. C. N. 62 (1932), and *Monasterio de Soriano v. Municipalidad de la Capital,* 169 S. C. N. 180 (1933). In both cases the Court held that such an act on the part of the government does not deprive the owner of his property without due process of law[22] and that he has a cause

erty may be taken by the government even if the owner does not accept the price offered, provided the executive has deposited the money with the Court. And fifth, the federal courts shall have jurisdiction to decide all controversies arising between property owners and the government relating to the expropriation of property for public use. *Colección de leyes nacionales,* II, 469.

18 Arguello v. Buenos Aires, 97 S. C. N. 408 (1903).

19 Lorenzo v. Buenos Aires, 97 S. C. N. 332 (1903).

20 Santa Fe. v. Senorans, 6 S. C. N. 67 (1886).

21 Article 19 provides that if the thing expropriated is not dedicated to the object which motivated the expropriation, the former owner may take possession of the property in the original state in which it was expropriated by returning to the government the compensation paid to him.

22 Citing J. Lewis, *A Treatise on the Law of Eminent Domain,* p. 1669, and *Ruling Case Law,* X, 177, the Court stated: "The judicial procedure to condemn property under the power of eminent domain and to determine its just compensation is a suit arising under the common law within the meaning of the law of federal pro-

of action if he suffers any damage on account of the act of the state.[23] In the first case Associate Justices Sagarna and Guido Lavelle delivered a dissenting opinion on two points: First, that the Argentine Constitution, unlike that of the United States, requires that the owner of the property shall be indemnified before the government condemns his property. The Justices said that according to the laws of New York, New Jersey, Tennessee, Maine, Pennsylvania, and of other states, the states have to pay the price of the property after it has been fixed. And second, that, as the property owner has acquired a property right by virtue of the judgment rendered in his favor, he cannot be deprived of such a right without violating due process of law.

The recent case of *Bianchi v. Gobierno Nacional,* 186 S. C. N. 151 (1940), is an example of the tendency of the Court to protect property rights in eminent domain proceedings. The national government had expropriated plaintiff's property after the payment of fifty-four thousand pesos, about half the value of the property. Later on the court declared the total value of the property to be eighty thousand pesos. The plaintiff demanded payment of the rest of the debt owed to him by the nation, but the government officials objected to the payment on the ground that under the provisions of Article 7 of Law No. 3952 [24] the judgment rendered against the nation as a juridical person had only a declaratory character, that is to say, that the judgment merely recognized the obligation of the nation to pay the debt but that it did not compel the nation to pay it by judicial decree. The lower court decided against the plaintiff and he appealed to the Supreme Court, contending that the statute as interpreted violated his property rights. The Supreme Court upheld his contention, saying:

It is impossible to deprive the property owner of the judicial means of obtaining what belongs to him since such an act would constitute a

---

cedure. And in order that a citizen may bring a case to the federal Supreme Court it is necessary that he should have been deprived of his property without due process of law in violation of the rights guaranteed by the Constitution."

[23] In Maloch v. San Juan, 171 S. C. N. 142 (1934), the Court held that if the government desists from expropriating a property and the owner suffers damages because of this fact the government is liable for damages to the owner of the property.

[24] *Colección de Leyes Nacionales,* XII, 397.

violation of the property rights guaranteed by Article 17 of the national Constitution. If this were permitted, the right of property would have no defense against the state, which by depositing a small amount of the total price of a property could take it from the owner, thus violating Article 17 of the Constitution, which provides that in order to expropriate property the government must previously indemnify the owner of said property.[25]

Equal Protection of the Laws

Long before the adoption of the Fourteenth Amendment to the Constitution of the United States, the Argentine Constitution had embodied the principle of equal protection of the laws as an essential means of protecting individuals against unreasonable governmental interference. The Argentine Constitution provides that all the inhabitants are equal before the law and that equality shall be the basis of taxation and of public burdens (Art. 16).[26] In applying the principle of equal protection in tax matters the Argentine Supreme Court has generally followed the precedents established by the Supreme Court of the United States.

[25] Another important protection of the right of property is that no armed body shall make requisitions or exact aid of any kind from any inhabitant. This provision, similar to the provision in the Third Amendment to the Constitution of the United States, is to protect the inhabitants against requisitions of money or of other property which before national reorganization the armed forces of the provinces used to impose upon the inhabitants. J. V. González, *Manual de la constitución argentina*, p. 131.

[26] In Gobierno Nacional v. Olivar, 16 S. C. N. 118 (1878), the Argentine Court defined equal protection of the laws as follows: "The principle of the equal protection of the laws, according to the letter and spirit of our Constitution, is nothing else than the right of a person not to be deprived of privileges or exemptions granted to other persons under similar circumstances. Therefore true equality before the law consists in applying the law impartially to all persons and things under similar circumstances." With the exception of cases dealing with taxation, the Court has never declared unconstitutional a provincial or national statute because it denied equal protection of the laws. The following statutes have been held valid against the objection that they violated the equal protection of the laws: A provision of the military code which provided a more severe punishment for the crime of theft than the national penal code, Gobierno Nacional v. Barrueco, 126 S. C. N. 280 (1917): a provision of the code of criminal procedure of Buenos Aires that in ejectment proceedings the defendant had no right to appeal except in cases in which the contract involved in the controversy is alleged to be fraudulent while the right of appeal was granted to the plaintiff without limitations, Ravinovich v. Lambeski, 127 S. C. N. 167 (1918); a law exempting from attachment civil and military pensions, Pravia v. Massa, 139 S. C. N. 145 (1923); Santoro v. Frías, 124 S. C. N. 127 (1916); a law which exempted women from military service, Lanteri v. Reinshaw, 154 S. C. N. 283 (1929); a statute exempting from attachment the damages awarded to commercial employees for wrongful dismissal by the employers, Leal v. Giménez, 184 S. C. N. 398 (1939).

In *Unanué v. Municipalidad de la Capital*, 138 S. C. N. 313 (1923), the Court laid down the general principles for determining when equal protection of the laws in regard to taxation had been violated by national and provincial legislation. The defendant municipality imposed an inspection tax of one hundred pesos for every horse on every stable taking care of race horses. The plaintiff attacked the statute as against equal protection since the tax was not imposed on stables not taking care of race horses. But the Court held the tax valid: there was a reasonable basis for classifying these stables separately, and the tax was equally imposed on all stables keeping race horses. Referring to the power of the legislature to classify, the Court said:

> The equal protection of the laws referred to in Article 16 of the Constitution requires that taxpayers situated in similar circumstances shall be equally taxed. With regard to the power of the legislatures to classify objects for the purposes of taxation the United States Supreme Court has declared that the equal protection of the laws does not propose to fix a rigid rule in tax matters; it only prohibits the legislatures from establishing distinctions with the purpose of burdening or favoring arbitrarily certain groups of persons or things, as, for example, if the legislatures should take into consideration the race, religion, or nationality of the persons, or should take as a basis for taxation other factors which have no relation to the duties of the persons as taxpayers.[27] Consequently, when a tax is imposed upon certain kinds of property or upon persons, there must be some substantial reason for classifying these persons or property into different groups for the purpose of taxation.[28]

The principles enunciated in the above case have been applied in cases dealing with various forms of taxation. Thus, *Jewish Colonization Association v. Santa Fe*, 150 S. C. N. 205 (1927), involved the constitutionality of a tax law which imposed, besides a real property tax, a special tax on property owned by persons not residents of the province. The plaintiff contended that classification on the basis of residence was arbitrary. But the Court sustained the classification as based on a sound economic and social policy, namely, controlling absentee capitalism. And in *Guardian Assurance Co. v. Gobierno Nacional*, 150 S. C. N. 89 (1927), a

[27] Citing Bell's Gap Railroad Co. v. Pennsylvania, 134 U. S. 232 (1890).

[28] Citing Cooley, *Treatise on the Law of Taxation*, 3rd ed., and Willoughby, *Constitutional Law*.

law of Congress levying a higher tax on insurance companies whose capital and board of directors were outside the jurisdiction than on those companies domiciled in the nation was upheld:

> The distinction made for the purpose of taxation between insurance companies whose capital and board of directors are domiciled in the Republic and those which are not does not violate the equal protection of the laws in tax matters as guaranteed by the Constitution. The fact that the insurance companies have their capital and boards of directors in foreign countries may have direct economic consequences for the nation of sufficient importance to justify Congress, in the exercise of its constitutional power to tax, in taking this fact into consideration for the purpose of imposing a higher tax on them than on domestic corporations.

The power of the legislature to levy a progressive tax on real estate based on the number of acres owned and on the value of the property has been sustained in *Morán v. Entre Ríos*, 171 S. C. N. 390 (1934), and *Díaz Vélez v. Buenos Aires*, 151 S. C. N. 359 (1928). In the first case the province of Entre Ríos imposed a progressive tax on real property on the basis of the size of the holding. The plaintiff alleged that this system of taxation was arbitrary and unreasonable because it did not take into consideration the value of the property. The Supreme Court upheld the statute on the ground that the number of acres is a reasonable base upon which to impose a progressive tax.[29] In the Díaz Vélez case the law in question was one in which the province of Buenos Aires imposed a progressive tax on real property on the basis of value. The plaintiff alleged that the law violated the equal protection of the laws because large property owners had to pay proportionally more taxes. The Court held the statute constitutional saying: "In the United States, the classic country of progressive taxation, the constitutionality of such tax laws has been upheld by the Supreme Court of the nation. This court has held that the equal protection of the laws to which the Constitution makes reference is not an exact or mathematical equality in

[29] The Court cited Bell's Gap Railroad Co. v. Pennsylvania, 134 U. S. 232 (1890), Gray, *Limitations of the Taxing Power*, Cooley, *Treatise on the Law of Taxation*, 3rd ed., Willoughby, *Constitutional Law*, and Seligman, *Progressive Taxation in Theory and Practice*.

taxation but a reasonable taxation upon persons and objects situated under similar circumstances." [30]

The principle that legislative classifications for the purpose of taxation which are unreasonable, arbitrary, or which demonstrate a marked hostility toward certain groups or classes of taxpayers violate the equal protection of the laws was applied by the Court in the following cases:

In *Grosso v. Mendoza,* 128 S. C. N. 435 (1918), the Court declared unconstitutional a statute of the province of Mendoza which divided wine producers into two groups, those who were members of co-operative associations and those who were not, and exempted the first group from special taxes.[31]

Compañía Nacional de Tabacos v. Corrientes, 175 S. C. N. 199 (1936), held unconstitutional a law of the defendant province which provided that an agent of a business established in the province should pay a license tax of one hundred pesos as against seven hundred pesos for an agent of a business located in another province.

Cruz v. Santiago del Estero, 179 S. C. N. 98 (1938), held unconstitutional a law of the province which provided that persons or partnerships engaged in the selling of coal should pay a license tax of a thousand pesos a year while co-operative societies organized under the laws of the state should pay only half that amount.

This Court has decided in several cases, in which it has followed the American doctrine enunciated by Story, that although the taxing power of the provinces is extensive, yet such a power is limited by certain principles inherent in itself. According to these principles the power of taxation must be exercised in good faith for public and not for private purposes, and the taxes must be based upon norms of impartiality and uniformity in order to distribute the burden of taxation with justice.

In *Rizzotti v. San Juan,* 150 S. C. N. 418 (1928), and *In re Melo de Cané,* 115 S. C. N. 111 (1911), the Court declared unconstitutional two provincial statutes which demonstrated a marked hostility toward certain classes or groups of persons. In the first case

[30] Citing Magoun v. Illinois Trust Bank, 170 U. S. 283 (1898), and Seligman, *op. cit.*
[31] Citing Connally v. Union Sewer Pipe Co., 184 U. S. 540 (1902).

the majority of the physicians of the province of San Juan formed a mutual association, the bylaws of which provided that its members would not accept employment in any public or private hospital unless they were paid two hundred pesos a month, and that its members would not assist sick people in consultation with other physicians except for a payment of fifty pesos and after obtaining the permission of the association. As a result of this agreement, San Juan enacted a statute which provided that every physician should pay an annual license fee of five thousand pesos, and that failure to pay this tax constituted a penal offense. The statute also provided that the physicians must render free medical service to the Public Health Administration, a public institution created by the province to give medical assistance to the poor. The conditions under which these services had to be rendered were such that the physicians had no time left for private practice. The Supreme Court declared that the intent of the guarantee provided by Article 16 was to prohibit the levying of taxes with the purpose of penalizing special classes of persons and also to prohibit arbitrary distinctions in the imposition of taxes, and stated:

> The power to tax is subject to certain principles inherent in such power. It must be exercised in good faith for public and private objects and must be impartially and uniformly exercised. Any tax which does not conform to these purposes is not a tax but an act of spoliation. In other words, the tax must not constitute an act of destruction, prohibition, or confiscation of the taxpayer's property.

In the second case the Court declared unconstitutional a law providing that the Catholic Church should pay a tax of fifty percent on any property received by inheritance.

> It is impossible to admit the validity of the fifty percent tax imposed upon the property inherited by the Catholic Church on the ground that the purpose of the statute is to obtain revenue, when it clearly appears that the idea and practical effect of the statute is to prohibit indirectly the receipt by the Church of gifts through inheritance. The exercise of the tax power under the present circumstances is incompatible with Article 16 of the Constitution.[32]

[32] Citing Gray, *Limitations of the Taxing Power*, Story, *Commentaries on the Constitution of the United States*, 5th ed., and Bell's Gap Railroad Co. v. Pennsylvania, 134 U. S. 232 (1890).

The Argentine Supreme Court has upheld local assessments and other special taxes against the contention that they violated the equal protection of the laws by distinguishing these taxes from those of a general nature. And the Court has held unconstitutional tax statutes which, although imposed as special taxes, had all the essential characteristics of general taxes.

The first case in which the Court upheld the validity of a special assessment tax was *Marchelli v. Tramway Metropolitano,* 102 S. C. N. 379 (1905). The municipality of Buenos Aires enacted an ordinance imposing a special tax for paving certain streets. The ordinance provided that tramway companies whose lines were situated in these streets were to pay one-third of the cost while the property owners were to pay two-thirds. The Court upheld the statute, stating:

> Neither Article 16 nor Article 17 of the Constitution is opposed to special taxes which have the character of a fee for services or expenses for the improvement of specific parts or sections of the territory of the Republic. The services or improvements benefit directly the taxpayers who pay for these services, either from the point of view of the safety of their property or of an increase of the value of the same. In the imposition of these special taxes the property owner is not deprived of his property without compensation nor in violation of the equal protection of the laws.

And in *Ferrocarril del Sud v. Draque Cía.,* 131 S. C. N. 105 (1920), in which the problem was whether the national laws exempting national railroads from provincial taxation also exempted them from local assessment, the Court held in the negative, and distinguished general taxes from local assessment:

> It is well known that in the United States, whose institutions are analogous to ours, the benefits received by local improvements of the property are paid through a special tax called local assessment. The paving of the streets is generally financed by these local assessments. The general rule in the United States is that the local assessment has peculiar characteristics which distinguish it from the general tax. The use of the term "tax" does not show prima facie the intention to include local assessment. In order that the local assessment may preserve its peculiar character and that it may not be converted into an ordinary tax, it is necessary that the tax should be equal to the benefit received

by the taxpayer. If the amount of the tax is higher than the value of the property, or the assessment of the property for the purpose of paying the tax is higher than the benefit, then it is not a local assessment and therefore is unconstitutional.

In *Pereyra Iraola v. Buenos Aires,* 138 S. C. N. 161 (1923), the legislature of Buenos Aires had enacted a statute authorizing the construction of a public paved road from the city of Avellaneda to the city of La Plata. The statute provided that those persons whose property was located within an area of fifteen hundred meters on both sides of the road should pay seventy percent of the total cost of the road and that the government would pay the remaining thirty percent. The law also provided a special method for determining how this seventy percent would be paid by the property owners. The plaintiff attacked the constitutionality of the statute on three grounds: first, because the tax was confiscatory; second, because the law had not taken into consideration the value of the property but only the cost of the road, arbitrarily fixed by the same law; and third, because the tax absorbed the total value of the properties affected. The Supreme Court declared the statute unconstitutional: "In order that a special assessment tax may be valid it must have two characteristics. First, the public work that is to be constructed must be a local improvement; and second, the tax imposed must not exceed the benefit obtained by the property owner." [33]

In *Caeiro v. Astengo,* 140 S. C. N. 175 (1924), the municipality of Rosario had enacted an ordinance providing for the paving of La Plata Street, the greater part of which ran through land belonging to the defendant and used for growing alfalfa and vegetables. The street was not an urban thoroughfare but a road leading to the city, although it was within the territorial jurisdiction of the municipality. The ordinance also provided that the cost should be paid wholly by the property owners whose property the road crossed. The tax to be paid by each land owner was to be determined in proportion to the number of acres alongside the road. The plaintiff claimed that the ordinance was not a special assess-

[33] Citing Norwood v. Baker, 172 U. S. 269 (1898); French v. Barber Asphalt Paving Co., 181 U. S. 324 (1901); Gas Realty and Investment Co. v. Schneider Granite Co., 240 U. S. 55 (1916); Monongahela Navigation Co. v. United States, 148 U. S. 312 (1893); Warner v. Leaser, 239 U. S. 207 (1915); Lockwood v. St. Louis, 24 Mo. 20 (1856).

ment but a general tax because the work to be done was not a local improvement, and because the ordinance deprived him of the equal protection of the laws. The lower court upheld the ordinance on the theory that it constituted a reasonable exercise of the police power, but the Supreme Court reversed on the grounds urged by the plaintiff.

In *Compañía de Electricidad de Buenos Aires v. Municipalidad del Azul,* 166 S. C. N. 417 (1932), the Court sustained a special tax on a public utility company for the use of the streets against the objection that it conflicted with the equal protection of the laws. The Court declared that the equal protection clause applies only to general taxes and not to special taxes or compensations charged to a public utility company for the use of the public streets which are the property of the municipality. The Court held that this was not a general tax imposed on all inhabitants of the municipality but merely a tax imposed on the company for the use of the streets by mutual agreement with the municipality and that this agreement could be terminated at any time by the will of the parties.

X: CONCLUSIONS

THE FOLLOWING conclusions may be stated concerning the role which the judicial function has played in the Argentine constitutional system, in the maintenance of the federal system, and in the protection of individual rights.

1. The Argentine Constitution, like that of the United States, is not a wholly original document; and just as the framers of the Constitution of the United States made use of English and colonial constitutional precedents in drafting the Constitution of 1789, the framers of the Argentine Constitution employed colonial and United States constitutional precedents in establishing the federal system created by the Constitution of 1853.

2. For the reason mentioned above, many provisions of the Argentine Constitution were directly taken from or modeled on similar provisions of the Constitution of the United States. The most important of these are the judiciary article; the power of Congress to regulate interprovincial and foreign commerce, to levy taxes, to enact currency and bankruptcy legislation, and to establish post offices and post roads; the military powers of Congress; the clauses dealing with full faith and credit, interprovincial citizenship, extradition of fugitives from justice, the guarantee to the provinces, by the national government, of a republican form of government, the obligation of the national government to protect the provinces against invasion and domestic violence, and the powers of the provinces to make compacts with one another; the division of powers between the national government and the provinces; and some of the constitutional rights.

3. Many provisions, including some of great importance, have no precedent in the Constitution of the United States, and their origins can be traced to the early constitutional development of the nation. Some of these are: the power of Congress to enact code legislation; the provision that the provincial governors are the natural agents of the federal government; some of the rights guar-

anteed by the Constitution, such as trial by natural judges, the purpose and conditions of the jails, the prohibition of special privileges in criminal trials, and the abolition of the death penalty for political offenses; the power of Congress to foster the prosperity of the provinces and of the nation; some of the provisions dealing with the power of Congress to regulate interprovincial and foreign commerce; and the amending procedure. The power of Congress to enact code legislation is one of the fundamental differences between the two federal systems. Through this power the Argentine Congress, unlike the Congress of the United States, can not only control the economic and social life of the provinces but also impose a limitation on the police power of the provinces. *Viñedas y Bodegas Arizú v. Mendoza,* p. 151.

4. The Argentine Supreme Court has recognized the eclectic composition of the Constitution by following two jurisprudential tendencies in interpreting the Constitution. First, to follow the decisions of the United States Supreme Court when interpreting clauses of the Constitution which have a precedent in the Constitution of the United States, provided that those decisions seem reasonable to the Argentine Court, *Avico v. de la Pesa,* p. 201; and second, to reject the application of decisions of the United States courts if the provisions of the Constitution in question have their roots in the constitutional history of Argentina and not in the Constitution of the United States. *Hileret y Rodríguez v. Tucumán,* p. 164, and *Ferrocarril Central Argentino v. Santa Fe,* p. 122.

5. The practice of the Argentine courts of following the decisions of the courts of the United States is due, not to blind imitation, but to theoretical and practical reasons. There is the fact that, as indicated above, many provisions of the Constitution are based on the Constitution of the United States. And as the Argentine Court stated in *Avico v. de la Pesa,* there is an immense advantage for the court in having the opportunity to use the interpretation given by the Supreme Court of the United States to those clauses which have been adopted in Argentina. Many Argentine statutes to enforce the Constitution have been patterned after legislation enacted in the United States for similar purposes. An example is the statute organizing the federal courts and establishing their jurisdiction, *Pereyra v. Pacific Steam Navigation Co.,* pp. 70, 41*n.*

This practice of the Argentine courts is based on the universal rule of statutory interpretation, that the courts of one nation when interpreting a statute adopted from another nation will look to the interpretation given to the statute by the courts of the nation from which it was adopted. There are many principles in modern federalism of which the United States has been the creator, and the Argentine Court is compelled to appeal to United States precedents when a question involving one of these principles is brought before it. Illustrations of this are the doctrines of intergovernmental tax immunity and the doctrine of judicial review, *Banco de Buenos Aires v. Gobierno Nacional*, p. 101; *Ex Parte Sojo* (p. 75). The last reason is that the social and economic philosophy of certain decisions of the United States Supreme Court agrees with that of the judges of the Argentine courts. This is particularly true of the decisions interpreting the property rights guaranteed by the Constitution. In this type of case the Argentine Supreme Court, following a technique similar to that of the Supreme Court of the United States, has, through the application of the substantive concepts of due process of law, declared unconstitutional legislative acts which in the judgment of the Court constituted violations of the rights guaranteed by the Constitution. The extent to which the Argentine Court, like the Supreme Court of the United States, has protected the rights guaranteed by the Constitution has depended, as a general rule, upon the economic, political, and social forces prevailing at the various periods of Argentine history.

6. Although the Fathers of the Argentine Constitution established a federal system of government, modeled to some extent on that of the United States, this does not mean that they intended it to be identical with that of the United States. There is ample historical evidence that the Founding Fathers intended to establish a form of a federal system of government somewhat different from that of the United States. Just as the Constitution of the United States was a political compromise between federalist and confederate tendencies, so the Argentine Constitution is a compromise between centralist and federalist tendencies. And in reaching this compromise the men of Santa Fe, like those of Philadelphia, acted with a political wisdom which has deserved the admiration of students of constitutional law and political science.

7. Even if they had intended to establish a federal system identical with that of the United States they would have failed, because the political, social, economic, and historical traditions of the Argentine people were somewhat different from those of the United States. This point is demonstrated by the different interpretations and applications given in Argentina and in the United States to the clauses which provide that the federal government shall guarantee a republican form of government to the provinces and the states, respectively. In the United States the political tradition of respecting the self-government of the states has tended to prevent the intervention of the federal government in the governments of the states, no matter how far a state may violate the principles of a republican form of government. In Argentina, with a practically identical constitutional provision, political tradition has actively fostered intervention by the federal government, and has thus placed the local autonomy of the provinces at the mercy of the executive and legislative departments of the government. But there are well-founded hopes that this constant threat to the very existence of Argentine federalism will disappear. Four distinct forces are making headway in Argentina which will tend to protect local self-government against unjustifiable encroachment on the part of the executive and legislative. These are: a growing spirit of local self-government, the economic development of the provinces, the spread of an enlightened public opinion, and the development of a sense of political sportsmanship which will prevent a political party from reverting to the process of intervention when it has lost the confidence of the people.

8. The Argentine Supreme Court, in maintaining the federal system of government and in preserving the rights of individuals against national and provincial encroachment, has acted with wisdom and vision which have won the admiration and respect of the Argentine people. The court has also demonstrated a profound interest in the protection of individual rights by creating such rights when they were not expressly conferred by the Constitution. Examples of these are the right of habeas corpus, *Ex Parte Tripulantes de la* Pilcomayo (pp. 165, 6*n*); the right of assembly, *Comité Acción Radical v. Jefe de la Policía de la Capital* (p. 191); and the right of bail, *Ex Parte Llanos* (p. 170). In the maintenance of the federal system, the decisions of the Argentine Supreme

Court show a marked tendency to enlarge and uphold the supremacy of the powers of the national government over those of the provinces. The court has accomplished this in three ways: first, by deciding that Congress has, besides the expressly delegated powers, implied powers, *Ferrocarril Central Argentino v. Santa Fe* (p. 116), and inherent powers of sovereignty, *Soldati v. Banco Muñoz Rodríguez y Cía.*, (p. 118); second, by preventing the provinces from encroaching or interfering, in the exercise of the powers of taxation and police, with the power of the national government to regulate commerce, *Mazzocone v. Mendoza* (p. 158), *Swift de la Plata v. Tucumán* (p. 153), and to make treaties with foreign nations, *García v. Buenos Aires* (p. 140); third, by refusing to interfere with the national government when it intervenes in a province, on the theory that such an act is of a political nature and not subject to judicial cognizance, *Cullen v. Llerena* (p. 90).

But although the court has inclined toward the enlargement of the powers of the national government, sometimes at the expense of the powers of the provinces, nevertheless it has tended to preserve the federal system as established by the Constitution. The court has done this, first, by holding that the national government cannot tax the instrumentalities of the provinces, just as the provinces cannot tax those of the national government, *Banco de Buenos Aires v. Gobierno Nacional* (p. 101); second, by permitting the provinces, through the doctrine of permanent concurrent powers, to exercise powers which by the Constitution have also been vested in the national government, *Griet Hermanos v. Tucumán* (p. 147); and third, by holding that one province cannot exercise its powers within the jurisdiction of another province, *Banco de Córdoba v. Caja de Jubilaciones* (p. 148).

The Court has demonstrated a profound knowledge of the constitutional law and history of the United States and has shown a wide range of technical proficiency in its applications of the decisions of the United States Supreme Court. In the performance of its functions the Court has served as a moderating force in the institutional life of the nation, and has been one of the leading factors in making constitutional government in Argentina no longer an experiment but a reality.

SELECTED BIBLIOGRAPHY

Adrados, A. E., El unitarismo y el federalismo en la constitución argentina. Madrid, 1927.

Alberdi, J. B., Bases y comentarios de la constitución argentina. Buenos Aires, 1920.

Aldao, C. A., Errores de la constitución nacional. Buenos Aires, 1928.

Alsina, H., La justicia federal. Buenos Aires, 1931.

Amuchástegui, N. R., La constitución nacional argentina. Buenos Aires, 1939.

Bas, A. M., El derecho federal argentino. 2 vols. Buenos Aires, 1927.

——— Derecho público provincial. Córdoba, 1909.

Bielsa, R., Derecho administrativo y ciencia de la administración. 3 vols. Buenos Aires, 1938.

——— La protección constitucional y el recurso extraordinario. Buenos Aires, 1936.

Del Valle, P., Nociones de derecho constitucional. Buenos Aires, 1910.

De Vedia, A., La constitución argentina. Buenos Aires, 1907.

Espil, F. A., La Corte Suprema federal y su jurisdicción extraordinaria. Buenos Aires, 1922.

Estrada, J. M., Curso de derecho constitucional federal y administrativo. Buenos Aires, 1895.

García, Victorica B., Orígenes de la organización nacional. Buenos Aires, 1912.

García Merou, M., Alberdi; ensayo crítico. Buenos Aires, 1916.

——— El recurso extraordinario ante la Corte Suprema. Buenos Aires, 1915.

González, J. V., Debates constitucionales. La Plata, 1898.

——— Manual de la constitución argentina. Buenos Aires, 1897.

González Calderón, J., Derecho constitucional argentino. 3 vols. Buenos Aires, 1931.

——— Doctrina constitucional. Buenos Aires, 1928.

——— Estudios y dictámenes en derecho público. Buenos Aires, 1937.

——— La función judicial en la constitución argentina. Buenos Aires, 1911.

——— Historia de la organización constitutional. Buenos Aires, 1930.

——— El poder de declarar la inconstitucionalidad de las leyes. Buenos Aires, 1914.

——— Por la libertad y el derecho. Buenos Aires, 1921.

González Iramáin, N., Por el régimen federal; El derecho de las provincias. Buenos Aires, 1938.
Guastavino, J. M., and C. A. Novaro, Elementos de derecho público argentino. Buenos Aires, 1929.
Herrera, L. A. de, La revolución francesa y Sud América. Paris, 1910.
Ibarra, E. A., Congreso constituyente de 1852. Buenos Aires, 1933.
Irigoyen, B. de, Justicia nacional. Buenos Aires, 1903.
Lafont, J. B., Historia de la constitución argentina. Buenos Aires, 1935.
Laurencena, E., Centralismo y federalismo. Buenos Aires, 1938.
Levene, R., A History of Argentina (tr. by W. S. Robertson). Chapel Hill, N. C., 1937.
——— Los orígenes de la democracia argentina. Buenos Aires, 1911.
López, V. F., Historia de la República argentina. Buenos Aires, 1883.
Matienzo, J. N., El gobierno representativo federal en la República argentina. Buenos Aires, 1910.
——— Juan Bautista Alberdi. Buenos Aires, 1910.
——— Lecciones de derecho constitucional. Buenos Aires, 1926.
——— Nuevos temas políticos e históricos. Buenos Aires, 1928.
Montes de Oca, M. A., Lecciones de derecho constitucional. 2 vols. Buenos Aires, 1902.
Padilla, A., La constitución de Estados Unidos como precedente argentino. Buenos Aires, 1921.
Pelliza, M. A., Historia argentina. New ed. Buenos Aires, 1923.
——— Historia de la organización nacional. Buenos Aires, 1923.
Ramos, J. P., Federalismo argentino. Buenos Aires, 1910.
Ramos Mejía F., El federalismo argentino. Buenos Aires, 1889.
Ravignani, E., Historia constitucional de la República argentina. 2 vols. Buenos Aires, 1927.
Rivarola, R., La constitución argentina y sus principios de ética política. Buenos Aires, 1928.
——— Del régimen federativo al unitario. Buenos Aires, 1908.
Rowe, L. S., The Federal System of the Argentine Republic. Washington, 1921.
Sánchez Viamonte, Carlos, El habeas corpus. Buenos Aires, 1927.
Sarmiento, D. F., Comentarios de la constitución de la confederación argentina. Buenos Aires, 1924.
Sommariva, L. H., Historia de las intervenciones federales en las provincias de la República argentina. 2 vols. Buenos Aires, 1929–31.
Varela, L. V., Historia constitucional de la República argentina. 4 vols. Buenos Aires, 1910.
Zavalía, C., Derecho federal. Buenos Aires, 1926.
——— Historia de la Corte Suprema de Justicia de la República argentina en relación con su modelo americano. Buenos Aires, 1920.

TABLE OF CASES

ARGENTINA

UNITED STATES

INDEX

COLUMBIA LEGAL STUDIES

EDITED UNDER THE AUSPICES OF THE

FACULTY OF LAW OF COLUMBIA UNIVERSITY

Edwin W. Patterson, Editor

I. The Historical Foundations of the Law Relating to Trade-Marks. By Frank I. Schechter, A.M., J.D., member of the New York Bar. With a foreword by Munroe Smith, J.U.D., LL.D., J.D., Bryce Professor Emeritus of European Legal History in Columbia University. 8vo. cloth, pp. xxviii + 211.

II. Legal Aspects of Commercial Letters of Credit. By Herman N. Finkelstein, LL.B., J.D., member of the New York Bar. With an introduction by Karl N. Llewellyn, LL.B., J.D., Professor of Law in Columbia University. 8vo. cloth, pp. xxviii + 390.

III. State and National Power over Commerce. By F. D. G. Ribble, A.M., LL.B., Jur.Sc.D., Professor of Law in the University of Virginia. With a foreword by Robert B. Tunstall, LL.B., LL.D., member of the Virginia Bar. 8vo. cloth, pp. xii + 266.

IV. Argentine Constitutional Law; the Judicial Function in the Maintenance of the Federal System and the Preservation of Individual Rights. By Santos P. Amadeo, A.M., Jur.D., LL.M., Jur.Sc.D., Professor of Political Science in the University of Puerto Rico. With a foreword by L. S. Rowe, Ph.D., LL.D., Director General of the Pan American Union. 8vo. cloth, pp. xii + 243.

Bei Fragen zur Produktsicherheit wenden Sie sich bitte an:
If you have any questions regarding product safety,
please contact:

Walter de Gruyter GmbH
Genthiner Straße 13
10785 Berlin
productsafety@degruyterbrill.com